BULLETS AND BOLOS

Bullets and Bolos

Fifteen Years in the Philippine Islands

By

John R. White

Bullets and Bolos: Fifteen Years in the Philippine Islands by John R. White.

©Copyright Constabulary Books, 2019.

This book or any portion thereof may not be scanned, digitized, reproduced or used in any manner whatsoever without the express written permission of the publisher except for the use of brief quotations in a book review or scholarly journal. All rights reserved.

First printing, 2019.

ISBN: 9781097503063.

Contents

I - Soldier and Policeman 7
II - Paymaster or Fighting Man? 16
III - Tastes and Odors of the Tropics 23
IV - A Ball—and Some Reflections 28
V - A Modern Don Quixote 34
VI - Genre Pictures of the Trail 43
VII - A Provincial Idyll 48
VIII - A Night Raid by Outlaws 54
IX - Jungle Trails 59
X - A Desperate Venture 67
XI - Deeper in the Jungle 74
XII - A Fight on a Mountaintop 78
XIII - Murder, Merriment, and Morals 86
XIV - Cholera in the Camp 94
XV - Floods, Amphibians, and Epidemics ... 99
XVI - Disintegration and Reconstruction 104
XVII - A Jungle Killing 108
XVIII - Damacio the Negrito 115
XIX - Race Prejudice and Cattle Stealing ... 122
XX - A Senior Inspector's Routine 127
XXI - More Routine—Including Murder 131

XXII - Bad Hiking and Worse Cholera 135

XXIII - American Pirates.. 140

XXIV - The Moro Problem..................................... 145

XXV - A Tragedy of Zamboanga............................ 151

XXVI - In the Spider's Web.................................... 155

XXVII - Riflemen from Mud 164

XXVIII - Bullets and Bees....................................... 170

XXIX - Life at Cotabato 177

XXX - A Night Alarm 181

XXXI - Saved by Cicadas....................................... 184

XXXII - Datu Matabalo.. 192

XXXIII - Oriental Eden Isles 198

XXXIV - Talking for My Life.................................. 205

XXXV - Sailing the Sulu Sea 212

XXXVI - Amok and Juramentado 219

XXXVII - Bud Dajo.. 225

XXXVIII - From Warrior to Warden....................... 236

XXXIX - A Doleful Colony..................................... 242

XL - The Iwahig Experiment................................. 247

XLI - The End of a Tropic Day 253

Appendix 257

I - Soldier and Policeman

On July 4, 1901, William H. Taft was inaugurated first American civil governor of the Philippine Islands. A temporary grandstand had been erected on the little plaza fronting the Ayuntamiento in Manila; and the rough board structure had been placed on huge blocks of stone that marked the foundations of a building begun by the Spaniards but never finished. Those unused foundations were symbolical of that Castilian social and political structure that had crumbled when Dewey's[1] guns roared over Manila Bay on May 1, 1898.

In front of that grandstand, I watched the ceremonies that transferred power from General Arthur MacArthur[2], the military governor, to the civil authority; and saw a big, blond, painfully hot man inducted into a position as full of difficulties and stumbling blocks as could well be imagined.

Few men have perspired their way into the Presidency of the United States and its chief-justiceship, yet on that Philippine Fourth of July William H. Taft started a career which took him from a hot and cheap grandstand on the other side of the world to the cool and stately seat of the Chief Justice of the United States—via the War Department and the White House.

The crowd of spectators was not dense. There were a thousand or two Filipinos who should have been enthusiastically hopeful but were merely apathetic; a sprinkling of frankly sarcastic officers and soldiers, regular and volunteer; with a few, very few, American civilians who were largely employed by the military government but many of whom now found themselves automatically transferred to the civil regime.

For the most part the civilian onlookers were unconscious of being part of a historical event; ignorant that they were the nucleus of a civil service that was within a few years to work great changes in the allegedly unchangeable Orient. And least of all did I imagine that for thirteen years to come I should take a hand in the game.

It was perhaps fortunate that none of us at that time had read Sir Edwin [sic] Arnold's thoughtful lines:

The East bowed low before the blast
In patient deep disdain;
She let the legions thunder past,
Then plunged in thought again.[3]

If we had known the history of Eastern nations or had studied the relationship between Europeans and Asians, we might have been discouraged. But we were all young and we belonged to a young and hopeful nation. With firm and strong young hands which did not tremble we took the reins of government from palsied Spanish fingers; little did we reckon that we knew nothing of the temper or the mettle of the team we were to drive: Occidental Democracy and Oriental Autocracy.

After two years as a private and non-commissioned officer in the regular army, somewhat unprofitably spent in a Turkish-bath chase after insurgents over and through the rice paddies of Cavite Province, I had been discharged to accept a clerkship under the military government. I was twenty-one and, after the hardship of provincial hiking and fighting, life in Manila was good and full-flavored.

For that was the epoch still affectionately referred to by old-timers in the Philippines as "The Days of the Empire," when thousands of soldiers, volunteer and regular, had transformed a sleepy old Spanish colonial capital into a fascinating palimpsest.

The principal business street of Manila, the Escolta, throbbed with humanity from every quarter of Europe, Asia, and America: officers and soldiers of the army, khaki-clad and often stained by the mud of trench and rice field; a diminishing number of Spaniards, flotsam of centuries of Castile's rule and misrule of the islands; blue-robed and long-queued Chinamen who controlled practically all business but would now be forced to compete with hustling American men of affairs; tall Sikhs, much employed by banks and business houses as watchmen, and towering above the Filipinos who, with white camisas (shirts) hanging outside their trousers, were swept along in a current that already moved faster than before the American advent.

Most of the Filipinos were barefoot. Now there are few in Manila who go unshod. In that statement lies one measure of the changes of twenty-seven years.

Down the Escolta, drawn by a pair of native ponies, crept a toy tram and it was accompanied by diminutive victorias, *quilez, calesas, carromatas,* and *carabao*—gigs, buggies, covered vehicles, and water buffalo carts.

In the little vehicles, soldiers on leave sprawled their easy lengths and, when necessary for comfort, projected their legs to the driver's seat. In many of the more pretentious victorias[4] sat women of all nationalities, with but a single thought—to relieve the soldiers of their pay, hard-earned among popping Mauser rifles but easily lost, amid the popping of corks, to the *hetaerae*[5] who followed the army as sharks follow a vessel at sea.

Money flowed as easily as the turbid stream of the Pasig beneath the graceful arches of the Bridge of Spain[6]. There was no American so worthless but that he could secure a job of some sort with the army or the civil government.

For a month or two after my discharge, I lived in a "mess" in the Walled City—Manila proper. The old nomenclature of the city will probably fall into disuse, but in those days, everyone knew the Walled City as Manila, in contrast with other sections of the city such as Quiapo, Tondo, Binondo, etc.

Among a dozen of us young fellows, products of the latest civilization dumped down among the ruins of an Old World structure, were two ex-soldiers like me who hailed respectively from Georgia and Kentucky.

They were employed as clerks in the "Office of the Commissary-General of Subsistence of Prisoners," or some such imposing title. Owing to the transfer of the Filipino prisoners to Guam, their work ran out, but their pay continued; and those two youths spent most of their time cooling their throats and searing their stomachs with highballs of rye and bourbon.

The superior merits of Scotch whisky as a drink for the tropics were in 1901 unknown to most Americans. However, when our national intelligence was focused on this subject a full knowledge of the brew of Bonnie Scotland was speedily acquired.

Anyhow, Smith and Brown, as we'll call them, stuck to the liquor of their forefathers, spending their hundred dollars or so a month apiece on what they would call "a good old American drink, gentlemen—rye!" A hundred dollars in gold meant about 250 of the Mexican silver pesos current in the Philippines. A lot of whisky could be purchased for that sum. They went at it hard for weeks and by good teamwork avoided the provost guard.

However, one day I returned early from the office to find Smith asleep and affectionately embracing an empty bottle while a noise in the back of the building led me to the tiled bath on the flat roof, where I found Brown scrabbling around under the impression that he was pursued by a gigantic lizard.

And through the long thirsty years of tropical life ahead of me, the thought of that naked youth in the grip of delirium tremens often acted as a warning when the whiskies and sodas or the gin pahits (cocktails) were passed around too freely and too long.

Soon after the inauguration of civil government the need of an insular police force became apparent. The army, scattered throughout hundreds of small posts over the archipelago, was still engaged in hunting down wandering bands of insurgents; but the insurrection had degenerated into guerilla warfare of a particularly irritating nature, which bade fair to drag on indefinitely.

The Puente de España, 1899.

The Bridge Renovated[7]

The army had broken the backbone of resistance to American authority; Aguinaldo[8] and most of the principal chiefs were captured, killed, or had surrendered; but scores of minor chieftains were in the field while the long-established bands of those brigands, with which the Philippines, like all Malay countries, was infested, had fattened during the insurrection and were now ravishing the fairest portions of the islands. For the army to hunt down these small swift bands was like shooting snipe with a rifle. A native police force largely officered by Americans was needed; in fact, the army had already organized such a force under the title of Philippine Scouts.

But the rub was that the civil government did not control the Scouts and there was much friction between the civil and military branches. The civil governor needed an armed force under his direct supervision, so on August 1, 1901, Act 175 of the Philippine Commission created the Philippine Constabulary. Even now, thirteen years after my retirement from that little army, the name conjures up a flood of tender memories—of fights and friendships from Aparri to Bongao.

The Philippine Constabulary. Just two rather long words to most people, but as I write them tears almost come to my eyes as the thrill of loyalty to the old corps still wakes an echo in my mind; and I see through the mist of time and years the epic and the drama which we youths were to play in the cultivated lowlands and in the wild mountain jungles of those myriad tropic isles.

The Manila newspapers gave full accounts of the new organization which was to stamp out brigandage; we saw fledgling officers strutting around in all the glory of their red- and gold-trimmed uniforms; several of my best friends obtained commissions as inspectors and urged me to join. But at first, I hesitated. The Constabulary was ridiculed by many army men and from what I saw of its first halting steps I doubted whether the service would be attractive. However, the longing for further adventure decided me, and on October 18, 1901, I found my way through the narrow streets of old Manila to the first headquarters of the Philippine Constabulary on Calle Anda.

Behind a big narra table sat an army officer in civilian clothes: Captain Henry T. Allen of the United States Cavalry, detailed as Chief of Constabulary with the rank and pay of brigadier-general in the regular army. A few minutes' interview with him, a look at my discharge from the army and other papers, and, lo, I was changed from a mere civilian to Third Class Inspector John Roberts White, P.C.

My salary was to be $900 United States currency per annum, which in my mind was quickly translated into its equivalent in Mexican pesos per mensis. I was promised an early opportunity to chase *ladrones* (brigands) in the Philippine bosques (jungles) and told where I could purchase a uniform of gray linen or *cáñamo* cloth, the gilt buttons, and the broad red shoulder straps with gold bars which were to adorn my youthful shoulders. I had just passed my twenty-second birthday and when I had donned those red shoulder straps the world seemed a very pleasant place.

Our uniform was gray *cáñamo* cloth because in those early days it was thought better that it should not too closely resemble the uniform of the regular army. Much water was to run into Manila Bay before the jealousy between the army and the upstart Constabulary would be wiped out by memories of many a combined campaign in the swamps of Mindanao and the jungles of bloody Samar.

In 1903 the Constabulary adopted a uniform similar to that of the regular army and with the same insignia of rank. But instead of the promised excitement of outlaw hunting my first work was humdrum in the extreme. For several days I addressed the little books of instruction for the corps, 'The Manual of the Philippine Constabulary,' which from a pamphlet of few leaves grew within a few years to a substantial volume in which a Constabulary officer might find information on any subject, from filling out a requisition for kerosene to shooting a runaway prisoner.

Within a few days I graduated from this subordinate position to that of clerk for the Chief, whose civilian amanuensis was sick. My two or three weeks at this work gave me splendid opportunity to see the inside workings of the new organization. Some Spanish papers which the Chief gave me to translate compelled me to brush up on the Castilian language, the rudiments of which I had mastered a few weeks earlier by visits to a Spanish Augustinian[9] friar who lived in the massive monastery that fronts Manila Bay.

Emilio Aguinaldo, c.1898

Emilio Aguinaldo in 1919

II - Paymaster or Fighting Man?

How interesting always are the first experiences, the first steps that count so much. Those were fascinating days in the office of the Chief of the Philippine Constabulary.

In and out passed the heterogeneous population of Manila: ex-soldiers and officers of the volunteer and regular armies seeking commissions; Filipino politicians establishing relations with the new branch of the government or forwarding the interests of Filipino members of the insular army; secret service agents with reports of new *katipunans* (secret societies) or the whereabouts of badly wanted brigand chiefs; army officers of high rank with complaints of usurpation of authority by agents of the civil government; Spaniards of all degrees, men and women, backwash from a wave that had spent its force, and who were now looking for employment or for passage back to Spain.

Early in the history of the civil government the Constabulary became a dumping ground for all work not clearly allotted by law to a particular bureau. All of these people the Chief urbanely met while at the same time supervising the task of organization with the distribution of men, supplies, arms, and ammunition throughout the forty-seven provinces of the archipelago.

The Constabulary was organized by provinces; a senior inspector commanded in each province from fifty to three hundred men with the corresponding number of officers. Within his province the senior inspector controlled the police and campaign work under the supervision of a district chief.

There were five districts each commanded by an assistant chief with rank of colonel and within his district the assistant chief had the authority vested in the Chief of Constabulary to see that brigandage, unlawful assemblies, and breaches of the peace were suppressed, and law and order maintained.

With some minor changes this organization of the Constabulary continues to this day and has worked satisfactorily. The principal modification has been the organization within provinces of companies of forty-six men each. This has facilitated supply, mobility, and keeping of records.

For a time yet I was to be retained in Manila, although I frequently requested the Chief to let me go to the provinces and take part in fieldwork. Every morning's mail brought to the Chief's desk scores of telegrams and letters reporting fights with outlaw or insurgent bands. As I read and distributed them, a great longing to get into the game again surged over me. I was eager to be doing things—not indexing and filing reports about those who did them.

One telegram would tell of a desperate fight in which the Constabulary came out victorious, killing many outlaws and capturing rifles, *bolos* (machetes), and ammunition. Another brief wire might say that Inspector So-and-So, perhaps commissioned a few days earlier, was shot or bolo-ed to death while fighting against odds. Yet another would tell of outlaw raids on the rich sugar haciendas (plantations) of some island far to the south and of Constabulary pursuit over mountains, up rivers, and through jungle. That was a fascinating mail bag, and it was a poor morning that did not report the capture or death of a score of outlaws.

With the inauguration of civil government, legislative alchemy had transmuted all insurgents into "outlaws," and woe to the officer who reported "insurgent bands;" but by whatever name, they gave the Constabulary many a good chase and sporting fight. We felt little or none of that hatred of the enemy bred by propaganda and trench warfare during the World War. Rather we felt, after we had chased an outlaw chief for a few months through the jungle, a spirit of not unfriendly competition. But I am getting ahead of my story. These accounts of fighting and adventure awakened previous experience of war's alarms, so that with all the ardor of youth I longed to be beside the gallant fellows who were almost daily meeting death.

One day a telegram came which read something like this:

Indang, Cavite, Nov. 20, 1901.
Chief of Constabulary,
Manila.
While riding from Dasmarinas to Silang with two men I was attacked by band of six outlaws armed with rifles and bolos. We killed all six. Sent back detachment from Silang to bury outlaws.
Knauber,
2nd Class Inspector.

Knauber got a Medal for Valor for that. Such deeds soon gave the Constabulary needed prestige and made the red shoulder straps of its officers respected by all classes of Americans and Filipinos throughout that green string of islands that stretches from Formosa on the north to Borneo at the south—athwart a thousand miles of sapphire seas.

The Chief's stenographer returned. My request for provincial service was met with the remark that, "We have plenty of men who can hike and fight but few who can be trusted to do clerical work."

So, I was made assistant to the quartermaster, a young lawyer, Herbert D. Gale, who later rose to be Judge of the Court of First Instance. For a few weeks I ran around Manila buying supplies and acquiring intimate knowledge of the price and whereabouts of lamps, blankets, leather goods, dried fish, rice, and the thousand and one articles needed by the Quartermaster, Ordnance, and Commissary Departments.

It was interesting enough to dicker with the Chinese, Spanish, and other merchants while visiting out-of-the-way corners of the city on a hunt for needed equipment. A job lot we got. Most of it was scrapped within a few months. But it served to tide us over until systematic orders for supplies could be placed in the United States.

That purchasing job brought a few temptations in my way. With pay of about eighty dollars a month, the extravagances of life in Manila during the Empire Days made extensive demands on my slim purse.

Often, I found handsome presents from Chinese merchants—a case of whisky, a bed, a settee or other useful article—at my quarters; but my recollection is that I returned practically all of the presents. Memory is, however, dim about the whisky. There was in the Philippines to tempt our officials an inheritance of native Oriental venality, as well as the imported Spanish variety.

About the close of 1901, the Chief called me to his office saying that he intended to make me paymaster of the First District. Vainly I expostulated that I knew nothing of accounts. I could learn, said he. As sop to my vanity, promotion to the grade of Second Class Inspector was thrown in and for a very small mess of pottage I yielded. Promotion gave me one more gold bar and ten dollars a month additional pay.

That morning I awoke wondering where I could borrow a few dollars to tide me over until pay day. That night I had a bank account of some eighty thousand pesos, with a safe in my office containing some thousands more of pesos in silver, all done up in sacks of matting. Not strange, indeed, that during the early days of our Philippine venture some young American disbursing officers went astray.

It was about that time that one young Constabulary officer situated like myself put a hundred-pound sack of government silver pesos in a carromata and boldly drove off down to the red light district. Of course, he ended in Bilibid Prison, as did a score or so more Constabulary supply officers, provincial treasurers, and other disbursing officers of the government.

The Spanish law applied to these crimes. The penalty for embezzlement of government funds was about fourteen years, one month, and a day—rather a long period in which to atone for one night's strolling down an apparently primrose path.

Bilibid Prison in 1900

It was a great pity that more care was not exercised in the selection of officers entrusted with money responsibility, for the Filipinos got the idea that we were no better than the venal Spanish officials with whom they had hitherto dealt. Yet there was this difference: the Spaniards went back rich to Spain; the Americans returned to the United States in the holds of our transports after serving some years of imprisonment in Bilibid.

Often in after years when visiting that same prison, I would see American convicts about their daily tasks and think, "There, but for the grace of God, goes John White."

My experiences as a disbursing officer were sufficiently interesting, for at the start I did not know the difference between a voucher and an account current. Indeed, my financial experience had hitherto been limited to the simple process of filling my pockets with money and emptying them again as soon as possible. But now I found a desk with wire baskets full of imposing papers which a friendly brother officer told me were vouchers waiting to be paid. It was a tall pile of vouchers left by my predecessor, who had himself absconded for parts unknown, taking with him as many Mexican pesos and United States bills as he could secure.

Hopefully, yet not without trepidation, I tackled that pile of vouchers. In after years the wall of many a Moro fort looked less high to me than that pile of vouchers, which came from every part of the island of Luzon, north of Manila. One voucher called for payment of fifty sacks of rice; the next was a payroll for a provincial Constabulary; yet another showed that an officer had hired a horse for a month at two pesos daily, and so on.

Regulations governing expenditures I had none; or if I did have, I did not know where to look for them. But I had a checkbook, almost unlimited credit, and the knowledge that poor devils of officers and men, sweating over the hills after outlaws, needed money and food. So, I buckled to the job.

I disbursed funds for about three months; and for about three years after my transfer I was kept busy explaining to the auditor for the Philippine Archipelago—a title as forbidding to us youngsters as it was resounding—just where the half-million pesos or so that I disbursed had disappeared.

If a voucher came in stating on the face of it, "Horse hire, $50," I paid it. And that unreasonable auditor wanted to know where the horse was hired, for what purpose, and I know not what details omitted by the officer who had rented the native pony.

Sometimes I was tempted to ask if the auditor did not want to know the age, sex, date of birth of the animal, together with its color, marks, and pedigree.

After I had left Manila and was campaigning against the babaylanes (fanatical outlaws) in Negros, I received from the auditor my first list of suspensions. It was for more than $50,000, Mexican currency. Then for night after night, following strenuous days in the field, I was kept busy with atlas and papers making up journeys for officers and men whom I had paid months before in northern Luzon.

Thus, I came to have accurate knowledge of that part of the islands long before I visited it; for the auditor was so insistent as to dates, places, and facts, that often I had to supply them from an imagination keyed by taking part in similar scenes, and with the help of an atlas of the Philippines. How I blessed the Jesuit priests who compiled that atlas! Without it I might have been in Bilibid Prison.

More experienced brother officers to whom I shall ever be indebted helped me and instructed me in the rudiments of bookkeeping. But after a few weeks I was ready to resign; so, I respectfully told the Chief as frequently as possible that he had promised to let me go to the provinces. At last he listened to my plea.

One day he took from his desk a bundle of papers and walked across the room to a map hanging on the opposite wall. It was a blueprint of the island of Negros, one of the Visayas group, about three hundred miles south of Manila and noted for its big sugar plantations. Papers in hand and often referring to them, General Allen pointed out the centers of brigandage, spoke of raids on haciendas by bands of outlaws known in Negros as babaylanes, said that it was one of the most serious problems confronting the Constabulary, and that organization in the province of Negros Occidental was just beginning.

Then he ended by saying that I was to go down there to assist Major Orwig, the Senior Inspector of the Province, and that he expected that I would take active part in suppressing the outlaws and thus justify my relief as disbursing officer.

Treading on air, I left the Chief's office. I was to become at least a supernumerary on the colorful stage of the Philippines, its properties the weapons of guerilla warfare, and its drop curtain often death.

As I threaded the maze of the Walled City back to my room overlooking the Augustinian monastery, the gray city wall, and Manila Bay, never had the streets seemed so full of happy people, the weathered tiles of the buildings so restfully red, and the tropic sky above those tiles so brilliantly blue. I was young and off on a great adventure.

III - Tastes and Odors of the Tropics

A FEW DAYS AFTER MY INTERVIEW WITH THE CHIEF, I handed over to my successor my balance of government funds, together with my blessing and a heap of unpaid vouchers. Whether the money responsibility or accounts were too much for him or what, I do not know, but within a few months my successor died; and I have often felt that a few more weeks of that financial strain might have killed me, while the *bolos* and bullets of the babaylanes and Moros passed me by.

Then one day I packed my humble belongings in a tampipe (straw suitcase), strapped a heavy Colt single-action .45 revolver around my waist, took a .44 Winchester repeating rifle in my hand, and started south. That Winchester was to shoot my way through many a tight hole. As I write it hangs on the wall, reminder of a score of jungle fights, and on the stock are several notches which, boy-like, I made when outlaw chiefs fell before it. Those who were not chiefs went unnotched.

I was off for the southern Philippines. First came the steamer voyage to Iloilo. Some old-timers may remember the good ship Francisco Pleguezelo, which in those days linked Manila with the Visayas Islands to the south. We were not then as critical of transportation as American supervision of the inter-island steamers has since made us, or we would have complained of the accommodations more bitterly and resultantly than we did.

She was a craft of some four hundred tons burden, and indescribably dirty. To sleep in her cabins was an adventure. Huge cockroaches, inches long, black, greasy, and evil-smelling, infested walls and bedding. At night they roamed over the somnolent voyager, and until he learned to go to bed with his socks on, they browsed between his toenails, so that paradoxically enough sore feet often resulted from a steamer voyage.

Although it was hot meandering down between the islands at a speed of from seven to eight knots an hour, yet the only way to get a bath was to arise early, stand on deck arrayed in short cotton drawers, and bribe a sailor to draw buckets of water from the ocean to slosh over a body fevered by a night in a stuffy cabin and irritated by the attacks of militant and mephitic vermin.

True, those Spanish boats had bathrooms, because the ships had been constructed in Scotch or English shipyards. But unhappy days had fallen on those bathrooms; they were now used for storing vegetables.

The discomforts of travel, however, might readily be forgotten while studying the interesting passengers. Two Spanish Recolleto friars, tonsured and white-robed, were returning under American auspices to the little Visayan villages whence they had been driven by insurgents a year before—and very lucky to escape with their lives. What tales those priests told me and how their conversation was sandwiched with epithets about the Visayan natives, particularly about the insurgent leaders! *Chungos* (monkeys) was their habitual reference to that class of Filipinos.

There were fat Chinese *mestizos* (half-breeds), businessmen, and *hacenderos* of Panay and Negros, always discussing the price of sugar per picul or telling of haciendas ruined by outlaw raids.

A few American businessmen of the sutler[10] type that follows an army and whose principal samples were brands of beer or whisky, held to themselves on deck or retired to their cabins to discuss their samples.

Half a dozen well-to-do Filipinos, some of them ex-insurgent officers, and politicians all, were returning from interviews with high officials of the new *gobierno civil*. They were voluble in their appreciation of the Constabulary that was to take the place of the army, which would resemble the old Guardia Civil of Spanish days, and would (so they hoped) rapidly suppress outlawry in their native provinces.

From the Filipinos I learned much of provincial conditions, of the causes of outlawry and cattle stealing, and of the means to take for their suppression. Before the voyage was over, I had exhausted my small stock of Spanish, but had added many new words to my vocabulary. I began to realize that I was embarking on a strange life; and that only by a working knowledge of Spanish and the native dialects could I come to an understanding of the world around me and the problems of a Constabulary officer's life.

At meals we gathered round a long table on the after-deck protected by double awnings from the sun; and there, cooled by the northeast monsoon and with a panoramic vista of palm-fringed islands slipping by, we ate the *sopa de arroz* (rice soup), the *cocido* (dish) of meat and vegetables, the biftek and *pescado frito* (fried fish), which made up the usual fare on inter-island craft.

The fish was always served after the meat course. All was washed down with a good grade of Spanish Rioja wine, and the meal finished with Edam cheese served in its red cannonballs, guava jelly in flat tins, bananas and other fruits, and coffee. To a hungry youth those meals more than atoned for the cockroaches in bed and the potatoes in the bath.

When the jolly Gallego captain was feeling particularly happy he would invite certain of the passengers to drink a cocktail, so called. An American bartender would have shuddered at the mixture which a Filipino major-domo placed in octagonal tumblers holding more than a half pint. It consisted of gin and water in equal parts, flavored by a liberal dash of Angostura bitters, with a tablespoonful of sugar and all beaten to a froth with an instrument that resembled a miniature broom.

But mighty good those cocktails were. The taste of them still lingers in my mouth, conjuring up the mixed crowd on the steamer, the warm smell of the southern sea, the dancing water of the narrow straits between islands verdure-clad from beaches of golden sand to rocky summits piercing the blue bowl of heaven.

All the "call of the East" seems sometimes held in those cocktails mixed on the old Pleguezelo and other ships on the waters of that fascinating eastern archipelago.

However, despite cockroaches and cocktails, forty-eight hours after leaving Manila we steamed between islets through the narrow straits that mark the entrance to Iloilo harbor. There I transferred to a diminutive steamer that plied between Iloilo on Panay Island and Silay on Negros Island.

Soon I had opportunity to observe that comfort is always comparative; for the craft was no more than a top-heavy launch, laden to the gunwales with a mass of native passengers, chickens in baskets, dried fish in bales, guinamous, which is venerable fish in liquid state, in earthenware jars, live *carabao* and oxen, and merchandise of every description.

The variety of evil smells on that launch equaled the number of brands of pickles put up by a famous house. The old Pleguezelo was by comparison a holystoned yacht. For several hours

I stifled in a crowd of Filipinos, Chinos, and *mestizos*, while, wobbling in the swell set up by a stiff northeast monsoon, we crossed the straits to Negros.

Soon the passengers became actively and enthusiastically seasick, giving me opportunity to make the interesting observation that a mestizo is always more violently nauseated than a pure-blooded native. The reason for this I cannot even surmise, but must leave to the explanations of trained ethnologists. It was indeed a pleasant little voyage. Yet, but for the smells, the sickness of fellow passengers, and the combinations of both, indeed despite it all, I enjoyed the crossing. Air and sea sparkled under the cooling influence of the northerly winds which make the Philippine climate delightful for three or four months of the year.

We passed scores of white-winged lorchas (small schooners) and paraos (outrigger canoes), laden with sugar for Iloilo and leaping over the foaming combers. It was the season of the sugar-cane harvest and long before we reached the Negros shore the smoke of haciendas rose against the green fields which sloped up toward the mountain jungles and crags.

At last we ran alongside a crazy bamboo wharf at Silay. Strong wharves are not built along the open coasts of Negros, because of the destructive typhoons; while a bamboo structure is as easily replaced as it is swept away. Disembarking, I stumbled along the creaking, swaying pantalon (wharf) and hired a carromata with two horses for the drive along the coast road to Bacolod, the capital of the province of Negros Occidental, where I was to report to the senior inspector for duty.

It was the dry cool season which lasts from December to April or even May and the roads were soft with white dust that also lay heavy on the fields of sugarcane which bordered them. We drove beneath groves of coco palms or crossed shallow streams where *carabao* were cooling after the day's toil in the cane fields, and at each crossing a ruined bridge testified to the wave of insurrection and disorder that had recently whelmed the province; although Negros suffered less from the insurrection and more from subsequent brigandage than any other island.

Negros is one of the wealthiest islands of the Philippine group, with rich volcanic soil. The World War so increased the price of sugar that many of the *hacenderos* must have made great fortunes.

I was astonished at the progressive appearance of the country, the substantial houses on the haciendas and in the village of Talisay through which we passed. When sugar was at five pesos the picul or more the *hacenderos* bought diamonds for their daughters or built fine houses of beautiful hardwoods, the mahogany of the islands, molave, ipil, and narra. When sugar dropped, they pawned the diamonds and mortgaged the houses.

A swollen orb sank blood-red behind the mountains of Panay beyond the straits, leaving its glory of gold and topaz to light the brief twilight of those latitudes. The air was heavy with the never-to-be-forgotten fragrance of sugar cooking from the vats of the hacienda mills.

Chinese settlers in the Philippines

IV - A Ball—and Some Reflections

IT WAS DUSK WHEN THE CARROMATA containing the big, young, and very green Constabulary officer rattled down the streets of the capital of Negros Occidental. From the massive church in the center of the plaza, dominating in Spanish custom the pueblo and its surroundings, rang the measured monotone of the vesper bell.

From house to house buzzed the hum of evening prayer, and through the low windows of the poorer dwellings or nipa (palm) shacks could be seen lighted candles or wicks floating in cups of coco oil faintly illuminating pictures of the saints or images of the Virgin before which women made their evening orisons.

From a tienda (store) at the corner of the plaza sounded the click of billiard balls; around little tables in the open air sat the *distinguidos* of the town, sipping their aperitifs of gin or beer. There were army officers, Filipino and American provincial officials, a Spaniard or two, and other Filipinos whom I later learned to know as prominent lawyers and merchants of the province.

Tied to posts stood several stocky ponies, heads drooping to the dusty road, flanks still wet with the sweat of the gallop in from nearby haciendas; for your well-to-do Filipino rarely rides his horse except at top speed.

The assemblage looked curiously at the passing arrival. I caught the glint of Constabulary shoulder straps. A young officer came forward to halt my carromata and offer his services in locating me for bed and board. At his invitation I joined the group for a drink that washed away the dust of ten miles. He had introduced himself as Third Class Inspector Walter A. Smith, the supply officer of the Constabulary of Negros Occidental, a somewhat imposing title which the organization and achievements of the Constabulary scarcely yet warranted.

After the drink we went across the plaza to the office of the senior inspector, and I reported to Major Orwig for duty.

Orwig had been major in a volunteer regiment and so had been given the responsible job of organizing the Constabulary of this outlaw-ridden province. He was an energetic and likable man.

But just now he was busy and could only greet me, for the governor-general of the Philippines, with a large party of high officials including our own Chief, had arrived on the gubernatorial yacht direct from Manila just as this very dusty subordinate officer of the government was crawling up the Silay road humbly to enter the town by the back entrance.

The governor-general had been received on the beach with music and banners. No music greeted me, but I got a bottle of beer from Smith at the tiendam, and if my welcome was less extravagant, it was none the less hearty, for Smith had said: "I'm mighty glad to see you. Things are in a devil of a mess down south and we've had no officer to send there."

Nevertheless, I've always amiably held it against the Chief of Constabulary that he did not contrive me passage on the governor-general's boat direct to Bacolod; for it left Manila within a few hours of my own departure on the dusty Pleguezelo.

I rather think that in those days the spirit of camaraderie had not been developed in the civil service and that some of the higher officials thought themselves—as they doubtless were—a cut above the ex-soldiers who constituted the hard-working and all-risking rank and file of provincial administration.

The bond of fellowship was yet to be created by the work of the years to come: those years when the ladronism of centuries was wiped out; when American health officers made the death rate in unsanitary pueblos drop twenty, thirty, and even fifty or more percent; when an ever-growing spider's web of permanent public roads and railroads crept over the provinces while American officers in cooperation with Filipinos worked by the hundreds, day and night, and died by the score, of bugs, *bolos*, and bullets.

And all for what? In the thankless task of making the Philippines safe, healthy, and prosperous. How could we, then little versed in history or philosophy, know that happiness would not follow? And that the Filipino people—or that element among them strongest-lunged—would rather be unsafe, unhealthy, and poverty-stricken under their own flag than everything that was good under the Star-Spangled Banner?

And yet the task was not thankless. It was worthwhile if only for the satisfaction it gave to racial pride and for the comradeship established both with Americans and Filipinos.

But that is of the perspiring years ahead. This is of Bacolod that night in March 1902. There was to be the usual baile (dance) in the provincial building to celebrate the arrival of the governor-general.

So, pulling a somewhat crumpled uniform from my tampipe, with light steps I accompanied Inspector Smith across the plaza to the official reception and ball. It was the first time in many years that I had attended a dance, for a soldier of Uncle Sam in the Philippines had all too few opportunities for wholesome social pleasure.

Different indeed was the treatment of soldiers in '98 from that given them during the World War. No YMCA's and society canteen girls for us in those days; only social ostracism for the enlisted man. From now on, however, bailes were to be as much a part of my life as expeditions against the babaylanes.

The people of Negros delighted in dancing. Rarely a week passed in any pueblo but that a baptism or a birthday offered excuse to get together a few guitars or a more pretentious orchestra, clear the polished hardwood sala (hall) of some house, and tread a maze of waltzes, polkas, and rigodons (square dances) from 9 p.m. to daybreak.

But now this first baile held for me absorbing interest. The long sala of the provincial building was as brilliantly lighted as could be managed with all the oil lamps in town, while palms and colored lanterns adorned stairs and approaches.

On chairs around the sala the Filipina and *mestiza* belles of northern Negros literally blossomed to the full. Their glossy black tresses were set with buds of fragrant ylang-ylang, gardenias, frangipani, or other heavy-scented flowers.

Later, when the room heated up with perspiring couples, the fragrance would be so sickly sweet as to compel an unaccustomed American to seek the open windows where a fresh night breeze blew down from the mountains to the sea. Even by American standards the girls of Negros were indisputably pretty; many there were whose features and complexion would not have been out of place in southern Europe; while a dash of Chinese blood in some faces, with the heightened cheekbones and slightly slanting eyes that looked so well above the sheltering fan, gave further piquancy of expression.

The darker beauty of the daughters of the soil set off the fairer charm of a score or so of American women, wives of army officers, or provincial officials. The white-and-gold uniforms of the officers gave another touch to the room. It was all fascinating to one who had but recently been a soldier of Uncle Sam, good for fighting but not for Society with a large S.

Soon the governor-general's party appeared, and the receiving line was formed. When my turn came I was rapidly shot along the line of American and Filipino officials and their wives; passed from the colonel commanding the Sixth Infantry to the Filipino governor of the province; on to the massive governor-general with Presidential aspirations just whispering in his brain; then on down the line of commissioners and minor officials, including our own Chief, until I was flipped off the end of the line to eddy with other guests in groups about the sola.

The reception over, the ball opened with a rigodon, a stately Spanish square dance that seems in some way to typify the social intercourse of the people as the two-step of those days might have been held to measure the easier manners of our world. The three-hundred-pound American governor-general led off with the ninety-pound wife of the Filipino governor.

The dance was on; and under Smith's tuition I was soon learning the Filipino dances, not so different, after all, from those of other peoples. The valse was merely a waltz in quicker time, the polka a jerky two-step, while the square dances all had figures which recalled boyhood efforts in a cooler clime. The Filipina girls made graceful and obliging partners; many of them already spoke a little English which pieced out my broken Spanish.

The official party left the ball early for a consultation between the governor-general and the provincial officials relative to measures to quash the outlawry which threatened to stop sugar production in Negros. Major Orwig told me to come to his office after the conference and receive instructions for the morrow. I gathered that at the meeting of the chiefs they would principally discuss the possibilities of enlisting a Constabulary sufficiently strong to suppress the outlaws and relieve the Regulars and Scouts now engaged in that uncongenial task.

Long after midnight I found the major at a table covered with blueprint maps of Negros. For an hour or more he sketched to me the political and police situation in the province. Soon my brain was muddled by a medley of names of places and outlaw chiefs. As he spoke his finger moved rapidly over the map:

"Here is Mount Canlaon, the eight-thousand-foot active volcano that you could see over from Iloilo. In the forests on its slopes are the bands of Dalmacio the Negrito and 'Gobernador' Francisco Abilo. They have about fifty men and operate chiefly on the haciendas between La Castellana and La Carlota, though they sometimes drop down over the other side of the mountains to the east coast and raid Escalante or San Carlos."

His finger traced the babaylanes' trails.

"Here, further south, is the valley of the Binalbagan River, the richest sugar-producing district in the island. This range of mountains to the east and south of the valley is the haunt of Papa Isio, the fanatical Pope of the babaylanes. He is the 'Papa' or Pope of the mountain folk, who are mostly criminals and ex-insurgents, though there are still numbers of the Bukidnons, the harmless wild tribes of the mountains on whom the babaylanes also prey and whom the Constabulary must protect.

"Papa Isio has probably two hundred men and forty good rifles. His principal generals in the south are Iping Daco, Iping Diutay, and Aguacil Cito. Rufo, one of his subordinate chiefs, recently surrendered to Colonel Kennon of the Sixth Infantry and now lives at Sipalay in the extreme south of the province, where we have a small Constabulary post. We have another detachment at Himamaylan, on the coast near the Binalbagan Valley; but we have no men in the valley.

"It has been policed by a company of Infantry at Isabela and the Scouts at La Castellana. But now the governor-general wants us to take over that part of the province, so I'm going to send you to Himamaylan with twenty additional men. You will command the post there, recruit more men, drill and instruct your detachment, and get into touch with Colonel Kennon at Isabela. Cooperate with him, and when he is ready you will receive orders to relieve the Sixth Infantry and control the military and police situation in the whole southern half of the province."

I listened with both ears. Possibilities and responsibilities were unfolding before me; I was to command an independent detachment and uphold law and order over a broad section of Negros. I was impatient to be up and doing, so thought it no hardship when Major Orwig closed with:

"You'd better get an hour or two of sleep before daybreak, as you will start early for Himamaylan. It is forty miles south of here. You can hike it in less than two days going easy. Smith will provide you with a horse. Your men will foot it. You will purchase rations on the road. Further supplies will be sent you by parao when Smith makes his bimonthly pay-trip. Goodbye and good luck! Don't be too rash," he glanced at my red hair, "and don't let the babaylanes get you. You get them, when the time comes."

V - A Modern Don Quixote

IT SEEMED THAT I HAD BARELY TUMBLED ONTO the canvas cot in Smith's quarters before that genial officer, responsive himself to an alarm clock, routed me out with: "Time to start for Himamaylan, White! Six o'clock, and your outfit is ready and waiting."

A few minutes later I was surveying my first command of Filipino soldiers, twenty weak, drawn up alongside the road. A small but wiry pony was held in waiting for el capitan, who was myself; for the Filipinos, accustomed to Spanish military titles in the Guardia Civil, did not wait for the orders which, a few months later, changed our appellations from inspectors to lieutenants, captains, etc.

A Constabulary officer of today with his neatly clad and uniformly equipped troops would hold up hands in horror at the appearance of my first command; nevertheless, I was as proud as if in command of a squadron of United States Cavalry.

But it certainly was a nondescript detachment; uniforms were of several grades of *cáñamo* (linen) cloth, made by local tailors after a general pattern to suit personal preferences; leggins the soldados had none; some were shod, and some went barefoot; some wore blue flannel shirts, others *cáñamo* blouses; hats and caps were of various kinds, favor being shown a wide-brim straw with red hat-cord.

Most of the men were armed with the single barrel Remington shotgun, a weapon frightfully ineffective against outlaws possessed of high-powered modern rifle. Only a few had Mauser or Remington rifles, relics of the Spanish Army. Ammunition was carried in pockets or in home-made belts of light duck; haversacks, also homemade, were stuffed to overflowing with all manner of non-uniform articles.

Cooking utensils dangled from shoulders or belts; and in the latter, *bolos* were stuck with a rakish, brigandish effect. The one really uniform article of equipment was the scarlet blanket which each man carried in a roll over his shoulder.

Altogether they looked as pretty a bunch of *ladrones* as could well be imagined and it was to be hoped that if we met any

Regulars or Scouts they would see me first—otherwise they would surely open fire on my detachment. We doubtless resembled the soldiery of a Central American republic.

But through the spectacles of youth and the telescope of opportunity I saw no flaw in my command, although it was with some misgivings that I bestrode the native pony. I am considerably over six feet in height; the little stallion was perhaps thirteen hands. I almost walked into the saddle and my feet dangled within an inch of the ground. Beside me Don Quixote on Rosinante would have appeared the knightly figure that his disordered brain conceived. However, with a farewell word of thanks to Smith, and a promise from him to bring needed funds and equipment to Himamaylan as soon as might be, I gave the word of command—"Detachment—atten-shun! For-r-r-ward—march!"

The column swung unevenly into line. Feet padded the dusty road; mixed accoutrements clattered and jingled a marching tune; a few sleepy-eyed Filipinos came to the shell-framed windows of their houses. I urged my fiery little brute to the head of the line, and we started south.

I sized up my men; and it is pretty certain that they sized up me. From now on what mattered most was the degree of confidence with which I could inspire them. Lack of arms and ammunition, improper uniforms, inadequate food and supplies, all mattered little as long as those small brown men believed in el capitan.

Many of the soldiers had seen service in the Spanish days, either in the Guardia Civil or in the various forces of native troops with which the Spaniards controlled, or failed to control, the Philippines. Some, however, were mere boys, enlisting for the fun of the thing—much like their commander, though, needless to say, the ensuing years sobered me down. I soon took due pride in the constructive work that we of the Philippine Civil Service were doing in America's interest in the Far East.

My sergeant, Melquiades Basubas, was a pockmarked Tagalo with a record of twenty years in the Guardia Civil. A corporal, Tomas Villanueva, promptly constituted himself my body servant and cook, turning out to be as amiable and useful a scoundrel as one might wish to encounter—or avoid. Tomas could always scrape up a meal for his chief. When more sophisticated in the ways and walks of Filipino soldiers I learned that it was not always well to investigate the manner of the scraping.

Let it now suffice to say that the pesos with which I furnished Tomas to purchase the chicken, eggs, rice, and bananas that were the staples of provincial diet usually remained, at least in part, in his pocket; while he fully enlarged on the rank, influence, and terrible wrath-to-be-invoked of his innocent commander to procure the necessary delicacies from browbeaten but perhaps slightly honored civilians.

Soon I learned to appreciate the cheerfulness of my men under the irritations of travel. They trudged through the dust which rose yellow underfoot; rapidly driven quilez and carromata passed, swirling up clouds that choked nostrils and eyes; the sun rose scorchingly above a fringe of coco palms bordering the coast road; but the men swung on, cracking jokes with passers-by, ogling soft-skinned girls pounding out palay (unhulled rice) under the palm-thatched verandas of peasants' huts or treading the road, straight and shapely, with market baskets of fruit and vegetables skilfully balanced on their heads.

When steps dragged some soldier would unswing a guitar to twang a brisk air that put new life into lagging feet. To help along the most heavily laden I dismounted from my Lilliputian steed and hung blanket rolls, haversacks, and miscellaneous accoutrements from the saddle; then footed it along with my men.

That noon we siestaed in the casa popular, or town-hall, of Valladolid, a considerable pueblo with many substantial stone and hardwood houses. There I was surprised to find two American women teachers, advance guard of that host of pedagogical Argonauts which, within a few years, was to make English the common tongue of those islands of Babeldom.

One teacher was a young and rather pretty girl already monopolized by an army officer who had ridden a score of miles to pay a call; the other, a sweet-faced, ringleted old maid, made me welcome in a cool room facing the plaza. How out of place she seemed amid those exotic surroundings—the heat, the luxuriant palms, and warm hibiscus beneath the window, the barefoot Filipino boys softly moving over the polished floor, carrying their lesson books and making goodbyes in broken English.

Rather she conjured up some cool New England village with old stone buildings and fences, with oaks and elms and a little white schoolhouse at the crossroads. What a spirit she had, and hundreds more like her, crossing continents and oceans, braving the dangers of insurrection and outlawry, to broadcast American ideas and education along our latest frontier.

The necessary rations for my men I purchased from Chinese storekeepers by means of vales. The vale, or IOU, was the Constabulary officer's right arm; it purchased anything from a horse to a ganta of rice, or even obtained cash to pay a detachment of men and meet an officer's personal expenses. It is good to relate that the Chinaman's trusting confidence was not often misplaced.

Sometimes an unscrupulous officer was transferred to another province or dismissed from the service without liquidating his vales; but usually he took them up when payday came, or the supply officer on his bimonthly trips would pay them if clearly issued for government supplies.

I believe, however, that the Chinos, accustomed under a previous regime to greasing official palms, were often surprised when American officers took up their vales. Those Chinese merchants of the provinces were our best friends. They stood for that law and order under which their business prospered and soon recognized the Constabulary as the most powerful agency in its enforcement.

Although the Chinos were often married to Visayan women, yet they lived in such manner that in each store and house there was a decided flavor of that oldest Orient—the Mongolian Empire. Occasionally a Chinaman would be met who had accepted the Roman Catholic faith, cut off his queue, and identified himself closely with the life of his town. But such cases were comparatively rare, notwithstanding that Chinese blood ran in the veins of many of the leading families.

Indeed, their names showed it; for the common Negros surnames such as Lacson, Locsin, Tiongco, etc., were merely the Chinese Lak-sung, Lok-sing, Ti-ong-ko easily adapted from ideographs to Roman letters.

The upper-class provincial population was divided into three groups, fairly distinct yet often merging through intermarriage: the pure Visayas, among whom were few wealthy families, the Spanish *mestizos*, and the Chinese *mestizos*. The latter was by far the most substantial class and early ranged itself in hearty support of the American Government.

Its members were largely merchants and *hacenderos*. The Spanish *mestizos* furnished most of the lawyers, doctors, and other professional classes—including the politicians. As a rule, they were less friendly to Americans. This was natural, as they were of the class which lost most prestige by the change of government. In the Spanish days a dash of Castilian blood ranged a man with the imperial race that held the islands, while his children were sought in marriage by Spaniards, either peninsulares, as those born in Spain were called, or by creoles, born in the Philippines.

If American control of the Philippines is early released the population would probably divide along the above lines. It is possible that the split would mean no more than political differences and struggles for ascendency; but it is likely that bloodshed and disorder would often result. Certain it is that the longer American control is exercised the greater will be the fusion of classes brought about by improved communications, by the public-school system, and by common friendly participation in government enforced by Uncle Sam. Whether we have any business burning our fingers while pulling Philippine racial chestnuts out of the exceedingly hot firs of Asiatic politics is entirely another question.

In Valladolid I met a Spaniard horribly scarred in face and body by cuts from *bolos* of raiding babaylanes. Within the past few weeks his hacienda had been assaulted by a band of Papa Isio's outlaws, his buildings burned, his cattle driven to the mountains, the younger women of his household carried off to be concubines for babaylan chiefs; while he had been left for dead.

The sight of this man made my blood boil; so that when I heard rumors that a band of babaylanes was at that moment raiding between La Castellana and La Carlota, pueblos of the interior a few miles from Valladolid, I decided to interpret liberally my instructions to proceed to Himamaylan and, instead of holding to the direct road along the coast, I swung my detachment inland and reached the pueblo of La Carlota at sunset.

It was a good twenty-mile hike to start my provincial career. The soldiers were foot-sore and very tired; but they smelled a possible encounter with the babaylanes and seemed eager to be put to the test. I was mightily pleased with them; and they seemed pleased with me.

At La Carlota we camped in the casa popular, the men curling up in blankets on the floor, while my superior rank procured a cot sent over by an American sergeant in charge of a small detachment of soldiers stationed there. The Constabulary was as yet unknown in La Carlota. Later on, when our reputations were made, the best houses of Filipinos and Spaniards in the town were thrown open to our officers.

I learned that the raiding band had been driven away by the Scouts stationed at La Castellana; but, as we were now inland, I determined to keep on south through the Binalbagan Valley and descend to the coast again at Himamaylan. My curiosity to see the famous valley which Chief Allen in Manila had pointed out as the "playground of the babaylanes" overcame any scruples about strict interpretation of orders to "proceed to Himamaylan"—the road being not clearly defined.

Before daybreak we were on the trail. Our way now led over rough cart tracks through sugar plantations with many a short cut over rolling hills covered with dense cogon grass. These green foothills are such a feature of Philippine physiography and Constabulary expeditions that a few words in explanation are due. A description of Negros will fairly well apply to other islands of the archipelago.

The backbone of Negros is a rugged chain of mountains running north and south, culminating in the center of the island in the eight-thousand-foot active volcano, Mount Canlaon. This cordillera (chain) is several thousand feet high, and densely forested, with but one or two passes at lower elevations.

On the lower slopes, a primeval forest thins out into bamboo jungle with occasional caingins, or clearings, where the hill folk have felled and burned timber to plant palay and camotes (sweet potatoes). Lower still are cogon-clad foothills billowing down to the coastal plain with its fat plantations of sugar and rice, where little whitewashed, galvanized-iron roofed pueblos, and haciendas dot green fields.

The cogon grass of the foothills is from knee-to-breast high, though in sheltered gullies it may be over a tall man's head, more of a cane-brake than a grassy sward. Winding up and down through the cogon, crossing rocky streams which issue from forest slopes above or diving into thickets of bamboo, wild guavas, or tigbao cane, are the trails leading from the plains to the mountains. It was down these trails that the outlaw wolves descended and up which the Constabulary hounds sweated in pursuit.

And now every turn of the trail opened pictures of Philippine country life. We passed through a hacienda: first the fields of ripe cane, arching overhead to cut unguarded face or hands, for the sugarcane like the taller cogon and tigbao grass will wound a careless wayfarer; then, nearer the central buildings, men were cutting the cane and piling it on carts drawn by *carabao* or oxen.

My little army wound between the carts, its barefoot members picking their way carefully over the sharp stubs of cane left in the ground. At the mill where the cane was pressed through rollers and the juice ran into boiling vats, the smell of cooking sugar savored the air and a generous Spanish mill-foreman gave us quantities of candy that women were pulling from the cooked sugar—long, toffee-like twists that I sucked as appreciatively as my men.

We tramped over the mulch of cane which, after passing through the rollers, was spread over the yard to dry in the sun before feeding the furnace; then, out through more cane-fields and into the cogon hills again, twisting, turning, tramping along, always south toward the Binalbagan Valley.

But on the haciendas not always did we pass through scenes of busy activity. More than once we came to blackened ruins where prosperous farms had stood. If there had been no other signs, we knew by this destruction that we were in the haunts of the dreaded babaylanes. From passing *taos* (laborers) or at little bamboo hamlets tucked away in the more fertile corners of the foothills my men sought news of the outlaws.

But evasive answers came; for the peasants of the hills dreaded more the wrath of the babaylanes than the arm of the law, then neither long nor imposing as represented by my dusty, ill-equipped detachment which must have appeared to the country-folk only less to be dreaded than the babaylanes themselves. Indeed, we often met men and women, the former carrying long spears and the latter heavy baskets of camotes and palay, who fled at our approach. Like rabbits they dived into thick cogon which quickly hid their passage.

My men jeered derisively that we were "Constabularies," not babaylanes. Sometimes the fugitives would return, shamefaced and trembling; but often they were stones cast in a pool, leaving but a ripple in the cogon to show where they dived. Sometimes we would find their baskets in the trail; and I doubt not that behind my back the soldiers would abstract a few camotes or ubis (yams) as provender by the way. Certainly, when we halted for lunch alongside a brook beneath a grove of bamboo, an extraordinary number of tubers was produced to roast in the ashes of our fires.

That afternoon we topped a steep cogon hill to see spread out below the small and almost ruined pueblo of La Castellana, while beyond stretched green and smiling the broad valley of the Binalbagan, dotted with haciendas as yet unburned, encircled by dark-blue mountains, and with the winding ribbon of its river showing silver and gold under the slanting rays of a westering sun.

Wearily we dragged our feet across the plaza to the apology for a municipal building which we knew as such only by its position fronting the plaza and by the sign 'Casa Popular" on a crooked lintel above ruined steps. My men were too tired to find fault with their quarters: yet I was relieved when an American officer of Scouts issued from a nipa (palm) house and invited me to pass the night with him. While eating a hearty supper of good army commissary rations, I learned much about conditions in the neighborhood and about the comparatively large army post at Isabela, ten miles further south, where the officer commanding the District of Southern Negros had his headquarters.

The Scout officer told me that a few weeks previously the babaylanes had raided La Castellana, surprising the Scout garrison under his predecessor, killing several soldiers, and capturing fifteen or twenty Springfield rifles which went to swell the armament of Papa Isio.

What with the devastated haciendas, the scarred Spaniard at Valladolid, and now the officer's tales of actual service against the babaylanes, it seemed that I was very close to the campaign. So before turning in for the night I inspected my men's sleeping quarters, placed them as securely as possible, and made sure that the sentries were alert.

A *mestiza* dons a Maria Clara gown, the Philippine national dress during the colonial era.

VI - Genre Pictures of the Trail

NEXT MORNING THE SCOUT OFFICER BADE ME FAREWELL. "Hope we get out on the hike together soon," he said. "I don't envy you going up against the babaylanes with that outfit—if you ever want real guns and ammunition, I'll help you if I can."

Poor fellow! He died by his own hand a few years later in the swamps of Mindanao and I was not far from him at the time. He was a good officer and showed none of the petty jealousy that some officers of the Scouts showed toward the Constabulary. But, as with many others, too much tropics, too much hiking, too much isolation, and too much responsibility, finally struck discord in a nervous system attuned only for more normal life.

From La Castellana we dropped through hacienda after hacienda into the heart of the Binalbagan Valley; and after thirteen years it still seems to me the fairest part of those fair islands. Nowhere else was the soil so fat beneath the plowshares, the sugarcane and rice so tall, the girls so pretty, the *hacenderos* so prosperous, and the peasants so apparently happy.

The swift Binalbagan, issuing cool from the slopes of giant Canlaon, ran its silver thread through an emerald field. Purling brooks rushed down to meet their mother and cooled our feet as we hiked along the trail. One hacienda followed another; and where the torch of the babaylanes had spared we found hearty welcome from the Spanish, Swiss, German, or Filipino *hacenderos*.

Who were we?

"The Constabulary? Oh, yes."

They had heard of the new corps which was to take the place of the Guardia Civil of other days. The Spaniards particularly were enthusiastic about our future and pledged me with many a gin cocktail and bottle of warm beer-terrors of the trail that did up as many young American officers as the outlaws' bullets. Advice I had aplenty.

"Ah! Senior capitan, it is necessary to set a ladrone to catch a ladrone. You must enlist some babaylanes; that is how the Guardia Civil handled these curs—these lobos who come from the mountains to steal and burn. Los soldados americanos? They are good—they are noble men! But they are not trained for fighting like this, in which one must creep through the bosque (jungle) for days to kill perhaps one babaylan. And they come and go, los soldados Americanos.

"They belong not here but in America. You? You will be of us, and soon you will know the mountain trails better than the babaylanes themselves. And your men, they are Filipinos who will know the tricks of the *ladrones*. Gracias a Dios, that you have come, for it is no longer safe to raise sugar in Negros. And with the price of sugar so low. Barely five pesos the picul—it is ruination if our cattle are driven off and our *taos* afraid to work in the fields."

All this over the cocktails; or, when we happened on a hacienda at meal-times, over plates of sopa de polio (chicken soup), cocido of meat, bananas, and garbanzos (chick-peas), with other dishes that savored well to a hungry traveler. Then, after the meal, a siesta on a cane-woven bed, with just a sheet stretched tight and two bolster pillows; but, after the hot glare of the trail, how cool and comfortable it was behind the louvered windows of a hacienda bedroom.

And so, we slowly wended our way through the valley until the white walls and galvanized roofs of Isabela rose above the cane fields. This pueblo in which I was soon to pass many happy months was situated at the very foot of the mountains that ringed the valley. Steep behind the town rose forbidding slopes of forest jungle. It was easy to see why Isabela was the garrison town; for, standing on a slight eminence, it dominated the haciendas below so that raiding outlaw bands coming from the south or west must pass close to the town before reaching their prey.

Isabela was the usual provincial pueblo: a plaza and a church; a casa popular for municipal officials and a cuartel (barracks) for the garrison; a few pretentious houses of stone or hardwood with tin roofs around the plaza, tiendas on the ground floor, residences above; for the rest, a scattering of less substantial houses of bamboo, coco, and nipa, radiating out to fields of rice and cane on three sides of the town, and on the other up the foothills to the jungle.

But beyond other Philippine pueblos that I have known, Isabela possessed a distinctive flavor; whether it was the carelessness engendered by the proximity of constant danger or because of the large number of *mestizos* and Europeans on nearby haciendas I cannot say, but Isabela was always gay. The babaylanes might be raiding the haciendas by day; but there would be a baile at night. Despite many years of insurrection and outlawry there was plenty of money in circulation. Let the price of sugar rise ever so little and the haciendas fairly ground out wealth from the black volcanic soil. Did the babaylanes burn the buildings? There was abundant bamboo in the foothills to be rafted down the river, and a camarine (storehouse) could be erected in a day or two.

A happy town was Isabela and full of happy people who so endeared themselves to me that after many years I write of them with affection and hope someday again to see the smiling valley with old Canlaon towering to the skies and brooding over all.

As we neared the town, I knew that I must explain to the military officer in command the reason for my trespass on his preserves. As Major Orwig had told me, there was an arrangement by which the army controlled the interior of Negros, while the Constabulary recruited and organized on the coast. Yet here I was, carelessly voyaging through the heart of the military territory.

It was therefore with no little fear that I drew up my pitiful command in the plaza, flicking the dust from a *cáñamo* uniform never too presentable but now stained and sweated, the despair of any laundryman. My poise was not steadied by the joking remarks of American soldiers lounging in the plaza who were critically surveying the arms and equipment of my detachment.

However, on presenting myself to Captain Atkinson of the Sixth United States Infantry with request for a night's lodging for myself and men, I met with a hearty if quizzical welcome. He smiled at my explanations of how I found myself in Isabela instead of Himamaylan and, as he handed out a telegram that was awaiting me, said: "You'll see plenty of the babaylanes before long, young man—and without bending orders too badly, either. Better read that telegram."

I did not find the officer commanding the District of Southern Negros wildly indignant at my trespass; indeed, I suspect that he regarded me with good-humored, if disparaging, tolerance. The army did not take the Constabulary very seriously in those days. But Colonel Kennon told me that the Sixth Infantry expected to leave Negros as soon as the Constabulary could be whipped into shape to relieve them.

He estimated that to control a situation which now taxed a company of infantry and another of Scouts I would need considerably more men and better supplies than I had in my callow detachment of twenty; and he gave me a good idea of conditions, stating that Papa Isio still controlled more than two hundred fighting men with forty or fifty rifles, but that he was hopeful of negotiating the Pope's surrender before the Sixth Infantry was withdrawn.

I have among my few Philippine papers a pencil sketch which Colonel Kennon drew for me that night to show that to keep the babaylanes out of the Binalbagan Valley and protect the haciendas when American troops were withdrawn, I would need more than one hundred men in three or four stations. I regard that sketch with pride because my original detachment of twenty men was but little augmented before the Constabulary smashed the babaylanes some fierce blows and made the Binalbagan Valley the safest region in the island.

From Colonel Kennon and other sources, I learned more about the outlaws of the mountains and of the remarkable old Visayan tao at their head, Papa Isio, who had been in the mountains for years before the American occupation of the Philippines, and had given the Guardia Civil many a hard chase. Originally a laborer in the lowlands, Dionicio Papa, as he signed himself, fled to the hills after committing a crime which was now wrapped in the hoary mystery of the years.

Although an uneducated man, he must have possessed character: for he quickly gathered a band of cutthroats before whom, by reason of a little dog-Latin picked up while sacristan of his village church, he posed as the head of a new religion. This was a clever scheme. The growing hatred of the Filipinos for the friars gave him recruits from among the discontented, while every fugitive from justice found welcome in his band.

Papa Isio posed as the friend of the oppressed. Of course, he knew nothing of English history, or he might have called himself the Robin Hood of the Philippines. During Spanish days the hacienda laborers were often unjustly treated by their masters and could be imprisoned for debt or required to work it out for the creditor. Among an improvident people, this law resulted in a mild sort of slavery from which escape was always possible by flight to the ever-waiting mountains. These conditions obtained more or less throughout the Philippines; but as the haciendas in Negros were larger and more prosperous than elsewhere, the "debt slavery" question was more aggravated.

Indeed, during my time in Negros, I was often called up to rescue *taos* from the clutches of their creditors or release them from unlawful imprisonment by municipal officials.

Now, if Papa Isio's bands had consisted only of such fugitives from debt and oppression there would Have been some sympathy among Americans for the babaylanes. But every scoundrel from the lowlands escaping from the wages of crime or too lazy to earn an honest living found easy refuge with the outlaws. The bands, also, were not content with laying tribute on the rich; they burned and pillaged where they listed; and often they inflicted unmentionable tortures on victims suspected of aiding the forces of law and order.

Such were the babaylanes and such was the problem which, so it seemed, I should assume the responsibility of solving. My interview with Colonel Kennon sobered me.

The following morning, I took my detachment over the rice fields and cogon flats to Himamaylan, resolving to so drill and discipline my men that when the time came the Constabulary should prove no unworthy successor to the United States Army in the valley of the Binalbagan. As I looked at my cheerful, sturdy, if uninstructed, soldiers, I knew that the right spirit was there, and fancied that lack of arms, ammunition, and supplies would matter little if the spark were in me to kindle that spirit into flame.

VII - A Provincial Idyll

HIMAMAYLAN IS A SMALL PUEBLO STRUNG ALONG a sandy beach under shady coco palms. The Himamaylan River, little more than a lagoon, throws into the straits that lie between Negros and Panay a crescent sandbar behind which shelter fishing *bancas* (canoes), trading *paraos*, or occasional sugar lorchas (small schooners) from Iloilo. An eighteenth-century stone church with a connecting monastery fronts the sea. The monastery, known as the convento, furnished quarters for me and my men.

The Spanish Recoleto friars had been driven away during the insurrection and had not yet returned. The building had been looted, but there remained a few articles of solid furniture. Until recently Inspector Smith had occupied the quarters and had left there a detachment of five soldiers who now went to swell my footsore score.

An American teacher also lived in the convent—which was big enough to shelter a dozen men and give each separate quarters—but he was a reserved individual who preferred to live and eat alone rather than pool with the only other American present. Smith had told me that the schoolteacher knew the price of eggs, chicken, and rice better than a Filipino and boasted of living on twenty centavos a day.

How we Constabulary officers laughed at the parsimonious pedagogues!

Like the ex-soldiers that we were, we scattered our money right and left; the schoolteachers, fresh from the economies of life in small American towns, saved three-fourths of their pay. They were the wise virgins, even if their stinginess did occasion unfavorable comment among the Filipinos. It was not good to see an American living and eating like a tao. Harsh criticism we of the Constabulary thought and voiced at that time; yet, now that the mellowing years have passed, I can see that those teachers were not necessarily avaricious.

Who knows what debts and mortgages on little farms back in Iowa and Kansas were paid off? Their pesos were hard enough earned, God wot, for they ran risks of death by disease and outlawry without the compensating excitement of the chase that we had. Maestros, we called the teachers; and the female of the species was known as a maestra.

The presidente (mayor) of Himamaylan was a young Filipino with a dash of Spanish and Chinese blood, by name Serafin Gatuslao. From the beginning he was the best friend of the Constabulary in southern Negros. At his house I took my meals; from him I quickly learned of all the malhechores (offenders) in and around the pueblo.

Although married and father of several children, Serafin was little older than myself. During the intervals between drilling and instructing my detachment I found him a boon companion. Together we went shooting to nearby rice paddies and ponds and loaded the little brown boys who were our retrievers with duck, teal, snipe, parrots, cockatoos, and I know not what other strange tropical birds.

On these expeditions we would talk intimately of provincial politics, of the babaylanes in the mountains, and of the cattle-stealing gangs in the lowlands which were beginning to be a more serious problem even than the babaylanes. Serafin was an exception in that I rarely found his counsels interested. The wealthier provincial Filipinos have so many parientes (relatives) and friends that their advice on conditions in their own localities must often be discounted.

But although Serafin administered a hacienda a mile or two from town, he had few political ties in the south; his relatives and friends were in northern Negros, and marriage to a girl of Himamaylan had brought him there to administer his wife's property. He had first been made presidente by the military authorities and later was elected by the people as a tribute to his honest administration.

Sometimes we would go on a picnic—a sunsuman, as the Visayas call it—up a river to Serafin's hacienda. The presidente's wife, some pretty girls from neighboring haciendas, a few youths, Serafin, and myself, made up the party. Embarking in bancas, we were paddled by Visayan boatmen up an estero (tidal creek) under overhanging mangroves through narrow passages where nipa palms fanned our faces. At the hacienda landing our lunch was waiting, the piece de resistance a suckling pig done up in banana leaves, all ready for the roast.

Beyond the landing we neared the hills; the estero became less swampy and soon our boatmen poled us up a clear stream that rippled over a rocky bed. We found a smooth spot beneath a mango tree and there the suckling pig was roasted whole. The liver was removed, pounded up with the leaves of a bitter herb growing near the river, and stewed into a sauce to pour over the roasted cracklings.

The taste of those cracklings can never entirely melt away; and the scene after lunch is easily recalled: the boatmen squatting in a circle around the remains of the succulent porker, the Filipina girls showing shapely legs as they paddled in the creek with many-colored skirts drawn up to knees, the young Filipinos splashing and flirting with the girls; beyond the bickering water a bamboo grove traced like giant maidenhair fern against a cobalt sky over which fleecy cirrus clouds drove with the steady northeast trades; a raucous-voiced, red-billed kingfisher perched on a waving frond of bamboo or diving to a pool unheedful of the picnicking crowd.

And beneath the umbrageous mango Serafin and I, smoking innumerable cigarettes, the cares of office not even lightly resting on our brows.

It was at such times as these that I learned to know the Filipinos and their kindly traits as one may only know them by life in the provinces, isolated from other Americans.

A man might live twenty years in Manila and know less about the Filipinos than by a few weeks' residence in Himamaylan. Yet living in Himamaylan he must be simpatico—he must have sympathy with the life of the people. That Spanish word simpatico is hardly translated by its English equivalent "sympathetic." When a Filipino says of an American that he is simpatico it means that he does not strike false notes in dealing with people of other races.

A man might be sympathetic, yet full of race prejudice; but if simpatico he is free from it; a Filipino can give an American no higher praise. A man may be able, honest, hard-working, and full of assorted other virtues, yet quite unable to get along with the Filipinos, if lacking in that touch of humanity which enables one to

Be to their virtues very kind,
Be to their faults a little blind.

Often in after years I thought what a pity it was that some American officials, I came to know could not have had the privilege of enjoying a sunsuman picnic with Serafin at Himamaylan. It might have made them simpatico—which they surely were not.

To describe the qualities that a Caucasian must possess for successful dealing with Asiatics, travelers and historians have used up a good many adjectives. There are not wanting even those who claim a measure of aloofness on the part of a Caucasian as an essential quality of success; yet I cannot believe that where two men are gifted with the possibility of intercourse by means of language and intelligence, barriers are necessary. It seems to me that all the necessary virtues may be summed up in that one Spanish word that is almost a phrase—simpatico. And that, after all, is the Golden Rule in one word.

But a distinction must be made between weakness, sensuality, and the capacity for being simpatico. It is possible, though it may not be easy, for an American to maintain his own racial standard of conduct and living, and at the same time be tolerant, understanding, and without arrogance of race toward the Filipinos, or other people of widely different race.

It is possible, but it is not easy. The easier course for the American of sympathetic nature was to acquire, by marriage or otherwise, what the Spaniard called a "sleeping dictionary," and then he would gradually be wafted over the gulf between the Malay and Caucasian races until within a few months or years his backbone changed from steel to rubber and his ideal existence was in pajamas and slippers. The Caucasian in the tropics cannot do as the darker-skinned races, immunized by the centuries, do.

Of course, life at Himamaylan was not all spent in learning the art of sympathy, if that can be learned. There were hours and hours, and then more hours, spent literally in sweating my detachment into shape. Up and down the hot narrow court in front of the convento I marched those devoted brown soldiers, teaching them to throw out their chests and pull in their chins and bring down their feet with the regularity of a German goosestep.

I taught them to handle their shotguns and the one or two old Mauser and Remington rifles that we had somehow acquired. Scraping together a little ammunition, we went to the hills outside the pueblo, and there, to the imminent risk of passing *taos* and grazing cattle, we held target practice.

Before long, my men could hit the bullseye with a Remington at two hundred yards or pepper a paper square with buckshot at thirty. That is, if the single-barreled Remington shotguns went off. They were rotten arms, somewhat more dangerous to the possessor than to the prospective enemy, and must have been a job-lot manufactured for some Central American republic by a kind-hearted American firearms company. I never saw a ladrone killed by one of those shotguns, though during the early days several Constabulary soldiers were killed or injured by bursting breeches. It was up to us to capture our own firearms from the outlaws.

Gradually my men worked into shape. They began to have confidence in themselves and their commander. I was itching to put them in the field against the babaylanes whose raids on the haciendas continued. But Colonel Kennon was negotiating the surrender of Papa Isio, and Major Orwig bombarded me with instructions to "sit tight and wait."

One day there was a little excitement. My bedroom faced the sea and at daybreak I heard a great hullabaloo on the beach. Thinking the babaylanes had raided the town, I jumped up. But the cause of the rumpus was a crocodile entangled in the bamboo fish corrals that spread fanlike over the shallow waters of the lagoon. Half the town was down to watch fishermen spear and rope the giant saurian, and just as the brute was hauled up on the sand, I joined the yelling throng.

The crocodile, entangled in ropes, bled from a score of wounds. It was as long as one of the bancas that had hauled it ashore; later I measured it—eighteen feet three-inches from tip of blunt snout to end of crenelated tail. When it was clear of the water a fisherman jumped on the broad back to drive a sharp maul into its spine.

Then the crocodile's death flurries burst encircling ropes and its threshing tail knocked over and badly bruised some of the bystanders.

When the last convulsive movements had ceased, the brute's jaws were propped open by a stick of wood, and a ten-year-old Filipino boy stood upright between them.

There was great rejoicing in the pueblo, for the crocodile was a well-known man-eater that had taken many victims in the Himamaylan River.

At times I would mount two or three soldiers on borrowed ponies and ride out into the hills behind Himamaylan to become acquainted with the trails and surrounding country. While returning one hot afternoon from such a trip, a terrific thunderstorm broke a long spell of dry weather.

Clinging, wet to our saddles, we rode into Himamaylan between rows of cocos and bamboo flailing wildly before wind and rain. As I drippingly dismounted at the convent door, Inspector Smith came down the broad stairway to greet me. He had come from Bacolod in a sailing parao, bringing with him also a Mr. and Mrs. Hopper, schoolteachers en route to Cabancalan, a pueblo a few miles further south.

Upstairs I found the new schoolteachers; and what a surprise it was to see a California girl in that old convent! The Hoppers were new types of pedagogues, bringing with them to war-worn Negros something of the sunlight and cheer of their own Golden State beyond the Pacific.

That night we had a jolly party for supper—four Americans gathered around the scarred narra (Philippine mahogany) table in the half-ruined convent, where white-robed friars had been more in keeping with surroundings. We were all young, and all intensely interested in the fascinating book of the tropics opening before us; in Negros with its Old World Spanish-Malayan civilization just receiving a few first dents from American ideas carried by the army, by the Constabulary, and now by the pedagogues who were to attempt to compress into ten years the education of centuries.

Smith paid my men, left a few supplies and many words of encouragement, then sailed off south along the coast to Sipalay. The Hoppers went on to Cabancalan by bull-cart and carromata. I dropped back into the routine of drill and post administration; but my first adventure with the babaylanes was at hand.

VIII - A Night Raid by Outlaws

ONE NIGHT WHEN A SILVERY MOON RODE HIGH above sleeping Negros, I was awakened by Presidente Serafin, who told me that a messenger had come flying from a hacienda a few miles inland with news of a babaylan raid. At ten o'clock, when the man left his hacienda, the outlaws were robbing the buildings and mistreating the *taos*.

While pulling on shoes and leggins I learned that the raiding band was small—only a dozen babaylanes with three or four rifles; further details came as I buckled on revolver and snatched up carbine. My men were already astir in their quarters beneath the convent; so that within a few minutes of the messenger's arrival I was on the trail with ten men panting behind me and the brown back of the half-naked guide basted with perspiration just ahead.

How we hit that trail inland! Half-walking, half-running, we passed through the quiet streets of the pueblo; under a grove of cocos where the ghostly light traced queer patterns through fronded boughs; over dried rice paddies where stubble crackled underfoot; up steep grassy hills, between groves of bamboo never more feathery and fernlike than when seen by moonlight. On, on, at top speed, until cartridge-filled belts rasped sweaty bodies, so that a halt was necessary for readjustment.

Then on again with the lope of wolves on a hot trail, always hoping that the babaylanes would not escape before we could give them a volley and show that the Constabulary was organized in southern Negros. Out from the bamboo groves to the rolling plateau that lies between Himamaylan and Isabela, until at last a dark mass ahead and some flickering lights were pronounced by the guide to be the Soledad hacienda where the babaylanes were at their midnight games.

To steady the men, I halted the detachment and disposed my forces. I sent a sergeant with four men and the guide to encircle the hacienda and block the trail leading from it to the dark mountains for which the babaylanes would break when disturbed. When the sergeant was in position I cautiously advanced toward the lights and the noise that swelled as we drew nearer the buildings.

Around the houses and camarines, men and women held resin torches which were scarcely needed in the bright moonlight but had been lit as fancied protection against those wild beasts of the night, the babaylanes. We crept nearer, taking cover behind clumps of brush or sugarcane until we could make out figures and hear the conversation of the disturbed *taos*, buzzing like a nest of bumblebees. Spears glinted in the torchlight and I had to restrain my men from firing.

Seeing no men with rifles, I told one of the soldiers to challenge. Answer came that the babaylanes had departed, taking with them two *dalagas* (young women) with much palay and sugar in bayone sacks of matting, some *carabao* and horses.

We went forward and were immediately surrounded by a gesticulating crowd of peasantry, anxious to relate the happenings of the raid. The outlaws had left about twenty minutes earlier, impressing a dozen *taos* to carry their plunder. Weeping parents implored me to save their daughters who had been carried off to become concubines of Papa Isio or his chiefs. Without waiting for details, we dashed through the hacienda out to the mountain trail. My force was swollen by several *taos* armed with spears and long talibong (fighting *bolos*); so, guides I had in numbers to follow the outlaws' tracks.

Hot on the scent, we fairly tore along the trail where breast-high cogon drenched us with dew that mattered not, as we were long ago wet through with sweat. Ahead, a pair of *taos* with spears ready poised set a pace that taxed us to follow. Mile after mile thus passed; now we dropped down to cross a stream and the cool mountain water was grateful to our scalded feet; then up a steep bank and on, always on, until the blue-black mountains took shape and a few trees dotted the slopes up which we toiled.

It was near daybreak when the foremost guide stumbled over something in the trail. It was a bayone of palay; and thereafter we quickly passed more, for the babaylanes were dropping their plunder to seek safety in more speedy flight. Forward! Forward! Ever more quickly forward! A challenging but scared voice ahead, a few dim forms, and behind me the soldiers rattled their guns and cartridges snapped into breech-blocks.

"Unload! Wait for orders! Esperan ustedes, soldados!" I shouted.

The forms ahead were the impressed laborers, who held up their hands, yelling words of friendship and beseechment.

The babaylanes were but a few minutes in front. So now added caution was demanded, for from behind any tree or bush or thicker clump of grass might come a rattle of rifle fire. My guides bent almost to the ground, but pushed bravely forward. More bayones of sugar and palay were passed, and then some friendly *taos* holding the *carabao* and horses which had been stolen a few hours earlier.

We had at all events made the babaylanes drop their loot; but still there were the two dalagas to take back to their wailing parents, and an accounting to be made with Papa Isio's scoundrels.

Just at daybreak we dipped to a stream at the foot of the steeper mountains. And there, quietly bathing their feet, we found two ox-eyed peasant girls, neither the worse for their adventure nor over-demonstrative at their rescue.

Perhaps the life of an outlaw's mistress held advantages over pounding out palay for stern parents on the hacienda. Quien sabe?

But now my men were about exhausted. Since midnight we had come fifteen or twenty miles at breakneck speed. We carried neither rations nor supplies for a more extended expedition. We were on the edge of the forest jungle, and although the babaylanes were but a few minutes ahead, they were aware of pursuit, and could easily scatter into the sheltering bosque.

Reluctantly I abandoned the chase and turned for home; not dissatisfied, however, at the results achieved, for we had recovered practically all the booty, and, it might be said, the beauty also, for the harried maidens padded contentedly along with my soldiers, who were not averse to this opportunity to shine as rescuing heroes.

A few days later I received from my senior inspector a letter that reproved me with some severity for making an expedition against the babaylanes, who were, so the letter said, negotiating with Colonel Kennon for surrender. I swore softly to myself and relieved my feelings by writing a communication to the senior inspector in which I stated that the babaylanes showed their desire to surrender in a queer way.

That little midnight hike was merely training exercise. Papa Isio did not surrender, and there was much work ahead for the Constabulary. Toward the end of April 1902, Colonel Kennon called me to Isabela to confer about Constabulary cooperation in a drive through the mountains against the Pope's headquarters, which was reported to be at Macabong, three days' march through the mountain jungle from Isabela. Two army and one Constabulary expeditions were to start from Isabela by different trails, converging on Macabong.

I was ordered to leave at midnight, April 22. Gathering together my best men from Himamaylan and from the sub-post at Payao, recently established near the scene of my first exploits against the babaylanes at Soledad hacienda, I prepared to show that the Constabulary could equal the army at hunting outlaws.

Indeed, the great truth was already dawning upon me that the way to hunt outlaws in the jungle was not in the army way of textbook strategy and tactics, of converging columns and large, slow-moving expeditions which arrived always to find the bird flown from the nest. I was beginning to understand that to hunt outlaws, babaylanes, pulajanes (fanatical outlaws), Moros, or any other malefactor of the hills and the jungles, it was necessary to learn from the enemy and beat him at his own game—mobility and knowledge of the country.

The time was to come within a few months when I knew southern Negros, plain, foothills, and mountains, as well as or better than the outlaws; and when I could gauge with nicety just how many men it would take to persuade them to stand and fight rather than run away.

With no army commissary from which to draw supplies, I purchased in the tiendas of Isabela rice, dried fish, canned goods, and a few bottles of "square-face" gin. I am not a believer in too free use of alcohol, particularly in the tropics; but my men were poorly equipped for cold nights in the higher mountains, and I must say that a swig of gin on reaching camp, wet and weary, often pulled us together to make ourselves comfortable for the night.

These supplies were done in sacks and bayones and loaded on twenty cargadores, or porters. The soldiers carried guns, ammunition, haversacks, and blanket rolls. I carried my Winchester carbine and a part of my own spare kit, the same as the soldiers, and found that by so doing I could get more out of them than if I hired special cargadores for a lot of personal baggage; though as rations were consumed, we all loaded our blankets and spare accoutrements on the sturdy porters.

Our guide was an old Visayan named Julian. He was reported to have been a babaylan whose daughter had been taken by Papa Isio as an additional concubine, and that Julian was now thirsting for vengeance. Certainly, he knew the mountain trails and took me safely over them on this and many a subsequent expedition.

This was the first of scores of expeditions I was to make in the mountains and swamps of the Philippines during the next four or five years, until I was severely wounded in the knee in Sulu in 1906. In the equipment and conduct of such an expedition there was a technique as different from warfare on the regular army plan as my barefoot constables were from a battery of horse artillery.

IX - Jungle Trails

At midnight we started from Isabela by the light of a gibbous moon. Before dawn we entered the open bosque of the foothills when an eclipse of the moon occurred, causing us to halt while darkness spread over the earth. It was ghostly to sit there in the long wet grass and watch a black shadow steal over Diana's face.[11]

Soldiers and cargadores were visibly disturbed; and perhaps considered it an evil omen until I remarked that just as the moon's light was put out, so would the Constabulary blot out babaylanism in Negros.

The eclipse passed. The short tropical dawn changed into glaring day, and we pushed on. The comparatively open foothills ran abruptly into a steep, densely-forested mountainside up which our trail led through thickets of bojo bamboo interlacing overhead. We were forced to crawl along a trail more frequented by wild hogs than by human beings, and out of the bojo thickets through a grove of buttressed giant trees which my soldiers said yielded almaciga. Indeed, during a halt, Julian dug from between the roots a mass of that fossilized gum which is the basis of varnish and shellac.[12]

Often, we clambered up slopes so steep that guns were slung over shoulders while we clung to the long rattan vines that grew everywhere. Although the sun was now high, yet in the depth of the forest all was cool and still, with the only sign of life an occasional flock of giant hornbills noisily flapping from our path, a wild hog dashing into the underbrush, or the booming of a big balud pigeon from the treetops.

Over the mountain ridge we slid down into the narrow canyon of the Guintubjan River, which roared over a boulder-strewn bed. After a late and hasty breakfast, we hiked up the river, jumping from rock to rock, wading the pool, and always keenly on the watch for signs of the babaylanes, for Julian assured me that any men we might now see would be "gente de Papa Isio"—outlaws on the trail for game or loot.

Once we sighted up a tributary creek three men with spears. With two of my swiftest men I gave chase; but the quarry leapt like mountain goat over the boulders, to disappear in the ever-sheltering forest followed by a bullet or two from my Winchester. I was still ignorant of the need of stealthy, catlike approach toward the outlaws.

Near sunset, when we were tired and sodden by hours of hiking in the water, we came to a spot where the river widened to form a sandy beach sheltered by an overhanging crag of rock. The ashes of many fires showed that it was a camping place often used by the babaylanes; and Julian said that the trail here left the river and that we had better camp for the night. Soon fires were blazing, clothes drying, rice washed and boiling, dried fish broiling, sweet potatoes roasting. The rice was cooked in hollow joints of bojo bamboo, quickly cut by cargadores from nearby thickets.

These natural cooking utensils were most interesting. A joint of bamboo, about three feet long and two or three inches in diameter, was filled with rice and water, the open end then plugged with a wad of grass, and the bamboo placed on the fire; and when the green bamboo was charred through, the rice was cooked.

It came out of the improvised pot a solid cylinder of cereal with a flavor of bamboo that hungry soldiers did not find objectionable. The rice, with a little dried fish, and a few camotes, made my men an ample meal. What an advantage in mobility this simple commissary arrangement gave compared to the heavy cooking utensils, cans of hardtack, beef, beans, and other impedimenta of a detachment of American soldiers!

How that night on the sandbar creeps back along memory's chain! The murmur of the rippling river and beyond the water a dark mass of trees with cicadas and bell-bugs stridulating their nightly song; fireflies flickering in the jungle; silver stars speckling the black velvet sky above the trees; our fires under the rock making chiaroscuro of the camp; soldiers curled in blankets near the warmth; a pile of packs with half-naked cargadores asleep atop sacks of rice; motionless sentries above and below the camp; and myself, with blanket over my shoulders, watching all, unable at first to sleep for the novelty of a scene which was to become as familiar to me during the coming years as is a crush at Brooklyn Bridge to a New York commuter.

At dawn we were off again, over more mountains, following ill-defined trails through virgin forest. But Julian unerringly sniffed his way along. I learned to love that squat, bow-legged, gray-haired old brown man, shuffling along just ahead of me, bolo in hand, slashing away at overhanging vines and brush, always with every sense attuned for danger. When in the jungle Julian was rather a panther on the trail than a human being. At home in the pueblo he was a mild and inoffensive old peasant.

After hours of such toilsome hiking Julian halted, whispering that he heard voices ahead. With ten men I crept to the edge of a caingin, which could be nothing but a lair of the babaylanes. We snaked through the undergrowth until within sight of two huts in the center of a clearing where corn, palay, and camotes were growing between fallen and burnt trees.

Before we could surround the huts three men bolted into the forest, their flight accelerated by loads of buckshot from my excited soldiers, who in a yelling skirmish line led by Julian and myself, and all slipping and jumping from log to log, closed on the huts. Bloody tracks showed that one babaylan was wounded. Inside the shacks we found palay, camotes, and other foodstuffs with several spears and *bolos* as well as documents proving that the occupants were babaylanes. Julian said that the caingin was known as Cabantaiang and was one of Papa Isio's outposts.

The rest of my detachment and the cargadores came tumbling into the clearing; soldiers and cargadores dug up camotes or filled their packs with heads of corn, all very happy at the pitiful loot as soldiers have always been and always will be

Till the war-drum throbs no longer, and the battle flags are furled, In the Parliament of Man, the Federation of the World.[13]

Often it went against the grain to destroy those mountain clearings hardly won by men from the ever-encroaching jungles; but if outlawry was to be stamped out, there was nothing else to do; each clearing was a refuge for the babaylanes, and honest folk could find land aplenty in the lowlands, without rivaling the eagles to place such aeries in the mountains.

Also, I suppose there are those who would criticize us for firing at fleeing men. Yet it is necessary to remember that those fugitives were criminals whom justice could reach by no other process than the bullet—swift warrant, subpoena, judge, and jury all in one.

When we came to clearings of the mountain aborigines, the Bukidnon, we scrupulously respected their belongings or, if necessary, to levy to satisfy our hunger, we paid in full for everything taken. On these first expeditions I did not visit any Bukidnon villages, but on later hikes found many of these attractive wild tribesmen with whom we made friends, and who, when the Constabulary showed stronger than the babaylanes, aided us with information against the latter.

And as far as the babaylanes were concerned, they had every advantage in the game. I understand that hunting out a wounded tiger in a nullah is dangerous sport; but it must be as tiddlywinks to football compared with chasing outlaws in the Philippine mountains, where they have every superiority of cover, knowledge of terrain, and opportunity to strike the first blow. Let any critic try the nerve-racking sport of hunting well-armed babaylanes, pulajanes, Moros, or "common or garden" *ladrones* before he censures the Constabulary for firing quickly—and to kill.

Refreshed by the outlaws' provender, we again swung on through the mountains; and after a time came out of the forests on the edge of a precipice. Hundreds of feet below was a large caingin with several huts scattered along a rivulet. Old Julian confessed that for once he had lost his bearings and thought that we had better capture a guide. Forms could be seen around the huts; but between us and them was the almost perpendicular cliff. Hand over hand, at imminent risk to life and limb, we scrambled down; and when we dropped into the valley I would not have made the descent again to capture Papa Isio himself.

Thick underbrush along the rivulet enabled us to approach within two hundred yards of the first hut before the babaylanes got our scent. Then five men and one woman harlequined through a window and leapt for the forest. My soldiers shouted that if they stopped, they would not be hurt, but our yells only served to make their flight swifter.

Opening fire, we pursued. The men escaped, but the woman received a slight buckshot wound in her calf and fell, lustily screaming. Nothing could be gleaned from her as to our whereabouts; and when I dressed her wound with first-aid bandages, she howled the louder.

Julian thought that if we went on down the valley, we would strike a trail with which he would be familiar, so we made the woman comfortable in one of the huts and proceeded. After several hours' hard hiking in the river bed we found a faint trace leading from the canyon, which ended, however, in an abandoned caingin with a ruined hut and overgrown camote patch. There we camped for the night, and the next morning wearily retraced our steps to the clearing where we had left the wounded woman.

It was clear that we must capture a man of the mountains for a guide, so I adopted a ruse which proved successful. When within a mile or so of the caingin, I picked out five husky cargadores who had shown themselves particularly hardy and venturesome. Promising a reward and arming them with captured lances and talibongs, I sent them ahead with instructions to approach the caingin, shouting that they were soldiers of Papa Isio.

With their spears and *bolos*, they certainly looked tough enough to be mistaken for babaylanes. They went on. We followed; and when near the clearing heard a great hullabaloo. Dashing forward, we found the ruse successful. The five cargadores were holding a struggling disarmed mountaineer. Seven more armed babaylanes, who were making to rescue their comrade, fled at our approach.

From the prisoner, I learned that the clearing was called Tugas, and was a camote patch to supply Papa Isio's main camp at Macabong, which, after persuasion, he said was six hours' hard hiking north. Of course, he did not define time by hours, but pointed to where the sun would be when we reached Macabong.

Now we had a guide who could supplement Julian's knowledge of the trails and take us into the heart of the babaylan country. The prisoner confessed himself a subject of Papa Isio, but not one of his soldiers; he had, however, been in the mountains for many years. I did not inquire into the circumstances of his flight from the lowlands, but treated him well and promised substantial reward for faithful service. We took the precaution of binding his arms securely behind with ropes of green rattan, though, and Julian took the leading rope when we started again.

Our prisoner confidently led us on a trail which, after traversing a few miles of mountain jungle, came out at a clearing on the western slope of a high mountain. There we fired at the disappearing babaylanes and rushed into the caingin, to emerge, for the first time in days, from encircling forests. Before us stretched miles and miles of mountains, sloping down to a strip of glorious blue sea, four thousand feet below; and beyond the sea was another island, gray-blue through the heat haze. We had crossed Negros; the sea was the Straits of Tanon and the distant island Cebu. Now Julian got his bearings and said that we were not far from Macabong. Retracing our steps, we crossed another high mountain and camped for the night in a gorge on the other side.

Next morning, we passed clearing after clearing, generally deserted by the babaylanes, who now knew that we were on their trail. But in one caingin we surprised several armed men and killed one of them, capturing also a boy of about seven years, whom we took along with us. He was a typical child of the mountains—only a G-string clothing his brown body.

A street in old Cebu

After being with our column several days he declared that he did not want to stay in the mountains. He attached himself to me so faithfully that I took him to the lowlands, where he became a loyal member of my household. Celedonio, as was his name, remained with me for nearly ten years; in fact, until I was married, when he went to live with another ex-dependent of mine near Manila. Burying the dead babaylan, we continued on to Macabong. We were now on a rolling plateau and the blanketing forest sometimes opened out into glades of grass and brush—second growth where caingins had been burned. Ahead was the smoke of a burning hut and on approaching it we saw a large body of armed men. Thinking it might be the main body of Papa Isio come out to give battle, I hastily formed a skirmish line; but the blue shirts and Stetson hats of a mixed detachment of American soldiers and Scouts showed up and soon we were fraternizing and exchanging experiences.

The army detachment, fifty strong, was commanded by a corporal of the Sixth Infantry, as the officer who started with the expedition and had fallen sick and returned to Isabela. They had as guide an ex-colonel of babaylanes, Marcelo. He said we were but an hour from Macabong, so, joining forces, we pressed on to Papa Isio's stronghold.

We came to the foot of a steep hill up which led a narrow trail; on either side was the almost impenetrable jungle. Marcelo said that Macabong was just on the other side of the hill, and his knees trembled as he spoke. It was clear that we might expect a fight, so with twenty men of both forces I clambered up the trail, the soldiers following in single file. There was no sound but the labored breathing of the men behind and the thumping of my own heart.

Up, step by step, every moment expecting a volley from above. The forest thinned out; a skyline appeared—we must be nearing the babaylan trenches. Still no shots. A last crouching upward spring! I was out on top and with a skirmish line of men streaming on either side swept into the little plateau, where refuged the Pope of the mountains. Macabong was deserted: there were two-score houses, a wooden church, and a large palm-thatched barracks, but only one babaylan, evidently left as outpost, who dropped from a house and made good his flight despite the rattle of bullets that followed him into the forest. The Pope had well chosen his pontifical seat. It commanded a magnificent prospect over the east coast of Negros, the sea, and Cebu Island; while immediately below snuggled a valley, hemmed in by mountains and dotted with caingins which supplied the babaylanes with food. It was their granary; and we were the rats to destroy it.

That evening just before dusk Lieutenant Young of the Sixth Infantry arrived with the third expedition, three days out from La Castellana. That night over a roaring fire, made of material from the babaylan houses, we swopped experiences of the trail.

Next morning, we sent out mixed detachments to destroy the babaylanes' food supplies in nearby clearings and in the valley below. At daybreak the following morning, we burned Macabong church, cuartel, and village, then gaily turned for home. Young and I set a hard pace, each eager to show that his men could out-hike the other's. We made the thirty or forty miles to Isabela over steep mountain trails in thirty-six hours.

I reported to Colonel Kennon the Constabulary's share of the round-up, telegraphed the results to the senior inspector, and hiked my men on to Himamaylan, well satisfied that they had kept the pace with Regulars and Scouts. And I had begun my apprenticeship in man-hunting in the jungle. It was dawning on me that in order to get a fight out of the outlaws it was necessary to proportion the expedition to the job in hand and not scare the bird by an unwieldy snare. In an old report of that expedition that lies before me I find that I ended thus:

The conduct of the detachment under my command was excellent, and they bore the hardships of the expedition without a murmur. Many of the men's feet were badly cut on the sharp rocks. At night the thin blankets were poor protection against the drizzling mountain mists. We ran short of rations, and were obliged to eke them out with roots, camotes, and corn. The distance traveled in the eight days I would estimate at one hundred and fifty miles, all over mountain trails of the worst possible description.

X - A Desperate Venture

SOON AFTER OUR COMBINED EXPEDITION TO MACABONG the Sixth Infantry was withdrawn from Isabela and returned to the United States for a well-earned rest after more than two years' service against insurgents and brigands. The Philippine Scouts were withdrawn from Castellana and I was ordered to assume responsibility for law and order in southern Negros: about 2,500 square miles.

With much regret at leaving Presidente Serafin I abandoned the station at Himamaylan and transferred my detachment of twenty-five men to Isabela.

They were still improperly equipped; but they were now well drilled and disciplined. Nevertheless, with my few Filipino soldiers it seemed difficult at first to substitute the American troops, whose superior organization and equipment gave them the prestige that we lacked. And to any armed force, particularly to a military-police force, prestige is worth more than numbers.

Now, although the people of Isabela received me cordially enough, they made plain their doubt that the Constabulary could police the valley and give protection against the babaylanes. Indeed, before the troops were withdrawn, many round-robin protests had been sent to Bacolod and even to the governor-general of the Philippines.

So, it seemed that I must immediately attempt some blow at the babaylanes that would give the Constabulary proper standing. Moreover, if Colonel Kennon's estimate of the numbers and arms of Papa Isio's bands was correct—which I had no reason to doubt—only bold action on my part would keep them from taking immediate advantage of the withdrawal of the troops.

I took station at Isabela about the middle of May. Ten days later, on May 26, 1902, to be precise, the Constabulary struck Papa Isio a blow from which he never recovered, for we fought him to a finish in his own mountain stronghold, five thousand feet up in the clouds.

After the previous expedition it became clear that the Pope must have some lair in the mountains more secure and better fortified than Macabong, where he had never intended to make a stand; for although Macabong was conveniently situated near rich caingins, where the babaylanes could obtain supplies of camotes, maize, and palay, it was too open for easy defense.

However, there were scores of peaks along the Negros cordilleras any one of which might be made into an almost inaccessible camp.

In Himamaylan, Presidente Serafin had told me that there were rumors of Papa Isio's headquarters on the summit of a high mountain, so strongly fortified that the babaylanes reckoned it impregnable; and often when riding between Himamaylan and Isabela I had surveyed the dark brooding mountains to the south and east and wondered which of the clear-cut peaks that rose above forested slopes held the aery of the pope.

No sooner were we settled in Isabela than I sent for my old guide, Julian Enserna. At dusk one evening he came shuffling up the wooden steps of my nip a house fronting the plaza.

"Now, Julian," I began, "where did Papa Isio go from Macabong?" The directness of question was foolish; but I had not then learned that the way to get information from a man of Malayan blood is to start a long way from the objective and close in gradually by concentric circles of thought. The old too moved uneasily, fumbling with bare toes at the split-bamboo floor, and it took much direct and indirect questioning to get out of him the information that I felt sure he possessed.

But when he was thoroughly convinced of my intention to hunt out the Pope, he broke silence, saying that he knew the stronghold but had not told me about it because he did not want me to be killed. Then he told me the name of the mountain on the summit of which the fortified camp was situated; it was Mansalanao, one of the highest peaks south of Canlaon; but he was quite emphatic about the utter impossibility of capturing Papa Isio's cuartel general. Had he been there?

Yes, he had been to the mountain years ago, gathering bejuco (rattan), but had never been to the top, as it was very steep—just like that, and he put up his hand almost perpendicularly. However, some Bukidnon friends of his had been to the summit, carrying supplies for Papa Isio, and they had told him about the babaylanes' trenches on the mountaintop, and how the approach was straight up to the trenches, and that all timber and brush had been cleared away to give open fire from above;

indeed, it was so steep that ladders of bejuco were let down from the trenches to the trail beneath.

Moreover, within the fortifications were piles of stones and sharpened hardwood, double-pointed throwing spears called planquetas, all ready to throw down on an attacking force.

Also there were huge rocks as much as twelve men could move, poised on the parapet wall and held by ropes of rattan so that the slash of a bolo would send the boulders crashing down the mountain; while, as the final dissentient, Julian lamented that there was only one trail up Mansalanao, and that one was narrow and sown with man-traps—suyacs (sharp pointed stakes) underfoot and balatigs (spring-traps) in the brush.

Furthermore, he informed me there were many houses on top of the mountain—which from his description I imagined to be an old volcanic crater—and many women and children, and that there were outposts down the mountain so that it was impossible to surprise the babaylanes; and as good measure, they had good rifles and plenty of ammunition.

Altogether it was not a cheering prospect and, as the narrative will show, every detail was correct. Julian begged me not to attempt to take Mansalanao; but assuming the greatest confidence, I told him to return to Payao and say nothing, but be ready to go with me when I sent for him. Also, I impressed him with the belief that I had an anting-anting (amulet or charm) stronger than Papa Isio's.

The Visayans are great believers in the virtues of anting-anting, which are no more than amulets to ward off the Evil One and preserve the wearer from *bolos*, bullets, or other misfortune. Papa Isio was strong on the dispensation of these charms, giving one to each of his followers which usually took the form of a scrap of paper covered with crude writing and figures, a cross, a few Ave Marias, some dog-Latin and the impress of a wooden seal, "Gobierno Revolucionairio de Negros," or some other high-sounding title. The bit of paper was sewn into a bag and suspended from the neck in locket fashion.

Sometimes a bullet or even a colored stone was the anting-anting or, for that matter, a bit of dried snake or lizard in a little bottle, or a piece of colored glass; and on one occasion I took from the neck of a dead babaylan the glass stopper of a bottle.

Poor, deluded folk of the mountains! How often have I seen their still bodies with anting-antings pierced by bullets. The mystery was how, with our frequent killing of the babaylanes, Papa Isio managed to sustain the prestige of his charms; but somehow or another he kept up the delusion, for we never killed a babaylan without finding the little bag around his neck, generally with the scrap of paper and Papa Isio's scrawling signature, "Dionicio Papa."

Quietly I prepared for the expedition to Mansalanao. But it is useless to pretend that I relished the job ahead. I did not, I was scared to death, and know that the chances against success were about a hundred to one. But pride of race and corps drove; while I knew that if I could defeat Papa Isio in his stronghold, the Constabulary would thereafter have a comparatively easy time. Moreover, it is usually sound strategy to attack first. The assumption of confidence has won many a fight against odds.

One night toward the end of May we left Payao, a village three miles from Isabela, at moonrise, about nine o'clock: seventeen soldiers, old Julian, fourteen picked cargadores, and myself. In Payao and Isabela I had given out that we were again headed for Macabong; and for several hours after leaving Payao we marched in a direction opposite to our objective. It was fairly certain that Papa Isio had spies in the pueblos and that news of our departure would speed through the mountains in the telepathic manner that word is conveyed among semi-civilized peoples.

By moonlight we crossed the rice paddies beyond Payao, forded two rivers waist-deep, and at daybreak were out of the cogon foothills and in the depths of the forest. Then we left the Macabong trail to cut our way by compass course through bojo bamboo thickets along a steep hogback—although Julian scarcely needed the compass to find the trail that led from Payao to Mansalanao.

As the sun rose, we suffered terribly from want of water. Canteens as yet formed no part of the Constabulary equipment, and as we had omitted to provide ourselves with bamboo tubes of water, we had drunk nothing since leaving the river overnight. After hours of hiking we finally emerged from the forest on a grassy upland where Julian found water in a little gully just as we were about exhausted; in fact, one of the soldiers, Private Cayetano

Amar, had succumbed from fatigue and thirst, being carried the last mile to water.

But when our thirst was slaked, we were soon revived by the cooler air of the plateau. We were now some two thousand feet above the Binalbagan Valley, whose smiling fields of green sugarcane and rice, dotted with little white pueblos, glittered under a high sun.

Ahead stretched the cogon upland, shimmering under the heat haze through which we saw a line of dark forest into which we must later plunge; while beyond and above the forest a mountain peak silhouetted clear against an azure sky. Julian grunted, "Mansalanao," and a quiver of excitement ran through my men. The mountain was twenty miles away in a beeline and that meant two or three days, hard hiking through the jungles over intervening ridges and ravines.

But there was Mansalanao, our goal or our grave or, perhaps, both. I marveled that I had never guessed that that particular mountain was Papa Isio's headquarters. It was plainly visible from Isabela and was the highest peak south of Canlaon, probably between five and six thousand feet in height.

Shaped like a cone truncated just below the apex, it plainly showed ancient volcanic action, and that it had at some remote period "blown its head off." As one fascinated, I gazed at it: how clear and commanding it rose above lesser peaks, how steep its slopes! Could we hope to win up there against great odds? I looked at my men. They looked at me. Then I smiled a confident smile that was perfect dissimulation of my feelings.

"Ha! mis soldados," I laughed in broken Spanish, "el Papa teme mucho los Constabularios! Miran Ustedea como se escode en los montes mas altos." (The Pope is much afraid of the Constabulary. See how he hides on the highest mountains.)

The contagion of my forced spirits ran through the easily influenced soldiers, though I noticed that one or two of the older Guardia Civil non-coms shook their heads in doubt. For this desperate expedition I had carefully chosen my men, picking the youngest and most daredevil soldiers, but including one or two old non-commissioned officers as ballast; and this tale will tell how youth won the fight, while age, with which comes too careful weighing of chances, lagged behind.

We siestaed beneath some giant rocks that cropped up hoary-headed above the cogon. Then up and on over a rolling plateau of country that was like a park, in sharp contrast with the dank jungles we had left behind. Tree ferns filled shady hollows and thorn trees dotted the cogon, which was nowhere tall enough to impede our passage. Now and then a frightened deer dashed off at our approach. It was a pleasant bit of trail. But ahead lay the gloomy forests.

Suddenly we came out on a broad, hard-beaten path, cutting a swath through the cogon, and curving ahead until lost in the forests in the direction of Mansalanao.

"Camino Real de los babaylanes," cried a soldier, and the others laughed at his joke. A camino real is the Spanish "royal road"—a highway. It was a fine broad trail, showing that there was much unsuspected traffic between Papa Isio's headquarters and the lowland pueblos. Julian grinned. The old scoundrel had long known this trail. But for months he had taken army expeditions in every direction except the one that led to the Pope's real headquarters. However, not much blame was his; for he doubtless fully believed that by attacking Mansalanao we went to certain death—unless my anting-anting was stronger than that of Papa Isio.

We pressed forward across the plateau; the wall of forest loomed nearer; at last the trees sheltered us from the setting sun. Behind lay the sun-washed cogon plateau; ahead loomed the dark, damp jungle forest. There was something forbidding in the contrast, something ominous in the shadowed depths into which we must plunge.

Julian ran over to where a giant bamboo drooped gracefully outward from the forest wall, and with a well-directed slash of the talibong bolo cut down a thirty-foot stem, while with a few more strokes he made a sharp-edged stick about two feet long. I asked him for what it was intended.

"Limatuk, po!" (Leeches, sir), he answered. We were to enter a belt of forest infested with these blood-sucking pests, so the soldiers and cargadores also cut bamboo scrapers with which to remove them from bare limbs. Then we dived into the forest.

The hard dry trail of the cogon was ended, and now underfoot was dank leafy mold with rattan and other vines crisscrossing the path, festooning trees, climbing up toward the life-giving sun that never penetrated the forest depths; and in the mold, on every twig and leaf underfoot, alongside or hanging from above, were the wretched limatuks, which, though scarcely longer and thicker than a pin, would after a few minutes' adhesion to human skin swell to the size of a man's little finger.

Every little while I called a halt, to let the cargadores scrape limatuks from their skin, while the soldiers and myself removed our shoes, often to find leeches that had wormed through eyelet holes or between folds of clothing. That is, some of the soldiers removed their shoes, for others were still barefooted.

Nothing kept the leech pests entirely out, though when the Constabulary adopted woolen puttees, we found them almost complete protection. I discovered, too, that salt liberally rubbed on socks was a specific; but as mountain hiking involved wading of rivers the salt soon washed off.

If the leeches got into nose, eyes, or ear, they were really dangerous. Their bite anywhere on the body, if not rendered aseptic, might result in a frightful tropical ulcer as big as a dollar and eating to the bone. I have doctored many such sores on soldiers and on brother officers.

On one expedition I was followed by a dog, but never repeated the experiment; the poor beast was so attacked by leeches as to be entirely blinded. They fastened on his eyeballs, and the first intimation of their attacks was that the animal wobbled helplessly from side to side, scraping his head along the ground. From his eyes we removed at least a dozen bloated leeches. His sight was ruined.

XI - Deeper in the Jungle

For two days we hiked through the forest; down one mountain, up another; across rushing rivers; along steep hogbacks; through thickets of bojo-bamboo—the steady, slogging hiking that tires body and soddens soul. Always the towering tree trunks were around us like cathedral columns, while verdure vaulted overhead so that we rarely saw the sun. We passed no clearings.

At night we camped in the jungles. The men cut bamboo and leaves of the anajao palm with which to erect fragile sleeping shelters. At dawn we rose, stiff and damp; at dusk we camped, tired and wet.

On the morning of the third day we were resting at a place where our trail turned from a river bed into the forest. Julian had advanced a few yards to make certain of the trail. Suddenly he ran quickly back and, with finger to lips, whispered that he heard men coming through the forest.

Babaylanes they must be; for we were now within a few hours of Mansalanao. Enjoining silence, I advanced up the trail with a few men, posted them in the brush and behind trees, and took similar shelter myself.

With Julian by my side, I crouched behind a bush, whence I could see a few yards up the trail. All was still; only the iterative cicada broke the silence of the jungle. Like Roderick Dhu's rebels we awaited the babaylanes who would soon find that...

> *... every tuft of broom gives life*
> *To plaided warriors armed for strife,*[14]

...though, to be sure, my poor, half-equipped handful of Constabularies was less romantic than Roderick's "full five hundred men."

Soon there was a distant rustle in the jungle, a low hum of voices coming nearer, a grunt as of a man bearing a burden; and then through the trees he came, padding heavily.

Naked save for a breech-clout, he was carrying an enormous load of bejuco. Sweat ran down his copper skin; yet in his right hand and serving as a staff was a long broad-bladed spear, while by a string around his naked waist hung a vicious talibong.

Behind him followed a boy and another man, similarly laden and armed.

They grunted under their burdens. But they grunted louder when I shoved the muzzle of my Winchester into the foremost man's face, while Julian and the soldiers quickly disarmed and secured all three before they could get the loads off their backs.

Other men, coming down the trail, heard the slight scuffle and fled up the mountainside. I sent five men after them. Several shots were fired.

One babaylan was killed and another wounded. We had surprised a "trade convoy" of Papa Isio's. Our prisoners were some of his Bukidnon cargadores taking bejuco to Payao and escorted by two babaylan soldiers, one of whom we killed.

The prisoners confessed that they were "gente de Papa Isio" on their way to Payao, ostensibly to vend bejuco but actually to obtain salt and other items of which the Pope stood in need. At the same time, they were to spy out the situation in the lowlands and size up the Constabulary forces at Payao and Isabela.

In a trice the prisoners' arms were bound behind with rattan from their own bundles.

We carried them along, unwilling guides, for they would be extremely useful when we approached Mansalanao and had to dodge the man-traps with which the trail was reputed to be sown. It was only to be hoped that the escaping babaylanes would not reach Mansalanao before us to give the alarm. To avoid this, we quickly took to the trail again.

Down the mountain, from where our river issued from Mansalanao's bosom, echoed the roar of a waterfall. After crossing yet another mountain we descended into the canyon of a considerable river; and as, knee-deep in water, we hiked upstream the canyon opened out. The banks became less precipitous and clothed with giant tigbao (cane) grass instead of forest growth. We splashed around a bend. And then the cone of Mansalanao was in full view, now quite close and towering straight up from a strip of level land that here bordered the river.

Standing in the stream with water swirling between my legs, I straightened out my straggling column. Then the Bukidnon showed us where a trail led up the river bank, but hidden by the giant tigbao grass, twenty or thirty feet high and with stalks resembling sugarcane. He said that we were near babaylan houses, so, creeping along a natural tunnel under the tigbao, we cautiously approached a pretty clearing with two huts.

As it was visible from the summit of Mansalanao, I kept my men under cover of tigbao and brush. The huts were deserted. The Bukidnon said that all the people of the clearing had gone to Papa Isio's camp for a fiesta. From where we sought shelter Mansalanao stood out like a lone pine on a ridge at sunset. A few hundred yards' distant the foot of the peak ran into comparatively level land along the river, but above the mountain rose at an angle of forty-five degrees. It was heavily covered with forest and jungle growth to within a couple of hundred feet of the summit or crater. On the rim of the crater were several huts which, so the Bukidnon said, were shelters at the trenches. The village was further back, over the rim. Among the huts moved antlike human forms who must be the babaylanes, and one of them might even be Papa Isio himself. We were near the end of our journey—perhaps in more senses than one.

Through my field-glasses I studied the mountain, the summit of which appeared about 2,500 feet above our resting-place. It was clear that the jungle-clad slopes offered no opportunity for approach except along the babaylanes' own trail, winding up a ridge which to the naked eye appeared a mere furrow down the mountain, but which the glasses revealed as a precipitous hogback, flanked by gullies hundreds of feet in depth.

It was late forenoon on May 26, 1902. I ordered the men to make a meal of the cooked rice and dried fish that had been prepared in the morning. I sat alone on a blackened log that had resisted the fires of many dry-season burnings and thought out my scheme of attack. Private Fernandez, who served as my cook and butler, brought a handful of cooked rice in a banana leaf, with a piece of red Spanish sausage: Chorizo de Viuda.

With my thoughts on the bloody work ahead I ate but little; even I felt slightly sick at the stomach, as I have often felt before going into great danger. It was not the impending fight against odds that mattered so much as the lack of medical care for such wounded as we were sure to have—including myself.

We were days distant over mountain trails from any assistance and everything depended on my own safety. If I were wounded or killed my recruits might stampede. Yet I must expose myself in order to carry them forward and win the day. The horns of the dilemma were equally sharp. It is easy to be brave when the contagion of courage is fostered by martial array and good comrades by one's side, as well as by the consoling thought of doctors and ambulances in the rear. But to put a man day-deep in the jungle, far from his own kind, and facing the prospects of horrible wounds and death, is some test of manhood. Yet by the score young officers in the Philippine Constabulary have stood that test.

The soldiers finished a scanty meal, sprawled around smoking their cigarillos, and frequently cast glances up at Mansalanao, where a thin column of white smoke rose from the babaylan trenches. That column of smoke fascinated me. The men there had every advantage of position. They even had better arms than the Constabulary. Was it any use to lead my men to almost certain death and possible torture?

But those were no thoughts for a Constabulary officer! My usual buoyant optimism, drowned for the moment by the fatigue of three days' hiking, reasserted itself. After all, the babaylanes were mighty poor shots, and my men would follow me to the death. Then the lust for physical combat strong within every healthy young male surged over me like strong drink and I snapped out an order.

The soldiers gave their haversacks and all extra equipment to the cargadores. With rifle and belt alone, we stood ready for the attack. I looked at the sun—for my watch had stopped when we forded a neck-deep river—and saw that it was just past the meridian. Three hours, I figured, would bring us to the fort, and that would leave several hours of daylight to decide issues with our friends aloft. "Alisto na!"

The men shuffled into line; in front went Julian and a Bukidnon guide; then Privates Fernandez and Montino, both good shots and daring youths, just in front of me, while behind me were Sergeant Basubas and six of my best men; then the rag-tag-and-bobtail and the *cargadores* brought up the rear.

XII - A Fight on a Mountaintop

THUS WE BEGAN THE ASCENT OF MANSALANAO and soon found the trail so steep that in places the babaylanes had cut steps in the yellow earth; and from these steps Julian scraped away mold and leaves which hid many suyacs—sharp pointed bamboo caltrops which would have pierced naked feet or even my own shoes, now soft and rotted by days of hiking in the water.

The Bukidnon prisoner, arms bound behind, stepped gingerly along and showed us all the traps, some of which he had doubtless helped set; and on a whispered word Julian halted us by raising his bolo; then, gliding into the brush, he slashed at withes that held a long sharpened stake to a bent sapling; the balatig spear (sharpened hardwood spring trap) was designed to dart across our path at the height of a man's breast. These traps were arranged to be sprung by our feet tripping on withes laid across the trail in natural manner.

In places the trail was only a foot or two broad, deep canyons yawning on each side. In such spots our progress suggested the idea of walking up a knife-edge canted to forty-five degrees. At a score of places, the babaylanes could have made a determined stand, but they were evidently relying on their trenches and pendent rocks above. At times I could see the winding column of our cargadores toiling up hundreds of feet below. It was a stiff climb to cap our three days' hike—and the immediate prospects of a rest on top seemed far from good.

About three o'clock Julian made a sign that he saw something ahead. The Bukidnon was dirty gray with fear, and trembled like the fronds of a coco palm tinder a north monsoon. Pushing past Fernandez and Montino, I saw on a ledge of overhanging rock almost immediately above me a little roofed platform, undoubtedly the enemy's outlook, but apparently unoccupied.

The trail wound steeply around the rock and as we clambered up, I began to think that we were going to take Mansalanao by surprise. But suddenly from far above came a challenge in the Visayan dialect. About two hundred feet beyond and above us I saw several heads, peering over the edge of a trench. As the challenge was repeated and the babaylanes showed that they recognized us, I took a shot at one of them.

Wild yells split the air. Pandemonium broke loose on the mountain and a hail of stones and rocks hurtled down on our heads. I scurried behind the roots of a blessed big tree, Fernandez and Montino shouldering me close on each side. Julian and the Bukidnon had vanished as if by wings, while Sergeant Basubas and the other men were behind the big outpost rock immediately below us.

The babaylanes cut loose their boulders, which crashed past down the mountain, carrying all before them. One smashed by within two feet of me, tearing down a stout tree as though it had been a twig. What with the yelling babaylanes and the soldiers' cries, the falling rocks, the crashing boulders, the rending of trees and rattle of rifle fire, it was terrifying enough. But the very narrowness of the trail saved us, for most of the boulders rolled harmlessly into the canyons on either side and reverberated down the mountain.

The babaylanes were in two lines of trenches, the first about two hundred feet above us, and the second on the rim of the crater, perhaps a hundred feet above the first. Upward, all herbage had been cleaned off, trees felled and rolled into canyons; but the trail broadened out a little and there were a few rocks and stumps for shelter.

From the comparative protection of our lucky stump, we potted at the heads in the first trench so successfully that within a few minutes the babaylanes had scrambled out to their upper breastworks. To aim better at the climbing figures, we showed ourselves for a moment.

Remingtons and Mausers cracked from the upper trench. But the babaylanes were poor shots and could not hit us at three hundred feet. On the other hand, we killed at least one babaylan. When shot he rolled at first as though he would tumble on top of us, but after vain clutchings at the rattan and other jungle vines, he tumbled like the boulders into the yawning canyon.

I called down to Sergeant Basubas that we must make a rush for the first trench and use it as our defense from the fire above. Exhorting my men by name, I yelled, "Sube! Sube! Avance!" and clambered from my protecting stump up, up the mountain, dodging from stump to rock and from rock to stump through a hail of stones and spears, until I reached shelter behind the wall of the first trench.

Fernandez and Montino were close behind me during that hazardous climb; and three other soldiers—Presquito, Lorep, and Cabo—gained the trench soon after us. We were all badly cut by spears or bruised by rocks. There we lay for more than an hour while rocks, planqueta spears, and bullets passed in a continuous stream overhead. My voice scarcely reached the soldiers below, as the din of falling rocks, cracking rifles, and agun (gongs) beaten in the upper trench drowned all.

But the trench above was clear cut against the sky and every time a head showed we fired; and once or twice a stricken babaylan leapt up, perhaps to get another bullet through the body. It was pretty shooting and took a quick eye.

The babaylanes continually derided us. My men told me that they said we could never get up and would all be killed. This seemed likely, as they had all the best of the argument. Papa Isio's voice urged them to resist and prayed for our defeat. But the five soldiers with me were not slow in responding with all manner of taunts and threats; and as the minutes winged away without serious casualties on our side, they grew bolder.

After an hour or more of such fighting and shouting we were no nearer the top. Although many babaylanes must have been killed and wounded, there were plenty more to take their places and the situation was becoming desperate, for with five men I could hardly hope to storm the fort, and the other soldiers would not leave their protecting rock.

So, I climbed out of the sheltering trench and stood on top of it, where my men below could see me. Then, between dodging rocks and spears, I berated them by name for cowards; individually and collectively I went into their ancestry and uncovered their pedigrees, exhausting my stock of expletives, in English, Spanish, and Visayan.

Nevertheless, fear overcame shame and the men below stuck fast. Rifles cracked merrily from the babaylan trench, and one bullet went through my shirt. Every bullet should have found a billet in my body at that distance—a hundred feet; but the rocks and spears were worse, and between exhortation and threats to my reluctant soldiers I dodged and twisted to escape the shower.

Despite much show of agility, I was soon bruised and scratched in many places. The five soldiers lying beneath me in the trench wanted to come out with me, but I bade them lie low and keep down the babaylanes' fire by potting heads as soon as they appeared.

At last I began joking with the white-livered gentlemen behind the big rock. I told them that I was like Papa Isio and that rifle balls would not touch me. I enlarged on the virtues of an anting-anting that I possessed; and asked them what they were afraid of and if they wanted to go back to Isabela to have their women sneer at them while they would adore Fernandez, Lores, et al, who, needless to say, between their shots at the babaylanes, gave me ample vocal assistance.

It was a case for psychological treatment to overcome physical obstacles which appeared insuperable. I worked harder with my voice than with my rifle. Indeed, although I started the fight with two belts of ammunition, I was already running short of cartridges. Once a rock about the size of a man's fist caught me full in the chest and knocked me from my perch, making me spit blood, and then a yell of delight went up from the babaylanes; but I was up again in a moment and the game of dodging and yelling went on.

At last my epithets and persuasions took effect. Sergeant Basubas timorously emerged with several men, who in the open became brave enough. I saw that the supreme moment had come. So, for the thousandth time I yelled, *"Sube! Sube! Avance! Viva los Estados Unidos!"*

The men joined in one wild fighting chorus and followed me madly up the steep mountainside. Then the shower of rocks from above ceased, the lull after a fierce storm. Nevertheless, the slope was so sheer and slippery that it was several minutes before we gained the hundred feet or so to the uppermost trench; and in places we hauled ourselves up by ropes and ladders of rattan hung down for the purpose and which the babaylanes in their hasty flight omitted to cut. Had Papa Isio's men kept their nerve, we could never have won to the summit without losing half the detachment.

Fernandez was first on top. As I crawled over the edge, I saw him brandishing a long spear which he plunged several times into the body of a dead babaylan whom Lores—himself an ex-babaylan whom I had enlisted—turned over with the muzzle of his carbine to recognize as Aguacil Cito, one of the Pope's most noted fighting chiefs. The trench was a sickly sight. It was full of blood and muck, but only two dead men, both shot through the head.

Another dead babaylan lay in the brush near the trench and yet another dying nearby, while trails of blood leading from the trench showed where those killed and wounded earlier in the fight had been carried off by their women. As the fight had lasted now for two or three hours, they had had ample time to remove the dead and wounded.

Beyond the trench there opened up a pretty little concave plateau, dotted with houses and gardens, on the further side of which, some four hundred yards away, many babaylanes were scurrying into the forest, carrying several wounded men. We gave them a volley and another babaylan dropped; while the rest, leaving their wounded, fled the faster. But we were now too exhausted to pursue. Moreover, our ammunition was low, and I was suffering from the effects of severe bruises.

However, I sent Sergeant Basubas with a few unwounded soldiers to make a round of the plateau, gather up the wounded, and clear out any lurking babaylanes, although I believed that they had received a drubbing that would keep them going.

We followed the trails of blood to the huts in the center of the plateau, where I called the roll in front of Papa Isio's residence. Miraculous to relate, not one of my men was seriously injured. Seven had nasty cuts and contusions about head and shoulders, but after a little rest would be fit for the trail. With first-aid packages I bandaged the soldiers' cuts and my own; then turned my attention to the wounded babaylanes whom Basubas brought in.

There were several of these; and the job of bandaging up your enemy's wounds, when every nerve and fiber of your own system called for rest, was not an unusual ending to a Constabulary officer's day.

The cargadores came up and we all quartered in the Pope's mansion, which was supplied with running water, piped in bamboo tubes from a spring further up the plateau. There was food and loot for all, as the houses were full of the babaylanes' plunder from half the haciendas of Negros—mirrors, women's dresses, china dishes, pots and pans, and I know not what, household truck and farming implements.

In the sweet potato patches pigs were rooting. A couple of fat porkers soon rooted no more, but were roasting whole over the coals of our campfire. It was sunset. Chickens were flying to roost on the ridgepoles of the huts whence my men ingeniously removed them by means of a long pole with a crosspiece at one end. This they would slowly push up under a roosting fowl, which, irritated at the disturbance, transferred its perch to the crosspiece, whence it was drawn gradually down the roof to within reach of a soldier's grasping hands.

The gardens yielded fresh ears of corn with camotes, ubis, melons, and other fruits and vegetables. What a meal that was! And how the soldiers gathered around the fire afterward, puffing cigars made from the Pope's choicest leaf tobacco that we found hanging under the eaves of his house, and sipping pangassi rice wine from his great earthenware jars!

White mists wreathing up the mountain before sunset hid the magnificent view of Negros which was to open on the morrow. At that altitude it was now quite chilly, and the assorted bedclothes found in the babaylan houses were distributed among the soldiers.

The Constabularies stretched around the blazing fire, recounting with many gestures the incidents of the fight; but soon fatigue and full stomachs drove them to sleep. I passed the night on a slatted floor, covered for additional warmth with an assorted lot of women's dresses; and despite the groans of wounded babaylanes beneath the house, my slumbers were those of a man with a good day's work accomplished.

The following morning when the sun melted the mists, a panorama of Negros opened many thousand feet beneath us. Isabela and the little towns of the Binalbagan Valley were white dots on a green carpet; the coastline of Negros was a ribbon unrolled for our inspection; Guimaras Island and much of Panay were in view beyond the blue straits; and even the summit of King Canlaon, forty miles to the north, seemed little higher than were we.

I can think of few happier hours than those spent that morning on the summit of Mansalanao, smoking the Pope's cigars, eating his roast suckling pig and sweet potatoes, breathing the cool mountain air, surveying lazily and contentedly a large slice of this glorious old earth of ours, and contemplating with all due gratitude to an inscrutable providence the sheer joy of being alive.

We buried the dead babaylanes and spent the day loafing on the plateau, healing up our wounds, and preparing for the return hike to Isabela. I was prodigiously pleased with the results of the expedition, for although Papa Isio had escaped we had dealt him a blow from which he would be long in recovering; and we had established the prestige of the Constabulary in Negros for all time.

The captured babaylanes said that the Pope himself had been wounded and that that was why their resistance had broken. Two babaylan leaders had fallen, Aguacil Cito and Felipe Dacu, while it was safe to estimate their total killed at a dozen.

Some years later, when I was superintendent of the Iwahig Penal Colony, I went to see Papa Isio, then a prisoner in Bilibid Prison, Manila. The old scoundrel had remained in the mountains until my successor in Negros, Captain Bowers, by clever work obtained his surrender.

I had a long talk with the Pope, but got little from him, for he posed as very stupid. However, I managed to get his shirt off, to see whether there was a trace on his leather skin of a bullet from my Winchester. I could find no scar. But the plight of the old brigand chief, cooped in his narrow cell after so many years of sweeping free through the mountains, excited my sympathy.

I felt no animosity; rather the friendly feeling that may be had for an antagonist who has brought forth one's best efforts; so I gave him some little luxuries and, soon, in conversation with the then governor-general of the Philippines, James F. Smith, took occasion to say a good word for the Pope, who was under sentence of death.

General Smith had once commanded in Negros, and knew the history of Papa Isio and his babaylanes. He commuted the death sentence to life imprisonment. But the prisoned eagle pined in confinement and soon died. He was a very old man of pure Malayan type, with nothing in his appearance to show the reason for his previous high estate.

On the morning of May 28, we left Mansalanao, first burning all the houses—except one for the wounded babaylanes —and with all the plunder that we could not carry away. The manner in which those soldiers and cargadores loaded themselves with loot was astonishing.

One cargadore had a large mirror on top of a pack that of itself must have weighed 100 pounds. We destroyed many tons of palay, sugar, and other foodstuffs, leaving the pretty plateau a burned and scarred sore on the mountain. That was hard but necessary, for we did not want the job of taking Mansalanao again.

As it was, I went back a few months later, on news that the babaylanes had returned. But it was a false alarm. The clearing was still a waste, although Nature, so generous in the tropics, had covered all scars with her mantle of green. The babaylanes, like wild animals, rarely returned to a lair where they had been disturbed. Despite wounds and stiffness, it was a joyful column that wound down the mountain. On the afternoon of the second day we reached the cogon upland beyond the leech belt, as a typhoon gathered over Negros and black driving clouds swept through the mountains; soon torrential rains descended.

With a few of the best hikers I pushed on to Payao, wading over miles of rice paddies knee- and waist-deep in water and mud and finally reaching the village at midnight in the middle of a terrific storm that was a theatrical wind-up to the expedition. The cargadores and the rest of the column did not arrive until the following morning. The storm, as is so often the case in the Philippines, was followed by a glorious sunny day, so that we marched into Isabela with leaping hearts. The populace turned out to greet us, incredulous at first that we had captured the babaylanes' stronghold. But our loot was the best evidence, and the townsfolk picked out belongings lost many months or years before. They gave us a baile to celebrate our victory and there were no more requests for the return of the regular army.

And from the day we took Mansalanao there were no more haciendas burned by the babaylanes in the valley of the Binalbagan.

XIII - Murder, Merriment, and Morals

THE RESULT OF THE MANSALANAO EXPEDITION was so far-reaching in establishing Constabulary prestige in southern Negros and in awing the lawless classes that presumably I should have considered my lucky star in the ascendant. But I have noticed that lucky stars rise in a man's particular heaven only when he pulls the strings of his own solar system. Of course, I was lucky, in one sense of the word. But no amount of good fortune could have made up for lack of care in drilling and disciplining my men; while slogging through the bosque and up Mansalanao seemed more a matter of endurance than chance.

Be that as it may, the Constabulary in southern Negros was by that one achievement lifted to an assured position. It was almost laughable to see the effect on my men. Their uniforms and equipment were still none too presentable; but they now bore themselves with a kick and a swagger which plainly said: "See who we are! The army and Scouts tried for months to find Papa Isio's cuartel general. We found it—we did!"

The effect might be noted also in the good-looking girls who joined the Constabulary forces, now being easily picked up by my young bucks. Some of them were married in the iglesia (church); some were hitched up by the Juez de Paz; while others neglected any formalities whatever. It did not do to be too particular about the marriage lines; and for that matter a soldier's querida (mistress) was often as faithful as any wife might be.

However, the Mansalanao victory did not mean rest for the Constabulary, although it staggered the babaylanes so that during my six months in Isabela they neither raided a hacienda nor committed other outrage in the lowlands. Papa Isio must have had a lot of anting-antings to explain away and his subtle old brain had to scheme, and plan means for reorganizing his bands.

Nevertheless, there were constant rumors of babaylanes to run down, trails to patrol, Bukidnon tribesmen to interview, maps to piece out, with all the local crimes to ferret out over several hundred square miles of territory.

It was not unusual for me to awake uneasily from a sound sleep at any hour of the night with my muchacho's (servant's) low whisper in my ear—"Capitan! Capitan! Capitan!"—sounding so faintly that it was loud in my subconscious dreams before my waking-self caught the meaning of the interruption.

It is a Malayan superstition that to awaken one suddenly is dangerous because the evil spirits always awaiting opportunity to enter a human body may slip in before the awakened person's own respectable soul can get back from wherever it may have gone during the sleeping hours.

When my soul finally returned, and my eyelids were propped open, out of the black night would come an excited municipal official or a hacendero with his story of murder, robbery, or what not, which meant work for the Constabulary.

At that time practically all crime was investigated by us or went unpunished; it was years before the municipal police, under Constabulary supervision, was brought to the point of accomplishing real work in the suppression of crime.

From a comfortable bed to the saddle was then a business of five minutes; though, as I got my non-coms trained, they relieved me of much of the detail work of investigations.

The Chinos, as I have said, were our good friends; but one day we caught one up in the hills peddling with the babaylanes and locked him up in the Constabulary guardhouse. That night I was awakened to hear that the Chino had committed suicide, or nearly so. He had broken the china plate on which his supper was served and with the jagged edge had almost sawed his throat in two; his breath whistled through the hole he had made, and he lay in a pool of blood. With the help of a Filipino practicante, or barber-surgeon I sewed up the gap with a needle and thread borrowed from a soldier's wife. The Chinaman recovered.

Murder! Rape! Arson!

The very words taste badly in the mouth of a person living in a civilized, law-abiding community, yet to me in disordered Negros they sounded as commonplace as "Yes, I take both sugar and cream, please."

Old Sergeant Basubas would come over to the house, climb the uncertain wooden steps, cross the shaky split-bamboo veranda, and stand at the open door to my combination bedroom and office.

"Que hay, sargento?" (What is it, sergeant?) I would rap out.

"Asesino, po! Hombre aqui viene de Magallon. Dice dalaga patay," (Murder, sir! Man here from Magallon says a girl has been killed) answered the sergeant in the mixed Spanish and vernacular that most of the soldiers spoke.

A few questions to the messenger would show whether the murder was a simple or a complex one. A simple murder, by our Constabulary standards, was one in which a peasant killed a peasant, while a complex one was when a peasant was killed by a *distinguido*, or one in which a wealthy citizen was in any way concerned. If two peasants quarreled and one killed the other, that was a simple problem; the laborer-murderer was so poor that there was none to do him reverence and the scales of justice were easily and quickly adjusted.

But if a prominent Filipino was mixed in the case as principal or abettor it might take a long time to get those scales on the balance—false oaths and affidavits, disappearing witnesses, false alibis, and many other chicaneries being thrown against the measured weights of justice.

Let a *hacendero* beat a laborer to death and it would take every ounce of a Constabulary officer's intelligence and energy to get a conviction. I remember one such case. A hacienda laborer was driving a *carabao* cart laden with sacks of raw sugar from the mill to the coast where it was to be loaded aboard a *parao* or *lorcha* for Iloilo.

It was midday. The *carabao* was faint for want of water and a mud bath; for the water buffalo of the East is a semi-amphibious creature which must wallow in water or mud several times daily or dry up and die. So, the *tao* unhitched beneath a shady tree, turned the *carabao* into one of those wallows which dot the waysides and fields of the islands, and composed himself to slumber on the green turf beneath his cart.

Of course, he took no count of the immutable laws which cause the revolutions of this sphere and the apparent rise and setting of our sun. Noon passed, and the shadow of the tree withdrew from the cart, leaving the crude sugar exposed to the full heat of an overhead sun.

Our driver, nicely sheltered beneath the cart, slumbered on until the sugar, liquefied by heat, trickled down upon his face, when he awoke with a start, crept from under the oozing cart, and beheld, instead of his five piculs of sugar, valued at as much as twenty-five pesos, a cartful of valueless molasses.

Well, thinks the reader, here is no tragedy but a comedy: the besmeared sleeper surveying his changed cargo, solid turned to liquid. But wait! Enter upon the scene the foreman of the hacienda, a *mestizo* and a *pariente* (relative) to the tune of about tenth cousin to municipal and provincial officials.

The foreman carries in his hand a palma-brava staff, a stout club made of the heaviest and hardest wood found in the islands. All foremen carry such a club, or did in those days. He sees the cart of ruined sugar; he upbraids the luckless driver; and as he tirades his rising anger feeds upon itself, until, blind with rage, he falls upon the driver and beats him senseless.

The tao dies within a few hours. The municipal doctor, himself a relative of the foreman, makes certificate that the tao died of calentura, or fever. That certificate is quite true—as far as it goes; the luckless carter had a temperature of 41 centigrade, as a man may well have when skull and ribs are driven in.

Of course, the doctor knew that the man was beaten to death; but then the foreman was his, the doctor's, relative, and a tao was only a tao —and that sugar was worth twenty-five pesos if it was worth a centavo, and it was completely ruined. So was the tao, and buried. Everyone was satisfied except, perhaps, the old and worn mother of the unlucky carter, who felt that the few pesos given her by the foreman scarcely repaid the pain of bringing her boy into the world and of rearing him to man's estate. Yet she knew full well the futility of expecting that the foreman should be made to pay the price for taking a life.

Let her appeal to the municipal president or justice of the peace; were not both also relatives of the foreman? And, in any case, could the foreman not buy a dozen affidavits to prove that the carter murderously attacked him, even if the doctor's certificate should not prove defense enough?

So here the case might well have ended had not the Constabulary somehow or another picked up a thread of the tangled skein of crime. And the unraveling of that skein cost me days of work. When, finally, the foreman was sentenced to six years' imprisonment for homicide it was only after I had succeeded in getting the provincial doctor to exhume the body of the luckless carter and prove that the fever was induced by a broken skull with other assorted internal injuries inflicted by a certain palma-brava club.

I would not, however, from the above example or from anything that I may write, arraign the *hacenderos* or wealthier Filipinos of Negros as a class of brutal, overbearing tyrants. The conditions were somewhat those of our own South before the war, when slavery fostered brutality where it existed. The gulf in intelligence between the hacendero and the peasant, with the consequent semi-feudal system existing in the province, gave opportunity for many abuses which when possible the Constabulary, as the only impartial agent of the law, corrected.

There was much in life at Isabela to make up for hard work and night alarms. The people were a happy, pleasure-loving lot; dances and other entertainments followed my expeditions in the mountains. The one other American in the town was the schoolteacher, a Harvard man of about my own youth, and just as willing to have a good time.

When no Filipino gave a dance, we gave one ourselves; and we were very much at home with the many charming senoritas of Isabela and vicinity. When account is taken of the fact that there were no American women within a score of miles, and that those of our fellow countrywomen whom we occasionally saw were mostly of that angular variety that devotes itself to pedagogy, is it to be wondered that the warm, soft charms of Encarnacion, Conchita, Consuela, Aurelia, Paz—the very names of the girls carry a seductive lilt—seemed real and not at all exotic to two youths whose hot young blood was stimulated by climate, food, and drink?

And really beautiful some of those Filipina and *mestizo*, girls were, with their soft olive skin, flashing black eyes, long glossy hair with fragrant buds of white tropic flowers coquettishly placed; their wide-sleeved, low-necked camisas of fine woven fabrics of pineapple fiber or hemp slipping back to show smooth, rounded neck and curve of bosom; their saya skirts close around their supple hips; their dainty feet encased in gaudy chinelas (heelless slippers); and the glow of youth, health, and passion flowing in a constant stream from their graceful persons.

That was the temptation to which every American officer in the provinces was subjected, so small wonder that many of them married Filipina girls; wonder, indeed, that more did not. Without entering into a discussion of the rights and wrongs of miscegenation, I may point out that an unfortunate feature of the American-Filipino marriages was that usually the American married a girl of the lower classes, and that generally it was the lower-class American who married.

But the maestro and I reckoned little of the temptations to which we were exposed. We enjoyed them. Pleasant it was on a night when the moon hung big and high to wander down the streets of Isabela to where some betel palms, bathed in silver, marked the entrance to the domicile of Senorita Encarnacion de los Reyes; then on the wide veranda, with the moonlight splashing through the palms, to watch Encarnacion's slim fingers tinkle the guitar or run across the harp, and hear her sing her Spanish songs.

Snatches of the verses come back: "Las orillas del Pasig, donde nace el sol," or "San Pedro no admite las mujeres al cielo."

There were several verses telling why St. Peter would not let women into heaven, and there was a laugh for us in every one of them. For by this time the maestro and I were pretty well acquainted with the Castilian tongue. Commend me to a pretty girl on a moonlit balcony as instructress in any language; by that method a man might acquire Volapuk within a month or so. To an American desirous of acquiring the vernacular the Spaniards used to recommend a "sleeping dictionary;" but the moonlit-balcony system was better for a moral youth.

The Presidente of Isabela, Senor Cenon Rosado, was a capable Visayan with a dash of Spanish blood in his veins. From the beginning a good friend to Americans, he gave me much information about babaylanes and cattle thieves. He was about the first Filipino in Negros to become a Protestant, doubtless thinking that a necessary first step in the adoption of republican ideals. He had picked up a little English and a little less knowledge of the United States.

I remember that one night at a dance, when the intoxication of the hour perhaps blended with that of the refreshments, Cenon began a eulogy of things American which ended by his raising a stout bumper of "square-face" Holland gin and ejaculating: "Come, capitan, I drink—you drink—we drink—health Estados Unidos! Great cun'ry, Estados Unidos—President Roosevelt—Philadelphia—hooray!"

Many years later, in 1914, when I was superintendent of the Constabulary Academy at Baguio, organizing the first class of Filipino cadets, I found, among the aspirants for a Constabulary commission, Cenon's son, whom I remembered as a barefoot boy at Isabela. It gave me much pleasure to write to my old friend, reporting the favorable progress of his boy, who was later commissioned a third lieutenant in the Constabulary.

The haciendas around Isabela kept open house for Constabulary officers, so that I often rode out to one or the other for some snipe or duck shooting, for a supper or a dance. Each hacienda was a community in itself—a feudal community of which the hacendero was the overlord. The hacendero's house, like a baron's fortress of the Middle Ages, stood in the center of the buildings and dependents' huts.

Many miles of almost uninhabited country might separate one hacienda from the next or from the nearest pueblo. The oxen, *carabao*, and horses to be seen in the fields or on the roads belonged to the hacendero; the broad acres of sugarcane and rice, the milch goats that fed beside the hedgeless roads, the long galvanized iron shed that housed the milling machinery, the paraos and torchas that loaded grass sacks of crude sugar at the landing on the river, the bamboo and nipa huts of the laborers; all were his.

Even the laborers, men, women, and children, tanned to darkest bronze by toil in the paddies and fields, might be said to belong to the hacendero, for they were usually so deeply in his debt for clothing and food advanced that escape was well-nigh impossible. And the hacendero would tell you that unless the peasants were in his debt they would not work. But this was an axiom of Spanish administration that American experience exploded; for we soon found that under fair treatment the Filipinos made satisfactory laborers.

In Negros the class of land-owning peasant farmers found in many provinces of Luzon, notably among the Ilocanos of the North and Bicols of the South, was lacking. Conditions in Negros approximate more closely to those which have brought bloody revolution to Mexico and Central American countries for so many years, for the land has been alienated from the peasants and is held in large parcels.

This has brought about speedy development of the province and apparent prosperity; but it has resulted in a social structure much less solid and safe than that of other provinces in the islands. Indeed, one of the most hopeful aspects of the Philippine question as a whole is the presence of such a large number of landowning farmers, a substantial middle class that should be the backbone of every country.

The wealthy hacendero lived in state. Fast horses carried him in carromata or quilez to the nearest town or to Bacolod when occasion offered. His daughters often spoke English or French, learned in a convent in Hong Kong or it might be Paris. His house was furnished with what passed for European furniture, but which was probably made in Hong Kong or Singapore; rococo pictures, vases, and other ornaments abounded.

Likely enough an orchestrion or other musical instrument of torture adorned his sola; for the wealthy Filipino sometimes shows an almost childlike fondness for large mechanical toys.

The life was a curious blend of Spanish and Malay customs. For instance, you might sit at a well-appointed dinner table, eating Spanish cookery off fine napery, drinking Rioja claret and Frontera sherry or even dry champagne; you would chat in Spanish, English, or French with your host's daughters, recently from Paris, chic and attractive enough to catch glances even on the boulevards; and if you had been able to see through the wall that divided the dining room from the kitchen you might have seen an old Visayan woman squatting on the floor, eating morisqueta (cooked rice) with her fingers or smoking a black cigar and chewing a red cud of betel. She was the mother of the charming girls with whom you were dining. In youth, and maturity, the wealthy Visayas are Europeanized— perhaps by now Americanized—but in old age they may revert to the more comfortable customs of their ancestors.

That picture, the old mother squatting on the floor in the kitchen while the daughters drink Champagne and talk French, in a manner epitomizes the chaotic structure of Negros society in 1902.

XIV - Cholera in the Camp

We've got the cholera in the camp, it's worse them forty fights;
We're dying in the wilderness the same as Israelites;
It's before us and behind us, and we cannot get away,
An' the doctor's just reported we've ten more today.

So sings Rudyard Kipling, high priest of the Anglo-Saxon religio-commercial crusade for the governance and reform of Oriental peoples. This dreaded Asiatic disease struck Negros while I was still at Isabela. We had marked its approach through the islands, from Manila where the infection started, brought doubtless by boat from Hong Kong. It appeared in Iloilo; and then of course it was a matter of time until boats carried it from island to island.

In later years strict quarantine measures in some measure stopped the spread of the disease. But the Philippine Bureau of Health had not then attained the marvelous efficiency to be brought about by the work of Dr. Victor G. Heiser of the United States Marine Health and Quarantine Service. A case or two of cholera appeared in Binalbagan, a coast town a few miles from Isabela; and the Isabelenos laughed uneasily, calling it the cholerina or "little cholera" induced by eating too heartily of green, half-cooked ears of corn when they first come in season. But the disease spread with appalling rapidity and the dreaded symptoms of synchronous vomiting and diarrhea were unmistakable.

Vainly the Provincial Board of Health broadcast circulars in English, Spanish, and Visayan telling the people to take quarantine measures, to boil all water, and to bury the dead in quicklime; as vainly the Constabulary threw cordons across the province in the hope of stopping the spread of the epidemic; for with inadequate forces to combat the ignorance and superstition of the populace the task was hopeless. In practically all towns drinking and cooking water was secured from easily contaminated streams and wells, while marketing was carried on in numberless open-air stores where fruit and vegetables were exposed to the deadly feet of flies from cholera droppings. The people were apathetic, relying for assistance solely on San Roque, the patron saint of the sick.

In each barrio (hamlet) and pueblo pathetic little processions paraded the streets, bearing banners and battered images of the saints and often headed by a band playing such a popular air as "There'll be a hot time in the old town tonight," a tune perhaps more appropriate at the deadly hour than was realized by the Filipino musicians. San Roque shamefully neglected his job.

For some months—until, in fact, the heavy typhoon rains of August and September washed the countryside clean—King Cholera reigned supreme and took his toll of from ten to twenty percent of the population. Owing to simple, sanitary measures such as boiling water and cooking vegetables, the Constabulary in Isabela was comparatively immune; but with men on patrols and expeditions it was impossible to be always on the watch and I lost one or two soldiers. And once I had a bad scare myself.

I was riding alone from Himamaylan to Isabela on a blazing hot day that parched me as dry as the proverbial bone. As I had no canteen of water, I stopped at a solitary hut beneath a shady mango tree, miles from other habitation. Before that occasion I had often stopped there to slake my thirst; and whether the isolation of the hut, force of habit, or the fatigue of the trail made me careless I cannot say, but I asked the old peasant woman who came to the door for a drink of water, which, with the apathy of her class and race, she silently brought to me in a goblet made from a hollowed coconut shell.

Raging thirst made me unheedful of the dirty receptacle, the questionable fingers that had dipped the water from an earthenware jar, and the source of the supply, so I gulped down the fluid; then I watered my horse, and not till then the thought of cholera uneasily crept into my brain and I questioned the woman, "May cholera diri?" (Is there any cholera here?) "O, po!" the answer came, "duha ka-patay sa balay." (Yes, sir, there are two dead in the house.)

Hastily I rode to Isabela and to cholera remedies. Galloping through a hamlet, I saw some bottles of native cholera mixture displayed on the bamboo shelf of an open-air store. I bought a bottle, swallowed the contents down to the last drop, galloped on again and, when I reached home, brewed a quart or two of strong tea and took that with a liberal dose of Dr. J. Collis Browne's Chlorodyne[15] and assorted other medicines.

Fortunately, there was work enough on hand to take my mind off my own condition, and the symptoms, expected and well earned, did not appear; but after that experience I was decidedly more careful.

However, one American officer in my district went down with the cholera and (which was quite the exception) recovered. Inspector Warren of the Telegraph Division of the Constabulary arrived at Isabela to build a telephone line that would link me up with the towns further south and with a detachment of Constabulary at Isio, a hamlet on the coast some thirty miles south of Isabela.

Warren went on south and from time to time would ring me up to report progress in construction; he was putting up a temporary line, mostly fastened to the coco palms, plantations of which line the Negros coast.

For a week or two I did not hear from him; then one day the telephone bell tinkled again, and I took down the receiver to hear a weak, thin voice say: "Is that you, White? I'm in Cauayan—I've had the cholera!"

Poor Warren had been stricken in about the most disconsolate, abandoned barrio in Negros with no fellow American within twenty miles and, of course, quite unable to communicate with one of his own kind; but a native practicante (pharmacist) had treated him and, marvelous to relate, had pulled him through.

I saw Warren a day or two later. He looked like a dead man and had dropped from about 170 pounds to but little over 100, such was the ravage of that disease, which seems, within a few hours, to deplete the system of half its blood and brawn.

When cholera started in Isabela some of the residents wanted to put in the evenings praying to San Roque instead of worshiping at the shrine of Terpsichore. However, the teacher, the Presidente, and I determined that cheerful spirits would supplement prayer as defense against disease, so we gathered the girls and youths and held a "Cholera Ball." Some of the senoritas and their escorts were loath to come.

We had to drive around to their houses in carromatas and even in *carabao* carts and almost drag them from scenes of despondent prayer to one of hopeful recreation. But despite all delays the dance was a huge success.

Perhaps there were more bottles of "square-face" gin, aniseed liqueur, and Angostura bitters consumed than was usual on such occasions.

The gaiety, at first forced, became spontaneous. I am sure that individual powers of resistance to the disease were strengthened by the spirits; both the bottled and the other kind. In fact, the only one of the dancing set in Isabela who succumbed was a girl whose parents absolutely refused to let her attend our dances, which now occurred more frequently than ever. She died. The rest of us lived.

Once we danced five nights in succession, never finishing before daybreak. Morning after morning I went home just as the first rays of the sun were gilding the summit of old Canlaon.

Some time afterward Major Orwig asked me what time I arose in the morning at Isabela so as to get my Constabulary work done. With a certain amount of mental reservation I told him that I usually saw the sunrise.

DR. J. COLLIS BROWNE'S
CHLORODYNE.

THE ORIGINAL AND ONLY GENUINE.

CHLORODYNE is admitted by the Profession to be the most wonderful and valuable remedy ever discovered

CHLORODYNE is the best remedy known for Coughs, Consumption, Bronchitis, Asthma.

CHLORODYNE effectually checks and arrests those too often fatal diseases—Diphtheria, Fever, Croup, Ague.

CHLORODYNE acts like a charm in Diarrhœa, and is the only specific in Cholera and Dysentery.

CHLORODYNE effectually cuts short all attacks of Epilepsy, Hysteria, Palpitation, and Spasms.

CHLORODYNE is the only palliative in Neuralgia, Rheumatism, Gout, Cancer, Toothache, Meningitis, &c.

From Dr. B. J. BOULTON and Co., Horncastle.
We have made pretty extensive use of Chlorodyne in our practice lately, and look upon it as an excellent direct Sedative and Anti-spasmodic. It seems to allay pain and irritation in whatever organ, and from whatever cause. It induces a feeling of comfort and quietude not obtainable by any other remedy, and it seems to possess this great advantage over all other Sedatives, that it leaves no unpleasant after-effects.

"Earl Russell communicated to the College of Physicians that he received a dispatch from Her Majesty's Consul at Manilla, to the effect that Cholera had been raging fearfully, and that the only remedy of any service was CHLORODYNE."—See *Lancet*, 1st December, 1864.

CAUTION.—BEWARE of PIRACY and IMITATIONS.

CAUTION.—Vice-Chancellor Sir W. PAGE WOOD stated that Dr. J. COLLIS BROWNE was, undoubtedly, the Inventor of CHLORODYNE; that the story of the Defendant, FREEMAN, was deliberately untrue, which, he regretted to say, had been sworn to.—See *Times*, 13th July, 1864.

Sold in Bottles at 1s. 1½d., 2s. 9d., and 4s. 6d. each. None is genuine without the words "DR. J. COLLIS BROWNE'S CHLORODYNE" on the Government Stamp. Overwhelming Medical Testimony accompanies each bottle.

SOLE MANUFACTURER:—

J. T. DAVENPORT,
33, Great Russell Street, Bloomsbury, London.

XV - Floods, Amphibians, and Epidemics

The advent of the rainy season somewhat abated the cholera epidemic, though it remained endemic for months or years, and I was still to have a remarkable experience with it in another part of the province.

The first heavy rain after months of complete drought is practically the only seasonal demarcation in the Philippines. In the tropics there is no spring with balmy breath and bursting buds; no autumn with first crisp frost to sere leaves and make the garden flowers droop their heads; there is only the quick transition from dust and drought to mud and moisture.

The change comes in a day. From January to June the country is parched, the earth cracks, the rivers fall lower and lower until they barely float the fishermen's canoes; only in the sunless depths of the mountain forests does any moisture persist.

The islands are athirst. Then one day clouds gather on the higher mountains and roll lower and blacker, while flashes of lightning shoot through and peals of thunder shake the very earth that yawns for water. The rain comes. At first big splashing drops are swallowed as they fall; follow such pent-up torrents as the temperate zone never knows. The dust in one's nostrils is replaced by that warm, conservatory smell of the hot earth after rain, when all nature seems to exhale humid thanks for the breaking of the drought.

Then the streams swell a thousand-fold overnight and the dreaded avenida—the freshet—wipes out rice fields and villages. But the Constabulary must keep the trail, wet season or dry. In the treacherous streams we have lost a dozen officers and many men. There was poor Manison returning on horseback alone, in a black night, to Batangas.

The rain had ceased. But the Batangas River, just outside the town, was in flood; and across the river were the lights of the army post from which strains of music floated out through the darkness. It was "hop" night—and Manison was young; so, he took a chance on the depth of the water, his horse stumbled, and he was swept away in the flood.

Like other Constabulary officers I have taken my chances on the flooded rivers—and was lucky. Between Isabela and the foothills hamlet of Mampahubug was a little stream, perhaps fifty feet wide, trickling between bluff banks; a rough cart track cut steeply down through the banks to a ford where, as a rule, the water barely wetted a horse's fetlocks.

One day in July 1902, I reached the ford with twenty men and as many cargadores on the first leg of an expedition against the babaylanes. The little stream was swollen to a turbid torrent running level with the top of its banks, ten or twelve feet deep and bearing along many snags, logs, and other debris.

Either we had to cross the flood or wait in a drenching rain for the end of the freshet which might run for days; or we might return to Isabela. I called for volunteers to cross the stream. One of the cargadores said he could swim it, a dangerous proposition with the current boiling down at least ten miles an hour, and the chance of being hit by a log. A rope was brought from the nearest barrio and the plucky cargadore safely carried it across the torrent, landing, however, quite fifty yards down from a point opposite his start. Then, with carbine and equipment slung over my back, I hauled myself along the rope and made the other shore. The soldiers followed.

Private Tobias, my company clerk, a pale-faced *mestizo* who had begged me to take him on an expedition, let go his hold in midstream and disappeared under the yellow flood. Below our crossing the stream doubled on itself, so with the soldiers already over I dashed across the neck of land in the hope of saving Tobias when he was swept around the bend; the river broadened here and was only a few feet deep on our side. We joined hands and I stood as far out in the torrent as was possible without being taken off my legs; and round the bend Tobias came hurtling down, turning over and over, vainly attempting to swim.

Nevertheless, the few strokes he made brought him nearer to us. I just managed to grab an arm, the line of men held firm, and after a few struggles we all got safely ashore. And now comes the most remarkable part of the incident: the same *cargadore* who had carried the rope across volunteered to dive and recover Private Tobias's carbine for five pesos. That fellow held his life cheaply; but I told him that I would deduct the sum from Tobias's next pay.

So, into the flood he went. Allowing for the current, he dived many yards above the spot where the carbine was dropped. We ran to the bend to pick him out of the river. But the human muskrat caught an over-hanging branch and hauled himself ashore. At the second attempt he got the carbine. Never was five pesos better earned. Of course, the Visayan is a Malay, and that race is semi-amphibious. In after years I saw remarkable feats of swimming and diving amongst the Moro pearlers in the Sulu Archipelago. But nothing equaled the courage and skill shown by that cargadore in groping for Private Tobias's carbine along the bottom of the muddy mill-stream.

On another expedition, when we were deep in the mountains, we camped on a sandbar in the canyon of a considerable river. Behind us was a precipitous cliff; in front the river, two or three feet deep. It was fine weather and apparently no freshet was to be feared. But there must have been a cloudburst further up the mountain, for just before dark we heard an ominous roar.

The soldiers yelled, "Avenida!" (flood). We gathered what we could of our impedimenta and scrambled perilously up the steep rock wall where lay our only safety. We lost in the flood some sacks of rice and other food and had to spend a comfortless night among the rocks.

The following morning the river had returned to normal flow. We continued our hike upstream and resupplied ourselves from the first outlaw village that we assaulted. But if the rains abated the cholera, the Fates still held chastisement in store for the unhappy Philippines. On the heels of man-disease came animal-disease. Epizootia[16] of cattle and *carabao*, surra and glanders of horses, now swept the province, and carrying off within a few weeks seventy-five percent, of the farmers' livestock.

The deadliness, the inevitability of the scourge may be imagined when I say that of fourteen horses in the Constabulary stables at Isabela, I could not save one for my personal use.

We had gathered quite a nice lot of animals for a mounted detachment that could patrol more country than foot-soldiers; some of the horses were bought by the government or by me personally (before the epidemic a horse could be purchased for from twenty to fifty pesos), while many we had recaptured from babaylanes and *ladrones*. All died within a few weeks.

The plague killed them almost mysteriously. There were few visible signs of disease. The horse ran a little at the nose and sometimes developed a protuberance on the belly, but he would eat heartily till the moment of death.

The native horse doctors doped the beasts with all kinds of decoctions and lit smudge fires of alleged medicinal leaves under their noses and sterns. If the smoke had kept away the flies it might have had some effect, for there is no doubt that the disease was spread by the bite of horseflies, like the tsetse of South Africa. When the epizooti-surra-glanders first appeared, I sent two favorite riding-horses to the foothills of Mampuhubug, miles from other hoofed beasts, unless it were the wild deer of the cogon hills. But, despite such precautions, the animals died.

With my own horses gone I was forced to make inspection trips on hired stock or often astride the gray, greasy, hairless hide of a *carabao*. Now, the water buffalo is built on substantial fair-fat-and-forty lines; it runs to breadth and solidity of structure rather than to curves designed for the rider's comfort.

The camel, it is said, requires careful navigation and his saddle-action will reproduce a fair imitation of a ship at sea, whence, I suppose, comes his name, "the ship of the desert." But the *carabao* will give all possible camel sensations of motion plus the exquisite experience of a circus rider who bestrides two horses at the same time. Yet even the performer does not attempt to sit down on two horses at once, as must he who ventures aboard the broad back of a full-grown female *carabao* a few months in calf.

Nevertheless, the *carabao* navigated well in the rainy season, when the dirt roads churned into quagmires and the dry season short cuts across the rice fields were impassable to man and horse. Aboard his gray hulk one could sail direct across country, splashing over rice paddies, through mud-holes, and swimming rivers.

Some of the hacienderos trained trotting *carabaos* for rainy season work, and when I managed to secure such beasts, I made the inspection trips in comparative comfort.

This plague on the animals seemed yet another drop in the already overflowing cup of the islands' miseries. Centuries of misrule, insurrection upon insurrection, internecine warfare, outlawry, and cattle stealing, agrarian disorders, cholera, animal diseases—all had now afflicted that archipelago so physically fair and favored.

It is indeed a tribute to the natural resources of the Philippines, and surely no less a tribute to constructive American administration, that within a few brief years the islands have been lifted from poverty and disorder to complete peace and comparative plenty. And to have played even a small part in such honorable reconstruction of a land and people makes one thrill with not unjustifiable pride.

XVI - Disintegration and Reconstruction

JOURNEYS OF INSPECTION TO THE TOWNS OF my district occupied such time as could be spared from expeditions—and dances.

Mounted on a *carabao* or a horse that might die under me before my destination was reached—once or twice this happened—and accompanied by a soldier orderly, I rode from Isabela south, through Binalbagan, Himamaylan, Suay, Cabancalan, where there was a Scout post and the Hoppers, and Himamaylan where Serafin always welcomed me.

It was a depressing little string of towns to visit. Grass-grown streets and plazas, tumbledown houses, unfinished churches with interior decorations and images left open to the weather; pariah dogs, often with loathsome sores and mange, roaming at will and howling at the passer-by; razor-backed swine rooting up such parts of the roads as yet held firm or, beneath every hut and house, performing the functions of a complete system of sewage disposal. After residence in the tropics the Mohammedan prejudice against pork is easily understood. The dogs, too, completed with the swine as sanitarians.

The inhabitants seemed paralyzed by the successive visitations of war and pestilence. They moved about their daily tasks with apathy and hopelessness, quite different from the attitude of the people on the haciendas around Isabela. The reason was to be found, I believe, in the fact that some of these southern towns were artificial populations gathered by the Spanish friars around the church, distant, perhaps, from the best arable lands.

With the departure of the friars the towns disintegrated, while new barrios formed on the edge of the rice fields rather than on strategic points of the coast or hills. The population regrouped itself on economic instead of theocratic lines; and during the period of redistribution the church-formed towns were pitiable, semi-deserted spots.

This sudden withdrawal of the friars had more to do with the chaotic condition in which we found the Philippines that has been generally supposed. It was the Spanish priests who gathered the nomadic tribesmen in permanent communities; it was the priest who directed the governance of the town even though the gobernadorcillo might possess apparent powers; it was the priest who easily swayed an ignorant populace by appeal to its superstition, and it was he who officiated at baptism, marriage, and death—the only notable events in the colorless lives of the peasantry.

Into such sloughs of despond as these pitiable pueblos, American schoolteachers, men, women, and girls, were often thrust. The work they did in heartening the people, instructing not alone the children in the three R's but also the adults in the principles of organization and self-government, interpreting the laws and the municipal code, pointing out the elementary principles of cleanliness and sanitation, while applying them by practical example, all that work of supererogation has never been appreciated in America, nor fully, I fear, by the Filipinos themselves.

My own work was to inspect the municipal police, investigate grave crimes, and get a general line on the politics and economics of the town and district as they might affect public order. I took with me as orderly a bright soldier or non-com and let him lounge around the stores, drinking a glass or two of tuba and picking up the town gossip, while I called on the municipal officials and inspected the police.

Such police they were! A few barefooted peasants clad in rags of uniforms, loafing around the Casa Popular, to be more often used as servants for the officials than in legitimate police work. To inspect them was a disheartening task; and no immediate remedy for such conditions was in my hands. The municipalities were autonomous; inefficient they might be and were; but the officials were exceedingly jealous of Constabulary interference.

Ten years passed before the continued worthlessness of the municipal police stiffened the arm of the provincial and insular governments so that the Constabulary was given sufficient authority to produce within a year well-uniformed, equipped, and instructed police forces in every municipality of the islands.

In Cabancalan I usually stopped for drink or a meal with the Scout officer stationed there. He was an ex-sergeant of the Regulars. His wife was with him, and Judy O'Grady found some difficulty in living up to the position of the Colonel's lady. They often quarreled violently.

One day I arrived at their house to find Mrs. Z. alone and only too willing to fill my ears with stories of her husband's illtreatment and unfaithfulness. She wept, became hysterical, and, imploring assistance, fell upon my shoulder.

Now, I was neither very old nor very wise. But something whispered that it would be wisdom to keep out of a family quarrel, so somehow, I escaped and rode on south. A few months later, when I was senior inspector at Bacolod, I received a telegram from a court-martial at Iloilo summoning me as witness in the case of United States vs. Lieutenant Z.

I flung the telegram to Lieutenant Smith and told him to answer it, saying that I was absent from Bacolod on an expedition. And so I was. I left immediately for the mountains—out of range of the telegraph.

I have already stated that the roads of Negros were bad; indeed, they were bad enough to merit a few further remarks on roads, good, bad, indifferent, impassable and engulfing, as were those dreadful highways in that stricken land.

Many years had passed since work had been done to repair the Spanish turnpike along the coast. Yet with a rainfall measured in inches daily instead of annually, constant supervision of roads was needed. But the insular and provincial governments were not thoroughly organized, and the municipalities, which could very well have done something to keep up the roads, of course did nothing. The municipal officials would daily walk around the mud-holes in the main street of a town, would answer "No hay dinero," (there is no money) if asked to fill the holes, or would cut a few banana and coco trunks to pitch into a cavity when even a *carabao* could not pull an empty cart through it.

More than once on the main coast road of Negros Occidental I have seen a *carabao* and cart so engulfed in mud that only the head, horns, and part of the neck of the animal were visible. At such holes carts were unloaded and the contents packed by drivers to the other side.

The repetition of this process a dozen times a day made transportation slow and hazardous. Through the lesser mudholes I rode or led my horse, coating myself above the knees, sometimes even to the middle, with black viscosity; while at the larger ones I detoured through the backyards of houses or out into the rice fields.

That was in 1902, and the conditions so inadequately described—inadequately because no words can paint the awfulness of those roads—obtained throughout the Philippines. Yet by 1913 there were thousands of miles of perfectly kept macadam highways that linked provincial capitals with outlying pueblos and with Manila.

That is just one among many activities of which Americans may be justly proud; and the chief credit is due Cameron Forbes, who initiated a road program when he was secretary of commerce and police in charge of public works, and continued it while he was governor-general, and until he was rudely and ungratefully removed in 1913 by President Wilson.

Then on top of all this filth and mud, this disorganization and disintegration of the towns, this falling to pieces of houses and of populace, was superimposed a severe cholera epidemic when the ambitionless, moribund natives went down like grass before a scythe; when the funeral bells tolled monotonously in the tumbledown church towers; and when pathetic, dragging processions to the cemeteries were scarcely ever absent from the roads.

Yet in the faraway barrio of Isio one night the people offered me a dance, which, despite thirty miles in the saddle and a score of mud-holes, I was nothing loath to accept. There were no modern houses in Isio. It was the first time I had danced on a split bamboo floor. Moreover, the senoritas were barefoot, only one girl possessing a pair of heelless slippers which were passed around to my partner for the time being. The room was lit by low-hung kerosene lamps of small candle-power as well as by nightlights, merely wicks floating in cups of coco oil.

The girls were brown, dark-brown, or chocolate; no *mestizas* in Isio but a pure Visayan strain. Nevertheless, they were young, buxom, and of a feline prettiness, so that we danced late into the night.

And let it not be thought that from a Constabulary standpoint the time was wasted; for during the intervals in the dance I drank gin with the distinguidos or elders of the village, and thus, when tongues were loosened, picked up many a hint on political conditions or the whereabouts of outlaws.

XVII - A Jungle Killing

Expedition after expedition I made into the babaylanes country. We had many minor encounters but after the Mansalanao lesson, they never attempted to stand.

It was now a case of still-hunting—quiet preparations for the expedition, stealthy tracking through the jungle, the surprise of a clearing at dawn or dusk, and the capture of occasional babaylanes in their beds or on the trails. It was very much as Kipling sings in the "Ballad of Boh da Thone,"

The word of a scout, a march by night,
A rush through the mist—a scattering fight ...

Perhaps a few typical incidents of the trail will serve to limn that strange life which, with all its risks, held much of charm for any young American with sporting blood in his veins.

While living the sheltered life it seems a rather awful thing to find "sport" in taking the life of one's fellow man; yet no such qualms then upset our view of things. It was kill or be killed, and it must again be emphasized that the enemy had every advantage. The following little morning's affair should make that point clear.

We were hiking through the jungle on my second trip to Macabong; Julian, as usual, just ahead of me. Following the rules of military expeditions, there should have been a "point" of two or three soldiers ahead; but I trusted so much to my own quick aim with Winchester or revolver that I was accustomed to precede my men. (Later, as I grew older, and consequently acquired the usual paradoxical view that my life was increasing in value, I threw out a point.) Julian bent forward, padding along with his head half turned so as to catch any suspicious sound.

Suddenly he stopped and bent lower, almost to the trail. I turned and halted, by holding up one hand, the column of soldiers and cargadores behind me; then with two soldiers crept on hands and knees toward the sound of voices in the jungle. A few yards of crawling brought into view a little rocky brook meandering through the forest which hemmed it close at every turn.

There, squatting like frogs, were several Bukidnon men peeling and stripping great lianas of rattan with which the jungle was hereabouts interlaced even more thickly than usual.

As we were always ready to capture or interview any of these wild hills men, we snaked cautiously nearer and nearer. They were chattering and working so earnestly that our approach passed unnoticed until we were some fifty feet distant—when they took the alarm and rose from their squatting posture, poised for flight.

We sprang forward; and at that moment from behind a large boulder between us and the Bukidnon and a little to the left of the trail rose a babaylan soldier, who discharged, at a distance of perhaps twenty feet, a Remington rifle full in my face. Scarcely had he fired when I put a .45 revolver bullet into his chest.

By firing too quickly he missed me and paid the penalty. It all happened so suddenly that a few seconds later I myself extracted the empty shell from his Remington rifle.

A remarkable feature of the incident—of itself an ordinary enough occurrence in Constabulary work—was that the bullet pierced a large anting-anting suspended on the babaylan's chest and consisting of a sheet of paper folded many times and sewn in a waterproof bag. On the paper was a scrawl in the Visayan dialect which my soldiers deciphered.

It was an absolution in full from Papa Isio for a murder committed by the wearer in the lowlands. Poetic justice, indeed, that the bullet pierced the false instrument of pardon.

My soldiers recognized the babaylan as an ex-guard of the provincial jail at Bacolod. It appeared that he had been guarding a prisoner at work in a field but had allowed him to escape. Rather than submit to the penalty for lack of vigilance, the guard shot an innocent peasant and carried the body back to the jail, alleging that it was his prisoner, shot while attempting to escape. Later, suspicion fell on the guard, and he fled to the mountains.

That was the story as some soldier told it to me. I never verified it; there were too many current crimes with which to concern oneself. But a precisely similar incident that happened within my own cognizance years later in Mindanao lends verisimilitude to the above story of the life and death of one babaylan.

On that expedition we were intent on crossing the island of Negros to the east coast. We paid a visit to Macabong, burned several babaylan clearings, and finally found our way into a delightful series of Bukidnon villages stretching for miles down the eastern slopes of the Negros cordilleras.

These pagan Bukidnon hills-men are a race distinct from the Visayas of the Negros lowlands; perhaps it would be more accurate to say that they appeared to be of distinct race.

Dr. N. M. Saleeby of Manila, who knows more about the origin of the Malayan Filipinos than any living man, divides the inhabitants of the Philippines into three classes: (1) the pagans or hill tribes, (2) the Christian Filipinos, (3) the Moros or Mohammedan Filipinos; and shows how the islands were peopled by successive waves of Malayan migration, coming from the Malay Peninsula, Sumatra, Java, Borneo, and the other Spice Islands of the Eastern Archipelago.

Those Malays were the Anglo-Saxons of the East. They had their Hengists and Horsas who sailed to conquest over the soft southern seas in their prahus, in ignorant rivalry of the Vikings who braved, in their shield-sided galleys, the icy waves of the Northern oceans.

The origin of the Filipinos is also traced by Dr. Saleeby etymologically back to the Sanskrit; so that, after all, the Filipinos and ourselves have a common origin on the plateaus of Central Asia.

Dr. Barrows says, "Another possible explanation of the many Sanskrit terms that are found in Philippine languages, is that the period of contact between Filipinos and Hindus occurred not in the Philippines, but in Java and Sumatra, whence the ancestors of the Filipinos perhaps came."

It is indeed interesting to reflect on those human streams issuing from the Roof of the World in the Pamir, one flowing west, ever west, its members growing taller and whiter among the mists and snows of the northland; the other running south, ever south, its men becoming smaller and darker under the Southern sun until at last American and Filipino meet—and I chase babaylanes in the Negros jungles or feast with Bukidnons in their mountain homes.

The first time I feasted with the Bukidnons, I was an uninvited and decidedly unwelcome guest at a marriage festival. It was on this same expedition that I have for the moment abandoned to chase an ethnological will-o'-the-wisp. We had been in the mountains for about a week, had run short of food, and had already eked out our rations with the ubud or edible pith of the rattan root.

In fact, that and a few sweet potatoes scratched from abandoned clearings had been our only food for forty-eight hours. We always figured on supplying ourselves from babaylan villages. But this time we reckoned without taking into account our previous work in destroying those sources of supply.

In Macabong we found nothing, and we plunged down the eastern slope of the mountains toward the Bukidnon villages that we knew lay between us and the coast. We were hiking for our dinner. At last we reached a bluff above a pretty valley where fields of corn and sweet potatoes with plantations of coco palms, coffee, cacao, and tapioca pushed back the jungle.

A village of a few houses—brown mushrooms on a green field—lay at our feet. Around the houses was gathered a crowd of mountain folk. My hungry soldiers murmured "fiesta" (holiday celebration); and old Julian added, "Seguro casamiento de Bukidnon" (a Bukidnon wedding).

Among the celebrants there appeared to be some armed men: babaylanes were attending the wedding.

So, we formed a skirmish line and advanced down a log-strewn clearing toward the village. But long before we reached the houses the crowd disintegrated: the celebrants eddied and circled for a moment, then incontinently fled. The presence of the babaylanes doubtless made the Bukidnon feel that they were also tarred with the brush of outlawry. I sent a few men after the fugitives to clear out any babaylanes and yell friendly greetings to the Bukidnon.

Then, with the rest of the soldiers, I turned to the marriage feast, spread out al fresco beneath a grove of coco palms. It was, indeed, a sight for hungry soldiers: there were two fat pigs roasting whole over a fire, just turning to a succulent brown.

A couple of soldiers took the spits within a minute after they were deserted by the Bukidnon cooks; there were roast sweet potatoes, ubis, gabis (edible roots), and other tubers; there were stews of chicken with vegetables and sili peppers; there were pots and pots of rice, cooked, hot and steaming, covered with banana leaves; and to cap the whole, there were two enormous earthenware jars of pangassi—the rice beer of primitive Malay society—

each jar holding five or ten gallons, ready to drink, and even provided with a number of bamboo tubes through which to suck the intoxicating liquor.

Picture a score of starving soldiers encountering, in the depths of the jungle, such a feast as that! As guardians of the law, I suppose that before attacking the spread we should have waited until we got permission from the Bukidnon owners. But hungry stomachs know only the law of appetite, and if the babaylanes had attacked us half an hour later, they would have found us loggy with food and drink. That pangassi beer was strong stuff; I took a few pulls through the bamboo tubes and all the fatigue of a week's hiking vanished. My guides and a soldier or two got too much, became hilarious, and were put in one of the huts under restraint.

How good that roast pork was! The fat cracklings crunched with great wedges of yellow yams, the handfuls of scented mountain rice accompanied by slices of tender melting fat, the great spoonfuls of stewed chicken, the tang in the mountain air, the sunlight dappling through the coco palms, together with the appetite—above all the appetite—that hiking and semi-starvation had given us. It was good to be alive that day in the Negros mountains.

The only inhabitant of the village whom we saw to thank for our meal was the bride for whom the feast had been prepared. This pretty mountain maid, soft, round, and brown, was so encumbered by the wrappings of her bridal finery that my soldiers found her in the jungle, and brought her to me. We treated her well, gave assurances of our friendship for the Bukidnon and enmity toward the babaylanes, then sent her into the jungle to bring back her relatives and friends, who were doubtless watching us from every vantage point.

However, they evidently feared to encounter men with such redoubtable appetites; we saw no more of our involuntary hosts; and I still owe a Bukidnon chief—name forgotten—the price of a hearty meal.

We were lucky in free meals on that expedition. From the village of our repast, we dropped easily and slowly down the eastern slopes of the Negros cordilleras, through one picturesque Bukidnon settlement to another, over grassy foothills and into the valley of a clear mountain stream which we followed to where it met the sea, near the town of Guiljungan, in the province of Negros Oriental.

The town was celebrating its annual fiesta on the day of its patron saint, so that people were gathered from far and near, and there was a banquet just beginning in the somewhat pretentious house of the presidente.

The people of Guiljungan had been not a little plagued by the babaylanes, so they welcomed us as deliverers. Footsore from the trail—I remember that my own shoes were falling from my feet and were only held together by strips of raw rattan, while my men were all barefoot—I was lodged in the place of honor at the president's right hand, and washed down an excellent meal with several bottles of warm beer, as well as a few glasses of claret. Truly, a Constabulary officer on the trail in those days encountered many dangers!

From Guiljungan we hiked up the coast to Valle Hermosa—the Beautiful Valley—where my expedition was accommodated at the hospitable hacienda of Don Diego de la Vina, an old Spanish *mestizo* and wealthy hacendero with a heart of gold; a table groaning under good food; a stable of fast horses, and the only caponized fowls I have seen in the Philippines.

Don Diego was a good friend of the Constabulary and had often hospitably entertained its officers and men. Just now he was in trouble. The municipal officials of Guiljungan, of which Valle Hermosa was a barrio, had so worked on the Filipino provincial governor and on the American Senior Inspector of the Constabulary of Negros Oriental to obtain the revocation of Don Diego's license to keep five rifles for the protection of his hacienda. He implored my assistance to obtain the return of his arms.

I promised my good offices, and later, through the district chief, Colonel Taylor, so managed matters with the powers-that-be that Don Diego's arms were returned. The gratitude of the old gentleman knew no bounds, and never thereafter did I visit Valle Hermosa but that the fattest capons were killed and everything else done to show his appreciation.

Years later, when I was severely wounded in Mindanao, I received sympathetic telegrams from the old King of the Happy Valley; while every step that I took upward in the Constabulary service brought from him a letter of congratulation.

From Valle Hermosa to Isabela runs a trail which crosses the only pass over the Negros cordilleras at a moderate elevation. Hiking along that trail, over open cogon flats instead of through dense precipitous jungles, was by comparison a pleasure journey.

But, after nearly two weeks' absence from Isabela, I was anxious to return to headquarters; there was no further danger from babaylanes, so leaving the main body of the expedition, I hiked fast with a few picked soldiers. I was in the pink of physical condition, and as I swung forward faster and faster man after man dropped behind until, at dusk, I trudged into the barrio of Magallon, nine miles from Isabela, with only one or two soldiers tagging behind me.

We had come more than thirty miles since daybreak, yet I felt I could make the nine miles further to Isabela that night; so, leaving my now exhausted companions in the village I pressed on alone.

Not far outside Magallon runs the Binalbagan River, a hundred yards wide and two or three feet deep, with a boulder-strewn bed. In the half-light I did not notice that the river was higher than usual, but plunged into the water, intent on reaching Isabela. Quite a freshet was running, and as I got further into the stream the water swirled up to my middle.

I slipped over a boulder and was carried down by the swift current, with difficulty regaining my feet. And several times before I won to the other side I slipped, fell, and recovered my footing there in the cascading, hungry stream, fighting alone the waters in the rapidly darkening tropic night. There was just the matter of a boulder, a log in the freshet, or an inch or two of water between me and death. It was a very ordinary experience in a Constabulary officer's life.

XVIII - DAMACIO THE NEGRITO

MY SOJOURN AT PLEASANT ISABELA WAS NOW drawing to a close. An opportunity was to be given me in a wider theater of activities than the towns, hamlets, and jungles of southern Negros.

In October 1902, I received orders from the District Chief to proceed to Bacolod and relieve Major Orwig as Senior Inspector of the Province of Negros Occidental. Lieutenant Bowers succeeded me in command at Isabela and kept up the hiking reputation of the Constabulary in southern Negros.

On October 10, my twenty-third birthday, I assumed command at Bacolod, a not inconsiderable command for a youth of my years: sixteen stations, a dozen officers, and two hundred or more men, scattered over a province several thousand square miles in area. However, I don't believe that I gave the responsibility a thought; there was work to do, much work, too much work to permit thinking about anything but the job immediately ahead.

Conditions in the province were bad; cholera and animal diseases had prostrated the people and further upset economic conditions that had not yet recovered from the insurrection. In the northern Negros mountains were bands of babaylanes which were focuses to gather in the discontented peasantry, while in the foothills were many bands of cattle thieves.

Fortunately, I had not now to worry about southern Negros. Rumors that Americans were responsible for the cholera by poisoning the wells and streams, were flying among the ignorant population.

Across the narrow straits to the east in Cebu, a wave of fanatical pulajanism was gathering, which threatened to be, and later became, the most serious disorder with which the government was faced after the insurrection; across the narrower straits to the west, Panay Island was seething with outlawry and fanaticism; and emissaries from both islands came to Negros to foment trouble. That Negros escaped in large measure the serious upheavals that occurred in Panay and particularly in Cebu, during the years 1903-4, was at least partly due to a lucky coup that the Constabulary made near Bacolod within a few days after I became senior inspector.

Scarcely had I warmed the chair of office and become acquainted with the Filipino and American provincial officials when most disquieting news reached me from Murcia, a town in the foothills, nine miles east of Bacolod, at the base of Canlaon Volcano. The presidente of Murcia, by great good luck, was an elder brother of my young friend Presidente Serafin Gatuslao of Himamaylan.

On such little things do a man's reputation and career sometimes hang. Serafin, of course, had written his brother Antonio about me, so that from the first the presidente of Murcia had confidence in my ability to control the situation which daily became more threatening; and without his assistance and hearty cooperation I could not have cast the dragnet and made the haul of outlaws which quieted northern Negros a few days after I took charge.

On the forested slopes of Canlaon Volcano behind Murcia roamed Dalmacio the Negrito, the most courageous and consequently the most feared babaylan chief in Negros. In the babaylan hierarchy he ranked next to Papa Isio; but his was a separate command and he terrorized the northern half of Negros even more successfully than the Pope's captains terrorized the South. Dalmacio was half Negrito. His mother was a woman of that rapidly vanishing race of primitive negroid aborigines.

The dwarf, kinky-headed Negritos are the original inhabitants of the Philippines, but successive waves of Malayan immigration have diminished their numbers and have driven them further back into the mountains. They are now found only in the most remote jungles of one or two islands. In the mountains of Sagay in northern Negros a tribe persisted, and Dalmacio's mother was doubtless a semi-slave taken from the tribe by coast Filipinos.

The army and Scouts had many times skirmished with Dalmacio's band. Even in southern Negros I had heard tales of his prowess and of his successful raids on the towns of Sagay and Escalante; so, I prepared myself and the Constabulary for a stiff campaign.

I rode out to Murcia, interviewed Presidente Antonio, went a few miles deeper into the foothills to get the lay of the land, and made my plans. I was already becoming a little tired of fruitless chasing through the mountains in pursuit of the outlaws, for since we smashed Mansalanao they would never make a stand. Dalmacio, however, was bold. It seemed likely that he could be lured to destruction. He was.

At Murcia there was a Constabulary station of a corporal and seven soldiers. To the corporal, Abasola, a trustworthy and intelligent Visayan, I gave orders to skirmish inland against Dalmacio, who now emerged from the deeper mountains to raid the foothill barrios of Murcia, and rallied to his standard, day by day, more of the discontented and criminal element. It became for me a nice calculation how far Dalmacio could be allowed to go—or come. The longer I delayed a decisive blow the larger his band became and the greater the haul of outlaws when I cast my net.

Corporal Abasola skirmished with Dalmacio almost daily. Following my instructions, he always retreated, thus giving the babaylanes the idea of easily gained victories. The recent withdrawal of the American troops from Negros also doubtless persuaded him that the American Government was breaking down.

Presidente Antonio helped my plan by keeping his head, steadying the peaceable inhabitants, and sending evasive answers to Dalmacio's frequent notes demanding the surrender of Murcia to the forces of the Pope. Dalmacio even addressed bombastic notes to other distinguished citizens and to the provincial government. Rumor had it that Papa Isio had joined forces with Dalmacio. Several of the notes were signed by the Pope, but if that dignitary had fled from southern Negros because I had made it too hot for him, he was out of the frying pan and into the same fire.

This minor strategy went gaily on for some days until, as Dalmacio grew stronger and bolder, Governor Locsin and Judge Yusay of the Court of First Instance became nervous and urged me to let them call on the governor-general for the assistance of the Scouts and Regulars to quell the uprising. Dalmacio was now reported to have over two hundred men with a cannon and many rifles. My total Constabulary force available was less than thirty men. Nevertheless, with my past experience of the babaylanes, I felt it sufficient.

I quieted the fears of the provincial officials and awaited the hour to strike. On October 29, Corporal Abasola skirmished with Dalmacio only a mile or so outside Murcia, and Bacolod became full of alarming rumors. Lieutenant Frank of the Scouts, who had had personal experience of Dalmacio's prowess, came to me begging that I would take some of his men to eke out my own scanty forces. He even offered, to save my face, to let them be dressed in Constabulary uniform and to say nothing about it to the authorities. I thanked him, recognizing a very real man whose Americanism was above petty jealousies, but I felt quite confident of myself and my men.

Looking back at it now, I rather marvel at that confidence. My men were not the trusted and experienced hikers of Isabela, but a new lot and comparatively inexperienced. However, I had one or two old faithfuls whom I had brought from Isabela, and they had doubtless disseminated the idea of my luck and antinganting. I always believed in taking a soldier or two with me from one station, province, or district to another; it was a cheap and easy way to take advantage of an already earned reputation.

Nevertheless. I was really over-confident, for on learning that the babaylanes were so near Murcia I left Bacolod at 4 p.m. on the twenty-ninth, with only six men to swell Corporal Abasola's detachment of eight.

On the road to Murcia we met a stream of people escaping as they thought from the babaylanes, many of them with all their household belongings on *carabao* carts. It looked like a rout before an advancing and victorious army. I sent back to Bacolod for Inspector Smith and eight more men. I arrived at Murcia soon after dark; Smith joined me at midnight. Presidente Antonio had a fine supper prepared for us, but he was pretty nervous. And well he might be, with two hundred babaylanes encamped on the outskirts of his town.

At daybreak on the thirtieth, Smith and I with twenty-two men and two volunteer armed guides, moved cautiously out of Murcia as the cocks were crowing; while sleepy-eyed Filipinos who had sat up all night in terror peered from the darkened interiors of their houses. The babaylanes had passed the night in a hacienda whose buildings actually joined the suburbs of the pueblo.

As we skirmished over the rice fields and gardens that surrounded the town, the outlaws fell back before us. The country was rolling and, where not cultivated in rice and sugarcane fields, covered with long cogon grass. As we topped one hill the babaylanes passed over the next, just out of range.

Dalmacio was maneuvering for position. Within an hour or so he took his stand on the further bank of the Caliban River where a swift stream rushed between steep banks, cut out to a depth of perhaps ten or fifteen feet. There was brush on the further side to conceal the enemy's already prepared trenches.

Under an erratic fire from the babaylanes, we advanced to within about two hundred yards. Their little cannon boomed and dropped almost at my feet a curious missile made of a piece of an old Standard Oil kerosene can and containing bits of iron, nails, bolts, and so forth.

Their bullets picked at the trail and raised little spurts of dust. We lay down behind a rise which gave us partial protection and opened fire. The babaylanes, well sheltered, gave us as much or more than we gave. Their yells of defiance rose above the crackling of rifles and the occasional harmless boom of the little cannon.

They were so bold and defiant that I found it easy to leave Corporal Abasola with a few men in front of them to keep up a fire which would continue to engage their attention while with Inspector Smith and the rest I cautiously withdrew a short distance.

We made a considerable detour and crossed the river a few hundred feet below the scene of the fight at a ford pointed out by the two guides who were natives of the barrio of Iglaon which here nestled by the river in a grove of bamboo. Unseen by the babaylanes, we crawled through the long grass in their rear, the bullets from Abasola's detachment clipping viciously above our heads.

There was a little gully up which we crept and when near enough we sprang to our feet and took the outlaws completely by surprise. Smith, the two guides, and I were the first to show above the gully. We were within fifty feet of the babaylanes when they turned in their trenches and opened fire on us. Their first shots killed the two guides who were between Smith and me. One bullet struck the muzzle of my carbine, almost knocking it from my hand. But Smith and I pumped bullets into them, the soldiers came up, and the babaylanes started to run. Nevertheless, for a few minutes it was warm work.

The grass seemed alive with the outlaws, who fired in our faces before they fled. Even then their numbers were such that had they boldly attacked us with their long fighting machetes they must have won, for many of our men were slow in getting into the fight. But the surprise had unnerved the outlaws.

The fight became a chase. Over the grassy flat beside the river the outlaws sprang toward the hills, diving for the gullies where the grass was longest and almost concealed them. The Constabulary split into small detachments and pursued. At about a hundred yards' distance I saw two men making off and gave chase.

They turned, fired at me, and ran. I stopped, fired, and followed. Thus, passed a frenzied mile chase through the long grass, during which I distanced the soldiers who started with me. I dropped one man, passed his body, and finally brought the other down with a bullet through the leg.

As I panted toward him, he was game and potted at me with a revolver which missed fire, so he flung it away and, trailing his broken leg behind him, pluckily squirmed toward me, bolo in hand. I had him at my mercy and withheld my fire, but kept him covered.

When within a few yards he threw down his bolo, threw up his hands, and cried for mercy. Among his pleadings I distinguished the words "Aco— Dalmacio!" (I am Dalmacio!)

What luck again! I had captured the dreaded outlaw chief. The skirmish was over.

I ordered some soldiers to carry Dalmacio to the river bank and sounded the recall for the others who had pursued and slain for miles. Then I counted the cost of the fight, when, needless to say, I was astonished to find that not a Constabulary soldier was killed or wounded.

Only the two volunteer guides who stood between Smith and me at the first assault had been killed. It was a cheaply gained victory. Seven dead babaylanes were found near the river, including three well-known and long-wanted leaders of outlaw bands.

Later we learned that the total number of babaylanes killed was twenty-one, most of whom fell in the pursuit through the long grass which hid their bodies. We captured some rifles, the cannon, and a great collection of spears and *bolos*.

The first news of the fight that reached Bacolod was a note that I scrawled to Presidente Antonio, asking him to send out two carts to carry in the dead outlaws. He sent the note on to Governor Locsin. In after years, the jolly little provincial governor often joked me about the carts for the bodies, and told what a relief it was for him to learn that babaylan bodies and not Constabulary were to be brought in.

The word of Dalmacio's capture spread like wildfire. In Murcia and on the way to Bacolod hundreds of people flocked to see the noted bandit chief who, a few weeks later, was sentenced to death. He died in Bilibid Prison, Manila, before the sentence could be executed.

Governor Locsin sent a eulogistic telegram to Governor-General Taft, who replied by sending me a telegram of congratulation and appreciation. The provincial board passed a resolution requesting my promotion and retention in Negros.

A few weeks later I was promoted to the grade of Captain, corresponding to the old rating of First Class Inspector.

XIX - Race Prejudice and Cattle Stealing

How lucky the capture of Dalmacio was I did not fully realize at the time. Looking back a score of years or so, I can now see that it released the Constabulary for the work of suppressing the minor bands of cattle thieves, which, although they sometimes acted in concert with the babaylanes, were often purely local organizations; that it enabled us to patrol the pueblos and barrios instead of spending weeks in the jungle; that it fired officers and men with new enthusiasm and energy during the dark months and years to come when the Visayan islands seethed with fanaticism and discontent due to disturbed economic conditions, to the aftermath of insurrection, and to the readjustments that American Government made in the heretofore hierarchically administered Philippines.

Of course, the Constabulary could not take all credit for the good conditions that obtained in Negros as compared with other islands. For one thing, Negros Occidental was exceptionally fortunate in the type of Filipino officials at the head of the provincial government. Governor Leandro Locsin, elected by the people, was a Chinese *mestizo* of character and ability, and a warm friend to the American regime.

Judge Estanislao Yusay, also a Chinese *mestizo* and a relative of Governor Locsin, was as able and honorable a man as could be found in the length and breadth of the archipelago. If there was any complaint to be found with either of them, it was rather a matter of relationships than personal character.

Throughout the province they had so many relatives in office and out of office that few cases entirely free from nepotistic features confronted them. In the Philippines the tie of family holds stronger than with us, and is, perhaps, an inheritance from the comparatively recent feudal days of the Malay chiefs.

In America we quickly lose sight of our second or third cousins. In the Philippines, the distant cousin seems to have a claim on the office-holder, even if it may be only for a more liberal interpretation of the law or government regulations.

With Governor Locsin I established a friendship which endured through the years.

The fiscal, or prosecuting attorney, of the province, Senor Manuel Blanco, was a Spanish *mestizo*, whose Spanish blood preponderated. His appearance and manner were wholly Castilian; and, while he was a good lawyer and could be energetic enough in prosecuting the babaylanes and other outlaws whom the Constabulary raked in, yet he was also adept at carrying water on both shoulders and often drove me into a frenzy by letting off notorious criminals too lightly.

In fact, except the Constabulary officers, all provincial officials trod warily and with circumspection. We hiked, killed, or arrested, often wearing ourselves out in an endeavor to "hustle the East" into peace, respect for the law, and consequent prosperity.

The Filipino officials were older; and they were very wise on such subjects as politics, prejudices, and parentage, of which we knew little. We pushed them. They appeared to yield with that Old World courtesy that sits so well upon them, but they interfered as little as possible with things as they were—with municipal officials incompetent and venal; with municipal police, tattered and inefficient; with *hacenderos* replenishing their stock of work animals from other herds than their own; and with all the chaotic conditions that change of government and greater change of ideals of government had brought about.

I was exceptionally fortunate in the Constabulary officers under me. Although without exception older than their senior inspector, they gave me wholehearted support. Inspector Smith, my supply officer and right-hand man, worked like a Trojan to supply and pay the soldiers, and was always ready to take the field against the outlaws if necessary.

Every two months he made a round of the province with *carabao* carts full of Mexican pesos, boxes of uniforms, ammunition, and other paraphernalia. It was no light matter to disburse all government funds in Mexican pesos. Our salary was fixed in United States currency, and we received its equivalent in silver pesos which were at a constantly changing ratio.

At one time a gold dollar was worth two dollars and sixty-four centavos in pesos, so that an officer whose salary was $100.00 in gold per month received $264.00 in silver. When, as was generally the case, pay had accumulated for several months, a man could hardly carry away his money. I know that once, in Isabela,

Smith paid me for salary and reimbursement vouchers a thousand dollars in silver, a sackful of coin weighing, I should say, nearly one hundred pounds.

A very brief experience in the Philippines in 1902 and 1903 would have cured the most ardent exponent of Free Silver theories.

Our Filipino officers, Inspectors Colmenares and Azcona, were Spanish *mestizos*, also much more Spanish than Filipino. It is a curious commentary of the progression of the Philippine government toward complete Filipinization to note that the *mestizo* officers who occupied a prominent place in the early Constabulary have almost disappeared, their places being taken by Filipinos or by *mestizos* in whom the white blood is submerged rather than dominant. That is, doubtless, as it should be, for the other men perpetuated, in a manner, Spanish traditions of the "ruling race," and they were usually harsher in their judgment of the Filipinos than were the Americans themselves.

Indeed, much of our early prejudice against, or perhaps it would be better to say criticism of, the Filipinos was due to ideas suggested by the Spanish *mestizos*, who at first made to us a not unnatural appeal of blood and physical appearance. Rizal, in his inimitable satires on Philippine social conditions during the closing years of the Spanish regime, depicts the desire of certain *mestizos* to array themselves on the side of their fathers and to depreciate the stock of their native mothers.

The word Americanista or anti-Americano were then constantly heard. We were urged to believe that a Filipino was either violently for or more violently against us. Not until later did we learn that he might be neither, but merely pro-Filipino. Many of our initial mistakes and much of the racial antagonism engendered was due to our acceptance of inherited prejudices.

These conditions were perpetuated much longer in Manila and other large centers where Americans and *mestizos* abounded than in the provinces where Americans and Filipinos met and fraternized, and learned that

> *There is neither East nor West,*
> *border nor breed nor birth*
> *When two strong men stand face to face—*
> *though they come from the ends of the earth.*

What a pity that the above lines are not more frequently quoted than the first part of the same verse, which alone is such a misleading epigram:

*For East is East and West is West,
and never the twain shall meet
Till earth and sky stand presently at
God's great judgment seat.*

If our sense of humor had been better developed and our perspective adjusted, we would have estimated at their proper value the constant allusions of the *mestizos* to the *Filipinos puros* as *chungos* (monkeys) or *monos* (apes). Such talk was ridiculous and soon made me as indignant as it made the pure-blooded natives.

There were problems enough for a senior inspector. His judgment should have been unclouded by such poisonous suggestions. The babaylanes, fortunately, had been crushed, so that they were never more than a somewhat remote danger to be attended to when time afforded opportunity. But the gangs of cattle thieves became more active as the epizootia swept the province, killing *carabao*, oxen, and horses, and increasing the value of a *carabao*, for instance, from twenty or thirty pesos in 1901 to one hundred and fifty pesos in 1903.

These cattle-stealing gangs operated over the maze of trails that led through the cogon, bamboo, and brush-covered foothills, behind which, when pressed too closely by the Constabulary, the mountain jungles offered them secure hiding places. Although the law provided that an animal should be sold only on presentation of its cedula (certificate originally issued by a municipal official and visaed at time of sale or transfer of the animal), the officials lent themselves to every kind of falsification and abuse in the sale and purchase of animals.

It is safe to say that half the municipal officers were venal and profited by the sale or transfer of falsified animal cedulas. The certificate described the animal minutely, giving its brands and other marks of identification. But brands could be erased, horns, ears, and nose cut, and an animal so changed that its owner might have considerable difficulty in recognizing it. Indeed, a female *carabao* might well be excused for failure to nuzzle her own calf after it had passed through the hands of a band of Negros *ladrones.*

We once discovered a complete plant for mutilating and metamorphosing stolen animals. There were brands and irons without number, sharp knives and *bolos,* even an apparatus for so steaming the horns of the poor stolen brutes, that they could be twisted into new curves. Small wonder that when we captured *ladrones—flagrante delicto*—with the four-footed booty of their crimes we often had difficulty in discovering the rightful owners.

At one time we had in Bacolod a score or more *carabao* that were left in charge of the Filipino sheriff; and I discovered that the said sheriff made a very nice perquisite by renting them out at a peso or two daily to Chinese merchants of the town. Thus, do our Captains of Industry begin!

However, within a few months we had practically stopped animal stealing in Negros. Scores of *ladrones* were captured, and many killed while resisting arrest; half a dozen municipal officials were arrested and one or two were sentenced to terms of imprisonment and heavy fines.

As Judge Yusay was related to some of the indicted officials, an American, Judge Powell, was sent to Bacolod. He was a fine old Georgia gentleman who gave us every assistance in cleaning the docket of accumulated cases of gang robbery.

Before Judge Powell we prosecuted the presidente and vice-presidente of the town of Guimbalaon, who were relatives of the provincial governor; and their conviction and jail sentence did more to discourage animal stealing than the death or jailing of a thousand *ladrones* recruited from the peasant class.

But it was hard work getting evidence against these prominent men. It meant for me nights of work with witnesses and over papers, following days in the saddle.

Often, I sent soldiers out at night in civilian clothes, with revolvers concealed beneath their flowing shirts, worn native fashion outside their pantaloons. By such tricks and by frequent patrols along the foothill trails frequented by outlaws, we threw the net over increasingly large hauls.

XX - A Senior Inspector's Routine

ANOTHER FACTOR MAKING FOR UNREST WAS the Aglipayan schism from the Roman Catholic Church. "Bishop" Aglipay visited the province and gained adherents in every town. At that time and subsequently, there was good reason to believe that the "National Church of the Philippine Islands," as the schism took name, was closely if intangibly leagued with the insurgent chiefs remaining as outlaws and with all the varied forces that opposed the American Government. I remembered handing out secret-service funds to "Bishop" Aglipay while I was a disbursing officer in Manila.

So, I knew that he was playing both ends against the middle and was a man to be watched. However, in Negros his propaganda was chiefly directed against Spanish friars who had now returned to some of the towns from which they had been expelled during the insurrection. In this way the towns were divided into two religious camps and soon came calls for the Constabulary, either to save priests from insult and the windows of their convents from stones, or to quell riots which started when rival religious processions met in a narrow village street. Now, competition may be the life of trade. But active competition between rival religions amid an ignorant populace produces highly inflammable conditions.

We were kept busy patrolling the towns and instructing municipal officials that the provision of the Constitution prohibiting abridgment of religious freedom, and handed on to the Filipino people in the historic Declaration of Rights in President McKinley's Instructions to the Philippine Commission, was not to be construed against the Roman Catholic Church. The majority of the municipal officials at that time favored the Aglipayan schism and welcomed the opportunity to give the friars a dig.

Yet another problem was gambling on a large scale. Its suppression gave us light, interesting employment free from the risks of hiking after babaylanes and cattle thieves. The Filipino, like all Malays, is an inveterate gambler and takes his whirl at cock-fighting, panguingue, or monte. Cock-fighting was legalized on Sundays and holidays.

Panguingue was a comparatively harmless game of cards largely played by the women and older men. But monte, like faro or poker, made appeal to full-blooded sports, *hacenderos*, municipal officials, and Chinese merchants. Big monte games were run in the principal towns, and when the stakes became large the fortunes of the game had a direct effect upon the law and order that we of the Constabulary were sworn to enforce.

A municipal official who made a big losing must recoup himself from the town treasury; a *hacendero* who staked and lost his *carabao* must abet the stealing of others to replace them.

So we raided the games when stakes rose too high. And they rose pretty high, even if Negros was then at low economic ebb. There was one *hacendero* who came to the game with a cart loaded heavily with sacks of Mexican pesos; the cart went back with the light load of its penniless owner sleeping off several days of gambling and debauchery. Our chief difficulty was in getting convictions even though we captured the gamblers with cards and money. According to the Spanish penal code, it was necessary to prove that one of the gamblers was getting a rake-off from the game. Unless we managed to persuade an aggrieved loser to turn state's evidence, the gamblers generally went free.

In one game that I raided at Bacolod, within a stone's throw of the provincial building, I made an unexpected haul, arresting an ex-American soldier who had served with me five years before in the Greek Foreign Legion. It was a rather theatrical arrest. We had heard that two American cardsharps were touring the province and matching wits, not unsuccessfully, even with the "heathen Chinee." One night, when they were gambling in Bacolod, I headed the raiding party myself. Securing a search warrant, we surrounded the house, made a quick rush, burst in the front door, dashed up the broad stairs and into the long sola, where a dozen prominent residents were busily sweeping up cards and money.

One Filipino, evidently either the banker or the winner, grabbed a fat sack of pesos and jumped out of the window like a harlequin through a hoop, followed by Inspector C. There was a crash of bodies and a tinkling of spilled silver money on the banana palms and shrubbery outside. I held up the other gamblers, while my soldiers removed weapons from the two Americans and gathered up the cards and money.

When everything and everybody was secured, I sent the prisoners to jail for the night and went to bed.

In my office next morning all the gamblers were lined up for preliminary examination. One of the Americans gave his name, an unusual one that tickled some corner of my memory. As I looked hard at him in an endeavor to link up broken threads, he smiled guiltily and said: "I reckon we served together in '97, Captain, in the Greek Foreign Legion. Do you remember Z., who joined just before the battle of Domokos?"

Negros and the tropics faded away. Instead I saw a line of ragged men in badly fitting, soiled green uniforms, with bandoliers of cartridges and old Gras rifles; I smelt the powder and dust of battle on the slopes of the Orthrys Mountains, and saw the dark masses of Turks in the plains below, opening out and advancing to the attack; I heard again the whine of Mauser and Martini bullets, the dull thudding of shrapnel, and saw its white cloud rings against the blue sky; I saw the men of the Legion fighting and falling, powder-stained and battle-crazy—the red-shirted Garibaldians darting forward through our broken ranks and driving the Turks back for the only time in that war; I heard the groans of hundreds of wounded men when night fell and I was helping the surgeons at their bloody work. I looked at Z. The robe of my office as senior inspector fell away, and I was again companion-in-arms with the gallant boys of the Greek Foreign Legion.

It was a curious meeting. Whether the evidence in the case was insufficient or other circumstances prevented the Constabulary from bringing the gamblers to trial I now refuse to remember. But Z., gambler and ex-legionnaire, went back to Iloilo the following day with money in his pocket and good advice which he followed. He is now a wealthy planter of oranges and grapefruit in—let us say— California.

Perhaps a matter that gave me more concern than gamblers, babaylanes, Aglipayans, or other disturbers of the peace, was the responsibility for government property scattered throughout many posts where officers and men were constantly changing. Smith was a genius at accounts. He kept the men supplied and paid as well as or better than could be expected with the difficulties that confronted us before uniforms and equipment were standardized and proper regulations drawn up. But although an agriculturist may make two blades of grass grow where there was but one, even Smith could not make two saddles out of one or two lamps burn where none existed, as government invoices and receipts said they should exist.

Our constant expeditions and changes of station resulted in wear and tear, and loss of equipment that was improperly reported at the time; while pressure of other work hindered proper accounting and inventories. Finally, there grew an enormous list of property missing, for which apparently I would have to pay unless the demands of the auditor could be satisfied. A lucky—and yet unlucky—happening saved my pocket.

On a Coast Guard launch I had made the round of Constabulary stations on the coast of the province, and had gathered up all the accumulation of worn-out, worthless property to bring to Bacolod for condemnation by the district auditor. I left the launch at some east coast town, to come back overland, inspecting stations en route. A somewhat worthless Constabulary officer was returning on the boat to Bacolod. The northeast monsoon was blowing strongly, and I had warned him not to overload the launch's rowboats when putting soldiers and supplies ashore. But he disregarded orders, and at Bacolod a boat containing supplies and soldiers upset, two soldiers were drowned, and everything in the boat lost.

Not long after this accident I received from the auditor a list of missing property for which I was accountable. The list contained a miscellany which ranged from shotguns to native horses, from lamps to office furniture. Among the items were one ruler, wood, and one paperweight, iron. It gave me much pleasure to endorse the list of missing property back to the auditor about as follows: "To the best of the belief of the undersigned, the within mentioned articles sank to the bottom of the sea when boats from the C. G. Cutter Rover upset off Bacolod, Feb. 11, 1903. The wooden ruler would doubtless have floated and been recovered, but that the iron paperweight was tied to it."

They told me afterward that the endorsement evoked so much laughter in the auditor's office that by unanimous vote I was relieved from further responsibility for those supplies.

XXI - More Routine—Including Murder

WE MAY HAVE LOST A CERTAIN AMOUNT OF government property through carelessness and more by reason of unavoidable circumstances connected with our campaigns and our high-pressure work by day and night. But we certainly made up for any such losses by dipping our hands in our pockets to buy food and equipment for our soldiers whenever government supplies failed us—which was often in those days of organization that sometimes amounted to disorganization.

There was scarcely an officer who did not purchase delicacies for sick soldiers, extra ammunition for target practice or for his own personal arms used against outlaws, or who did not spend his pay freely on entertainments for Filipino officials and in the thousand and one other ways that contributed to build up the corps and the prestige of its officers and men.

It was about this time (1903) that the titles of Constabulary officers were changed from inspectors of various grades to designations of military rank. At first, we were called lieutenants and inspectors, captains and senior inspectors, but later the suffix inspector was dropped, and we blossomed into full military rank.

Nevertheless, we were given little or no increase of pay to uphold our rank in competition with officers of the regular army and Scouts, whose pay averaged for the same grades about 25 to 30 percent, more than ours, while their commissions carried certainty of ultimate pension, which ours did not. We ran greater, far greater, risks of death or disablement in action or by disease. We had little or no opportunity for rest in garrison between field operations. We had no cheap commissary and quartermaster supplies with which to eke out our scanty pay.

It would have been much better if the military rank had been withheld from us when we might have been resigned to more economical life and have saved money to provide for a future that the government failed to guarantee. In order further to lure us on there was formed a totally inadequate "Pension and Retirement Fund" for the Constabulary; how inadequate may be imagined from the fact that for total disablement, such as loss of eyesight or both legs, an officer might receive the princely reward of twenty dollars per month.

Yet, inadequate as it was, the Pension Fund kept many of us in the service with the belief that future legislation would improve our conditions. Realizing the work, we were doing in establishing peace in the islands and playing a prominent part in building up a Civil Service that did credit to the United States, we could not believe that our only reward would be the consciousness of work well done. Age and experience were to disillusion us.

At Bacolod I had my first experience with beriberi, the dread tropical disease that science has later shown to be due to an insufficiency of nitrogenous food in the diet. Two soldiers whom I sent to the Mambucal Hot Springs near Murcia soon died there; while if I had kept them at Bacolod and fed them on beans and bread instead of rice and dried fish, they would doubtless have recovered.

Soon after the death of these men I learned from Filipinos that mongo beans (a species of lentil) would cure beriberi and by dieting soldiers who became afflicted I cured them.

A few years later at the Iwahig Penal Colony I cured scores of the convicts by change of diet. That was about the time that investigations by Japanese naval surgeons and by Dr. Victor G. Heiser in the Philippines resulted in the official discovery of the cause and cure of beriberi. Those hot springs at Mambucal, springing from the slopes of Canlaon Volcano, made one of the most attractive places I have seen in the Philippines. A cleft in the mountain opened into a pretty, grassy dale down which dashed a cold clear stream. On either side of the brook were bubbling springs of hot sulphur water in natural rock basins, so conveniently arranged that by rigging bamboo pipes it was possible to convey cold water into them, tempering to bathing point.

Towering lauan trees dotted the valley, giving it the appearance of an English park. In their branches were flocks of balud (fruit) pigeon and hornbills. Once or twice while at Bacolod, I stole a day or two to visit Mambucal, and my soldiers built several comfortable huts there.

In November 1902, not long after our fight with Dalmacio, an American was murdered near Bacolod. Mr. Montgomery, an American superintendent of schools, was attacked by a band of *ladrones* on the main road between Silay and Bacolod, and was stabbed to death. On the night of the murder there was a dance at Bacolod. The provincial treasurer came up to me saying that he could not understand why Montgomery had not arrived, that he had expected him to stay at his house, and that a telegram from Iloilo had advised of Montgomery's departure for Silay that day.

We talked it over and determined that the steamer had arrived at Silay late and that Montgomery had remained there at the house of the American schoolteacher. But next morning, just at daybreak, the treasurer and the provincial governor awakened me with the information that some peasants had brought word that Montgomery's body was lying in the road only a couple of miles from Bacolod. He was murdered while we were dancing and talking about him.

The facts that were later brought to light showed that Montgomery started late that afternoon from Silay on horseback with a Visayan youth carrying his suitcase containing some two hundred pesos in Mexican silver; and when at dusk they had reached the loneliest spot on the road they were halted by a band of six armed robbers who demanded the American's money.

The youth dropped the suitcase and fled, but Montgomery drew a pitiful little .32 caliber revolver. Spears, daggers, and *bolos* flashed, and he fell from his horse, dead. To us the murder afforded another argument against Free Silver, for if Montgomery had not stopped in Talisay to purchase some little things and pay for it in pesos taken from the heavily laden suitcase, in all probability the *ladrones* would not have been on his trail.

There is little doubt that a member of the band saw the silver or learned from the porter the weight of the suitcase and that plans were then laid to intercept him at dusk at the loneliest place on the road. There was more than a suspicion that the murder might be attributed to hatred of Americans engendered by stories of our poisoning the wells and causing cholera. As there were dozens of other defenseless American men and women, schoolteachers and others, throughout the province, it was necessary to take stringent preventive measures.

I interviewed Judge Yusay and Governor Locsin, who were, if possible, more indignant at the crime than were we Americans. The fine old Visayan gentleman gave me carte blanche, and although nothing was said about the suspension of the writ of habeas corpus, yet I came to an understanding with Judge Yusay that the courts would not hamper the Constabulary.

Within a few hours constables, usually in civilian clothes, were raking the foothills, towns, and barrios to gather up the criminal element; ladrone after ladrone was captured or killed while resisting arrest, and the bodies of the dead were brought to Bacolod and placed in front on the municipal building as an earnest of "the price of a white man slain."

Leading Filipinos who loved not the American Government fumed and fulminated in the local and Manila press against the "barbarities" committed by the Constabulary. Despite the fact that no men were killed except notorious outlaws or *ladrones* who resisted arrest, but against whom evidence had hitherto been hard to procure, the discontented element believed that too great a price was being exacted for the death of just one American. However, the strenuous exhibition of the arm of the law made such an impression that all hands, and what was more important, tongues, were against the murderers.

One night, Governor Locsin came to me with a man who had heard the murderers boasting of their crime when tongues were loosened by too free indulgence in tuba (palm-wine); and, strangely enough, it was on or near the governor's own hacienda at Silay that the assassins were located.

Several of my best constables left Bacolod that night in civilian clothes, with revolvers under their shirts, surrounded the house where the murderers slept, killed two, captured one, and let two escape. They brought back the toy .32 revolver and other effects of poor Montgomery. After that there were no more Americans killed in Negros. The province was purged and purified of its outlaw element in a manner that would have been impossible if in each instance we had had to invoke the processes of civil law.

XXII - Bad Hiking and Worse Cholera

IN MAY 1903, I DETERMINED TO MAKE AN expedition around the east slopes of Canlaon Volcano, a journey that, so far as could be ascertained, had never been made by others than babaylanes and Bukidnon. The surrender of a babaylan chief, Francisco Abilo, gave me an unwilling guide who knew the trails, deny them as he might; so, with eleven soldiers, ten cargadores, and a week's provisions, I set out.

Leaving Murcia at daybreak we passed through the scene of our fight with Dalmacio at the ford of the Caliban River and hiked up the grassy slopes to Mambucal Hot Springs, where we fortified ourselves for a week on the trail by a plunge in the springs.

In the cool of the afternoon we wended our way from Mambucal over the cogon hills on the northern slopes of Canlaon, and before dusk dropped down into the canyon of the Bago River, a considerable stream, confined between broken precipitous walls hundreds of feet in height. The river rushed tumultuously over huge boulders. It was late, and the crossing looked difficult, as there was no ford, and we had to get from boulder to boulder as best we might, so I ordered a halt and we camped for the night on a sandbar.

In the occasional pools of the river were myriads of duck and other waterfowl which we obtained by sneaking from rock to rock, often half underwater, until near enough to blow their heads off with bullet or buckshot. Also, in crannies in the rocks my men found crawfish as big as lobsters, and fat eels. Supper that night was a feast.

Breaking camp at dawn, we crossed the river more than waist-deep in rushing water, the sacks of rations being passed from hand to hand to the other side. Next, under a blistering sun, we climbed the grassy slopes of Mount Pandanaon and welcomed the cool forests into which our trail finally led beyond the summit. Here we found clearings of a Bukidnon tribe with whom the Constabulary had cemented friendship.

The chief, Captain Aquilanon, was away on a deer and pig hunt, but his fourteen sons lined up to welcome me. As there were quite a number of men who had not presented themselves at Bacolod to receive the Constabulary certificate that we issued to peaceful mountaineers, I scribbled temporary passes on scraps of paper. We were trying to keep track of the mountain folk and to prevent their clearings being used as refuges for criminals and babaylanes in the fashion of past years.

More hiking under the torrid sun and we dropped again into the Bago Canyon, now deeper and steeper than at the morning crossing. A thousand feet we perpendicularly descended, and then waded up the swift stream where the men often slipped over boulders to tumble head over heels into the water. Up and across the river, steeply up the other side of the canyon, and we came into a forested country where the mountains seemed freakishly piled on top of one another. It was bad hiking. When at sunset we reached a Bukidnon clearing named Bidio, many of my men were near complete exhaustion. At Bidio we found a number of aborigines, only one or two of whom had seen a white man. All gathered around me like small boys around a circus elephant. In all probability there are still Bukidnon in Bidio who tell their more ignorant brethren of the still deeper mountains that all white men are over six feet tall and have flaming hair!

As Francisco Abilo persisted in denying knowledge of the trail, we took along as guides two men of Bidio. They led us, next morning, over one of the worst trails I have ever traveled, a succession of slippery ascents and descents through the thickest kind of tropical forest, un-traveled for many months.

Trailing plants and vines crisscrossed in network before us. Moss orchids and ferns hung from the trees. Guides and soldiers hacked their way along. We crossed seventeen rivers, a few hundred yards one from the other. It is from this eastern slope of Canlaon that the two great rivers of Negros are fed.

Finally, we crossed the watershed between the Bago and Binalbagan rivers and neared an inhabited clearing. Then Francisco Abilo, seeing further obstinacy useless, told me that two babaylan "generals" with several rank and file lived in the clearing, which we approached by a circuitous route through the jungle along a secret trail known to Abilo.

As we emerged from the jungle some women and children yelled and fled, and two armed men with lances, who had come out of the forest on the other side of the clearing, turned to flee, refused to halt at our cries, and were fired upon. One fell at the edge of the jungle and the other had a narrow escape, for we picked up the blade and hilt of his bolo, smashed from his side by a carbine bullet. The dead man was identified by Abilo as Luis Tarangay, a notorious *carabao* thief, while the man who escaped with the loss of his bolo was Marianao Dapdap, another ladrone.

That night it rained hard. In the filthy huts of the babaylanes we had little opportunity to dry ourselves. Before morning we almost envied the dead man, comfortably interred and with a cross bearing his name, "Luis," engraved by some thoughtful soldier, likely enough a distant relative of the deceased—for I had several—babaylanes among my constables.

Next morning it rained still harder, and only after hours of hiking through the dripping, soggy jungle did we emerge on the well-known cogonales or grassy slopes over which wound the Valle Hermosa-Castellana trail. I was almost back in my old stamping grounds near Isabela.

When we intersected the main east-and-west trans-Negros trail we met at the ford of the Maslug River a patrol of constables awaiting me with a letter saying that Lieutenant Colmenares and five soldiers were down with cholera at Valle Hermosa. After days of hard jungle hiking, I was ready for a rest. But with three men I somewhat wearily turned toward the east coast.

After several more hours or hard hiking, during which we were lashed by typhoon rains, we slid down the eastern slopes of the cordilleras to the Happy Valley, now most unhappy and cholera-ridden. Colmenares was well cared for by the always hospitable Don Diego de la Vina. But the soldiers were weltering in their own filth in the nipa barracks, while two bright young Constabulary officers were drinking gin and making merry in a house some distance away. Those two officers were brilliant exponents of the "Don't Worry" attitude toward life.

They made little or no attempt to better the conditions of the sick and dying soldiers. In fact, their only anxiety seemed to be lest a boat be dispatched to San Carlos for a new supply of gin might not return before their bottles were emptied. Hilariously they greeted me and generously pressed a drink from their failing supply.

"Gin! Gin! Glorious gin!" was the stuff to keep the cholera away, so they swore. I took the drink—I needed it after a week in the mountains and the long hike of that day through the rain!

Then I left the fuddled pair to their orgy, and, by the light of flickering lanterns turned to the job of doctor, nurse, and hospital orderly in one. The details of the cleansing of that barracks I dare not divulge. But anyone who has seen just one cholera patient will be able to imagine the condition of several left practically to care for themselves for days. With the assistance of Filipino soldiers, as yet untouched by the scourge, I burned, boiled, scrubbed, disinfected, and administered such medicines and stimulants as could be secured. This job, coming on top of a week's hike and hardship, about finished me.

The two gin-soaked officers—one was an Englishman and the other a Hollander—belonged to the Constabulary of Negros Oriental. I had no authority over them. They rode off south next morning along the coast; before very long they were dismissed from the Constabulary.

That hike around Canlaon, the forced march to Valle Hermosa in the typhoon, and the overwork looking after cholera patients, broke my constitution, which I had come to consider as resistant to time and abuse as that of the United States. On my return to Bacolod I went down with a severe attack of malaria, which, at first neglected, became cerebral in type.

For two or three days I hovered on the border ground of the unconscious; Smith, splendid, loyal fellow that he was, managed to get a doctor and a supply of ice from Iloilo by special boat and saved my life. And some months later a heartless auditor tried to deduct the cost of the boat, ice, and doctor from my pay.

However, my senses returned when the ice cooled off my fevered brain, and I rapidly recuperated. In July I obtained a month's leave of absence, ran over to Hongkong, but was back again at the siren work of a Constabulary officer long before the month expired.

My work in Negros was nearly done, and I was to go still further south, to a part of the archipelago even more interesting, even more palpitating with the hot life of the tropics, than Negros. In August 1903, I was ordered to Mindanao, as adjutant of the Fifth Constabulary District recently organized, to form a Constabulary among the Moros.

On leaving Negros I had the satisfaction of knowing that the babaylanes had been thrashed so that they no longer menaced public order, that animal stealing had been practically stopped and the bands of *ladrones* comminuted, and that the Constabulary of Negros Occidental was second to none in organization and efficiency. The credit for this I cheerfully give to the loyal officers and men who supported me through dark days.

If these reminiscences deal almost entirely with my personal experiences and achievements it is because those are naturally freshest in my memory; while if I attempted to chronicle the deeds of my companions-in-arms I should soon exceed the limits that the reader would endure.

XXIII - AMERICAN PIRATES

COLONEL WALLACE TAYLOR, the Chief of the District of the Visayas, had a little job for me to do while en route to my new station at Zamboanga, Mindanao. A certain Constabulary captain, by name Herrman, stationed at Cagayan as senior inspector of the province of Misamis, had been gambling, drinking, and otherwise cutting didoes prohibited by Constabulary regulations. I was to investigate and report upon his conduct at Cagayan as well as at his previous station at Tagbilaran, Bohol.

During the first two years of Constabulary existence there was much winnowing of chaff from wheat, but there were still many officers who disgraced the service, and our District chiefs were so overworked that they could not be everywhere, inspecting and eliminating. So, Colonel Taylor sent his Coast Guard cutter Scout to Bacolod and I embarked for Cagayan, with a roving commission to go wherever the trail of Herrman's misdeeds might lead.

Very pleasant it was—sailing over those placid blue seas and straits past green islands over which often hung the smoke of mountain clearings; very restful to lounge in a deck chair and watch the coast of Negros slide by, and to identify mountain peak after mountain peak where I had hiked and fought during the past months. At sunset Negros became but a darker cloud on a topaz horizon.

At daybreak the mountains of Mindanao, the second largest island in the archipelago and by far the least known and most romantic, rose above the dawn mist.

In Cagayan I spent a day or two investigating and inspecting, to find the Constabulary in pitiful condition of inefficiency and disorganization. Captain Herrman, a German-American with a foreign tang in his speech and manner, was a disgrace to the Constabulary; his speech and manners were those of the barroom.

Lieutenant Johnson, Herrman's supply officer, was a callow youth entirely under the older man's thumb. It took little time to persuade me that both were unfit for the service. Moreover, at Cagayan there had developed a license and immorality not among

Constabulary officers alone, but which affected almost every member of the small American colony; drinking, gambling, and prostitution were rife.

Johnson's money and commissary accounts were in bad condition, but before my arrival he had borrowed sufficient funds to make up most of his shortage. I had no authority to do more than investigate and report to the District Chief, and charges against Herrman for misconduct at his previous station at Tagbilaran on the island of Bohol were still to be investigated.

So, I gave no intimation to him or to Johnson of my censure on Cagayan conditions, but sailed for Tagbilaran to get proof of graver crimes committed by Herrman while Senior Inspector of Bohol. Herrman's successor there as senior inspector had formulated charges against him of which Colonel Taylor had sent me a copy.

Had I suspected that Herrman and Johnson would become desperate, would seize a steamer and desert from the Constabulary to become pirates and wanderers on the Sulu Sea, needless to say I should have remained at Cagayan. But I am anticipating.

At Tagbilaran I found ample evidence that Herrman had been habitually drunk, that he had tortured prisoners, and that, in a fit of blind passion while on an expedition, he had killed a guide. I cabled the result of my investigations to Colonel Taylor, recommending the immediate suspension and trial of Herrman, and then set out for my prospective station at Zamboanga.

On arrival there, some forty-eight hours after leaving Tagbilaran, I learned that Herrman and Johnson had fled from Cagayan, impressing a steam launch and carrying with them several thousand pesos of government funds, with rifles, ammunition, and other supplies.

Years later, I had reason to suspect that Herrman learned the contents of my cable to Colonel Taylor and knew that his game was up. There was a cable direct from Tagbilaran to Cagayan, and my message was probably routed that way on its journey underseas to Iloilo, Colonel Taylor's headquarters—and operators sometimes talk, especially at remote stations where all Americans meet and drink together.

I was scarcely ashore at Zamboanga before Colonel Harbord, my new chief, sent me off in pursuit of the renegades, this time on the cutter Ranger.

Across the enchanted Sulu Sea, I sailed to Sandakan in British North Borneo, there warning the British officials that two American pirates were loose on the seas.

From Borneo ports, I touched at other islands to which the pirates might have run, but getting no news of them I returned to Zamboanga, to learn that the Victoria—the impressed launch—had put into Baliangao on the north Mindanao coast for coal, and had then headed for Negros and Cagayancillo, the latter a remote island in the north Sulu Sea.

So off I went again over the turquoise seas until the coco palms of sandy Cagayancillo showed behind a white line of surf where the waves beat on the atoll wall of its lagoon. There was a hazardous landing through the surf, a visit to surprised Filipino officials who saw strangers but once a year and who had barely time to don clean white shirts and find the tasseled cane of office, but who gave assurances that the pirates had not come to peaceful Cagayancillo.

Then the Ranger was headed back to Negros. After two or three weeks of investigation, excitement, and pursuit, I was almost back at my starting place.

Dawn found us off Sipalay, and there I picked up the fugitives' trail of blood and misery. Herrman and Johnson had taken their launch as far as Bayauan in southern Negros. There the launch—probably guided by its impressed Filipino skipper—had run on a sandbar. The pirates boarded a parao which proved unseaworthy, so they transferred to another larger and better-furnished craft which had a crew of six men and a nipa-roofed cabin, as have so many of the trading outrigger craft of the southern islands.

In this parao they set sail for Cagayancillo, and but for the happenings of their voyage, I might have encountered them there—with interesting results. They were now at sea: the two desperate Americans, one faithful misguided private of the Cagayan Constabulary, and the six sullen, unwilling Visayan boatmen.

The first night out from Negros Johnson was sick with a fever and Herrman kept watch, fearing the boatmen, but on the second night Johnson had so far recovered that Herrman, leaving him on guard, ventured to snatch some sleep. Then that lonely parao on that lonely sea became a bloody shambles.

Johnson, still fever-ridden, dozed. The boatmen seized the awaited opportunity, set upon the Americans with daggers and *bolos*, mortally wounded Johnson, cut off half the face of the Constabulary soldier, then stabbed through the palm-thatched cabin roof at Herrman, now awake and groping in the dark for his loaded Krag carbine.

Before he secured the gun, Herrman was slashed on the legs and about the head and shoulders. But when his fingers closed around the carbine he quickly took revenge, killed outright four of the sailors, while the other two, panic-stricken, jumped overboard into the dark night, the engulfing sea, and the waiting sharks.

Johnson soon died. Herrman was left on the ensanguined parao with a dying private of Constabulary, and himself bleeding from many wounds. At dawn—what a dawn!—the mountains of Negros showed just above the eastern horizon and Herrman set sail as best he might for shore and comparative safety.

The hours passed, the sun blistered and dried the blood on deck, the dying soldier groaned and tossed; the parao lurched drunkenly through the swell, until at last Herrman ran his tragic craft ashore south of Sipalay, where, after burying Johnson and a sack of pesos in the sand and leaving the wounded and apparently dying man to the care of natives, he embarked in a canoe and paddled south along the coast, half-crazy and wholly desperate.

At Sipalay I learned some of the foregoing facts, and down the coast I pursued the unhappy man. While entering the little bay on the shores of which Johnson had been interred, I saw that other pursuers were ahead of me. At anchor was the Coast Guard cutter Marinduque with Colonel Taylor and Captain Haskell aboard, both eager to wipe out the stain which Herrman had left on the Third Constabulary District.

Together we continued down the coast.

At Bayauan we caught up with the fugitive, who had sought refuge on the hacienda of a Spaniard whom he had known in happier days. On our approach Herrman fled to the jungle. We hiked after him, but found no traces. However, his apprehension was now but a matter of time, and I felt that it would be delicate of me to leave his capture to the officers of his own district, so I sailed for Zamboanga.

The following day Herrman was captured by Captain Haskell. A few weeks later he was sentenced to fifteen years' imprisonment—and very lucky indeed not to be hanged for a murder committed in Bohol and for slaying the six soldiers on the parao, though, to be sure, it was then kill or be killed.

However, I had not seen the last of him. Eight years later I was on my way back to the United States on an army transport when one evening a steward brought me a note from a passenger in the steerage.

It was from Herrman, pardoned by the governor-general and deported from the Philippines; so on a lower deck of a transport nearing San Francisco, I finished an acquaintance that had begun in Cagayan in Mindanao. Herrman seemed a changed man.

Soberly and with a sense of responsibility, he told me how bitterly he had expiated his crimes and how he had availed himself of opportunities in Bilibid Prison to learn a trade, to read and study.

The unhappy episode at least was fortunate for me in one way. It gave me an opportunity to become better acquainted with my previous District Chief, Colonel Wallace Taylor, of whom I had seen little while in Negros.

Panegyrics should be saved for the dead, but I must at least speak of the impression that the Bayard of the Constabulary made on me. Our work almost daily provided acid tests which showed up men in whom there was too much base metal, so we did not lack brave officers; yet Colonel Taylor was as conspicuous as a newly minted five-dollar gold piece in a handful of old copper cents.

Wherever the pulajanes were thickest, wherever the hiking was hardest, wherever the odds were greatest against the Constabulary, there he was to be found, inspiring by his courage but no less by his courtesy and fine manner of life.

No greater praise could be given him than was voiced whenever two or three junior officers were gathered together—"Colonel Taylor, he's white all through."

It is something to have served a man like that; and I often think that our best and perhaps only reward for Philippine service will be the satisfaction of work well done and friends "grappled with hoops of steel."

XXIV - The Moro Problem

ON MY RETURN TO ZAMBOANGA FROM THE pirate chase I took up the duties of adjutant to Colonel James Guthrie Harbord, the forceful army officer who was organizing the new Constabulary district, and who was later to win such a reputation in the World War.

A few weeks earlier, General Leonard Wood had assumed command of the Department of Mindanao, becoming also the first civil governor of the Moro Province and shouldering the considerable task of bringing order out of the disturbed conditions that had prevailed in Mindanao since the American occupation of the Philippines in 1898.

In the Christian-Filipino provinces of Luzon and the Visayas, the American Government had at least the wreckage of Spanish administration out of which to construct a government; but in Mohammedan Mindanao and Sulu the Spaniards had left little or no heritage of constructive government; they had held but a few fortified towns on the fringe of Moro populations still steeped in piracy, slavery, and superstition.

On the coast and on the lakes and rivers of Mindanao, on every island of the Sulu Archipelago, strung like a necklace of emeralds from Mindanao to Borneo, were Moro sultans, rajahs, maharajahs, datus, panglimas, or hadjis, each ruling his little band of gaudily dressed and weapon-adorned fighting men.

There were chiefs whose followers could be numbered on the fingers of one hand; there were others who mustered thousands of retainers armed with modern rifles in addition, of course, to the sharp kris or barong thrust in the sash of every Moro gentleman.

But the leader of five men was as touchy as the lord of five hundred; as quick to defend his ancient prerogatives of life and death over his dependents, and especially over the pagan hillmen who inhabited, side by side with the Moros, the jungles of Mindanao and the larger islands; as ready to die to defend his right to keep slaves and exact tribute from Subanuns, Bilanes, Manobos, Bagobos, or Bukidnon. Those are the names of a few of the dozens of pagan tribes that inhabit the Mindanao mountains.

Mindanao, an island about the size of Ireland, was almost a land unknown. Its rugged ranges of mountains culminating in peaks 8,000 and 10,000 feet high, its inaccessible and swampy lakes, its rivers flowing through trackless jungles, its shores fringed by mangrove swamps and coral reefs, its gloomy forests and its glorious sunlit grassy plateaus were mapped only in outline or by Spanish draftsmen with vivid imaginations.

Here and there a Jesuit priest or a captain with some flickering flame of conquistador spirit had journeyed into the interior to return with tales of magnificently retinued Moro chiefs or tribes of man-eating savages. One thing the Spaniard had done—and there were not lacking gallant pages in the doing of it. They had stirred up the nest of human hornets that inhabited the archipelago south of the eighth parallel of latitude.

And now we were to persuade those hornets to return to their burrows. But, despite fumigatory legislature, patience, and constructive administration, a good many Americans were to be stung to death before the buzzing Mohammedan swarms calmed down; while even now an occasional hornet escapes and the American public reads, over its breakfast coffee, or more often fails to notice, that "some renegade Moros in Sulu have been subdued by the Constabulary with the following casualties..."

Off and on for nearly ten years I served in Mindanao and Sulu, a minor actor in a bloody racial drama not un-lightened by incidents of heroism and self-sacrifice and amid scenes where the most backward and barbaric East clashed with the most advanced and energetic West.

Doubtless we might have profited more than we did by the experiences and experiments of other nations dealing with similar problems, from the Dutch in the East Indies and the British in the Malay States. But from the first our work was handicapped by the impermanence of army and other officials, the unsettled future of the Philippines, and the consequent difficulty of building up a corps of civil service employees who understood the Moro tongue and, what was even more important, the Moro tang.

It is not an exaggeration, I believe, to say that nine-tenths of the fighting and the killing in Mindanao and Sulu, the past twenty-five years, might have been avoided if those of us who knew the Moros had been encouraged to remain among them by adequate pay, permanent positions, and authority, and an eventual retirement and pension.

Zamboanga! The capital of the Moro Province and largest town in Mindanao. The name bears its own attraction of easily flowing syllables; the place exercises its charm over everyone who has been there.

Old whitewashed Spanish buildings squared around a sun-splashed plaza; palm-thatched Moro huts flung along a sandy beach where native outrigger boats of many-colored sails are tied up at back doors; groves of coco palms soughing under the steady monsoon breezes that keep Zamboanga cool and pleasant throughout the year; avenues of scarlet-blossomed "fire-trees," green rice fields sloping back to darker green, and purpled hills and mountains from which issue streams of clear water rushing down through the streets of the town into the sparkling blue Straits of Basilan. All the warm colors of the tropics are lavishly splashed on the palette of Zamboanga, and its surroundings of land and water.

Zamboanga—so quaint and picturesque under its coco palms and wild almond trees that it almost seemed like a stage setting for a comic opera. Yet racial and religious eddies swirled around that painted town where the physical surroundings were those of the beauteous South Sea Islands but the social atmosphere that of an East Side gangster war. Christian clashed with Mohammedan, Moro with Filipino.

It was there in the southern Philippines that two great currents of race and religion met. It was little wonder that there was a social and political whirlpool.

In 1519 Magellan sailed west across the Pacific, to discover the Philippines, and during the sixteenth, seventeenth, and eighteenth centuries a succession of Spanish soldiers, priests, and administrators streamed across the ocean from Europe or from Mexico. They imposed upon the northern islands of the Philippines at least a veneer of Latin and Christian civilization.

About the time that Christian missionaries were starting west, Arab priests of the other great missionary religion of the world, the Mohammedan, started east from Mecca, through India, through the Malay Peninsula, through Sumatra, Java, the Celebes, and Borneo, and so on to the Sulu Islands, Mindanao, and the Philippines.

Upon the Malay seafaring folk of the southern Philippines, the Mohammedan emissaries washed an even thinner veneer than that with which the Spaniards coated the northern Filipinos. Another racial distinction must be borne in mind. The Filipino of the North, whether Tagal, Ilocano, Visayan, or Bicol, is of more mixed blood than the Moro of the South, who is of pure Malay strain, the leading families alone having some of the blood of the Arab missionaries with a very occasional infusion of Chinese.

The Filipino, even at the time of the Spanish Conquest, was of mixed race, Malay and Indonesian diluted with Chinese and other blood; and since the Spanish Conquest, the Filipino of the North has further attenuated the Malay strain. But the Moro is almost pure Malay. His leading characteristics are those of the Malay: fierce personal independence, lack of respect for life and property, combined with much dignity, pride, and courage.

Just as the American of the Western frontier in the nineteenth century expressed the quintessence of the Anglo-Saxon racial characteristics—individuality, adventurousness, and the desire to build from fresh material—so the Moro was the Malay frontiersman of the Far East; in him the Malay traits blossomed into a virile race with a leaning toward warfare and piracy as national professions.

A high-strung, energetic child may be led to maturity along paths which may lead to vice or virtue. The Moros had, prior to American occupation and by the natural stimulation of religious rivalry, followed the road which had made them the best professional pirates in the world.

To compose the differences between Christian and Mohammedan, between Moro, American, and Filipino; to turn the energies of the Moros from savage warfare to agriculture and industry, was a task that called for a man who understood all three races; and for a permanence of administration which would permit the man to do his job.

Despite the fine pacifying work done by Generals Wood and Pershing, little progress was made in Mindanao until Frank W. Carpenter became governor in 1915. Army officers naturally worked upon the Moro problem merely as a stepping-stone to higher things; whereas it was the work for a man's lifetime, or for several men's lifetimes.

In a few years Carpenter brought Moro and Filipino amicably together for the common weal, and substituted order and trustfulness for bloodshed and suspicion.

In September 1903, under adverse conditions, we organized the Moro Constabulary, an experiment that the Spaniards and Filipinos looked upon as further proof that Americans were crazy. They warned us that the Moros could never be trusted, and quoted many instances of Spanish officers murdered by their servants or at the command of Moro chiefs in whom they had misplaced confidence.

However, in the American way we went ahead doing the impossible. A nation that had harnessed Niagara and bound the limitless prairies with bands of steel was hardly likely to find insuperable obstacles in Mindanao. And our faith in our own destiny was justified, for the Moros, in American hands, made fine soldiers. Only one of our officers was treacherously murdered by his own men. That was Captain Hayson, who, at the time of which I write, was Senior Inspector of Zamboanga and, with myself, the first officer to enlist the Moros.

Hayson was a fine specimen of Kansas manhood, who had worked his way up from coal miner to lawyer, from lawyer to captain in the United States Volunteers, and now to a responsible position in the Constabulary. His death is another story, and occurred two years later.

I had been in Zamboanga but a few weeks when Hayson and I had an interesting little adventure together.

The Portuguese explorer Magellan[17]

XXV - A Tragedy of Zamboanga

Hayson had rapidly recruited his Constabulary with a nucleus of Filipinos brought down from the headquarters troop at Manila and among whom were two of my old Negros soldiers. To these he added many Zamboanguenos (Filipinos of Zamboanga and vicinity) and a few Moros, sifting these in gradually as baking powder is sifted into flour to make a cake. His detachment was about twenty strong when an outlaw band developed in the environs of Zamboanga under the leadership of one Eduardo Alvarez, lately a prominent citizen of the town, now an outlaw with a price on his head.

As a matter of fact, the outlawry was more a matter of Zamboanga politics and feuds than an outbreak against the American Government; for Alvarez was an ancient enemy of the actual presidente municipal, who had the ear of the American provincial governor. Two American miners had been murdered by Subanun tribesmen in the mountains a few miles north of Zamboanga. The crime was fastened on Alvarez, although in the light of my hardly-won knowledge of Philippine men and manners, I doubt whether he was responsible. But evidently he expected little mercy or justice from his enemies in power, so he fled to the ever-waiting mountains.

Colonel Harbord was away, and General Wood summoned me to receive orders for Constabulary pursuit of Alvarez. It was my first official meeting with the general, whose courteous and kind manner toward a junior Constabulary officer has never been forgotten: and it was almost my first opportunity to learn that the bigger the man the smaller the "side."

It was at the time when General Wood's name was in every mouth. He had come to Mindanao fresh from his successful administrative regeneration of Cuba; behind him the glamor of the Rough Riders; around him the aura of President Roosevelt's intimate friendship.

The newspapers were full of Senator Hanna's fight in the Senate against confirmation of the general's commission as major-general in the regular army. He was a national figure; I was a junior officer of the Constabulary. Yet before I had been with him five minutes I felt as if I had known him a long while and he was actually asking my opinion on the subject of hunting down outlaws in the jungle, a game at which two years' practice had made me fairly proficient.

I remember years later in Mindanao another general of the regular army who called me in about a matter of rounding up some outlaw Moros; and who, on a map, showed me how he was going to do it, and talked at me for an hour or two. He neither asked for nor listened to advice. He did not get the outlaws. The Constabulary got them later.

For several days, army and Constabulary detachments raked the beautiful countryside of Zamboanga as well as the dense jungles and swamps surrounding it until at last we received from the municipal president definite word of the location of "outlawed" Alvarez, who was accompanied by his mistress, a pretty mestizo, of Zamboanga. They were said to be in a canoe in a mangrove swamp near Taluksungay, a few miles from town.

Hayson and I gathered a dozen men and out we hiked, eager to be the capturers. But the foxy presidente, with a personal feud against Alvarez, had sent his police force ahead, and as we passed through a field of corn that bordered the mangrove swamp we heard yells and shots—then silence.

Plunging into the swamp, up to the middle in stinking mud and slipping on the roots and "knees" of the mangroves, we made our way to the tidal canal, where a tragedy, which might have been prevented by our earlier arrival, had been enacted. Yet we had hiked fast, several of our soldiers had fallen out exhausted, and Hayson, who carried too much weight about the belt line, was puffing and panting at each step.

On the canal, under the overarching mangroves and nipa palms, was a little outrigger canoe; around it waist-deep in muddy water were the presidente's bloodhounds, with rifles and shotguns still pointed at the tragic occupants of the native craft—Eduardo Alvarez coughing out his life-blood, and a pretty girl sobbing and wailing over him.

A revolver beside Alvarez was undischarged but gave the police grounds to say that he resisted arrest. Alvarez died as we approached, and Hayson and I, with a couple of constables, took charge of the canoe, paddling down the canal toward the open sea, which we reached near a Moro village just at sunset.

Here we exchanged the dugout for a larger craft, and as a full moon rose, we sailed and paddled along the coast back to Zamboanga, some fifteen miles away. Amidships was the body of Alvarez, decently laid out; beside it sat and mourned the comely *mestiza*; and hunched close on one side was Hayson and on the other myself. We conversed across the body of Alvarez.

As the parao slipped over the water, the Moro boatmen at prow and stern chanted a native song; the paddles dipped and splashed in the phosphorescent sea; the sail flapped lazily, keeping time with the bamboo outriggers which rose and fell to a slight swell; the palm-fringed coast with Moro fishing villages built out on piles passed in silvered panorama; and over the body Hayson and I exchanged reminiscences of many men and places. Both of us were dripping wet with mud and water.

Before leaving the village, we had fortified ourselves with a bottle of vile gin, purchased at a Chino's store; and this unloosed our tongues and warmed our chilled bodies. It can be uncomfortably cold even in the tropics after sundown when one is sitting still in wet clothes. The fair maiden took a drink or two that we pressed upon her and soon felt her woes sit more lightly; and it will doubtless be a relief to the reader to learn that investigation at Zamboanga a few days later showed that she had been able to replace her outlaw lover by one not proscribed by the authorities.

We were wet to the skin, tired after a hard day's hike, and we had an outlaw's stark cold body and a warm and weeping maiden between us. But we were young. We were officers of the Moro Constabulary. And—we had a bottle of gin. Therefore, Hayson, a wonderful raconteur, was stimulated to tell some of his best tales; and between fantastic stories he joked in Spanish with the girl, pressed the gin bottle upon her, and otherwise solaced her so successfully that before we reached Zamboanga she was avowing that the dead man had deceived her, and was evidently in the mood to entertain his successor—American Constabulary officer preferred.

So, we sailed on through the incandescent night until at midnight the gray walls of the old Spanish Fort Pilar that guards fair Zamboanga reflected back the moonlight, and my first expedition in Mindanao was ended.

We turned Alvarez's body over to the municipal authorities, who doubtless chuckled at the ease with which they had staged and played their little tragedy of the Southern seas.

XXVI - In the Spider's Web

Colonel Harbord soon organized the Constabulary of the Moro Province. He was the kind of man who would cheerfully have taken up the task of organizing the devils in hell. And he would have organized them even if opposed by his Satanic Majesty himself. To be associated with him as adjutant for nearly a year was an inestimable privilege.

Other officers arrived from the north and were sent to organize the Constabularies of Lanao, Sulu, and Davao. One or two of these new men brought great reputations as "fire-eaters," gained in combat against insurgent and ladrone bands in the northern islands; and it was amusing to see how quickly some reputations were punctured by the spears and krises of the Moro warriors already on the rampage in the districts of Lanao and Sulu. The difference between hustling a ladrone band over the rice paddies of Cavite and facing a fighting throng of Mohammedan fanatics was about the same as that between stalking a stag and bearding a tiger in his lair.

My training under Colonel Harbord was an excellent thing for me. That able officer had the recipe for making "riflemen of mud," and one Provincial Constabulary after another was officered, organized, equipped, and put into the field against those Moros who refused to bend the knee to any form of government that curbed piracy and slavery and operated for the rights of man as opposed to the privileges of petty chiefs. It was twentieth-century democracy versus medieval feudalism, with unlimited complications of race, language, customs, and governmental impermanence. It is not surprising that Mindanao has run with blood for a quarter of a century.

Only one thing could have prevented the continuous misunderstandings and conflicts. A corps of well-paid, permanent American civil servants, firm while sympathetic with the Moros, might have avoided at least nine-tenths of the difficulties. General Wood saw that, but his efforts to organize such a corps were defeated by lack of understanding or interest in Manila and Washington.

The tragi-comic expedition by Hayson and myself against Alvarez was undertaken when the Moro Province Constabulary was in swaddling clothes. But almost before short pants substituted those swaddling clothes, other officers had gallantly led their raw constables against well-armed Moro clans.

The speed with which we organized, equipped, and drilled into shape only shows what can be done by a cranky machine when an expert drives; and in General Wood and Colonel Harbord, the Constabulary of the Moro Province possessed a pair of very capable chauffeurs—perhaps as capable as America could have produced.

It was good to work in Mindanao in those early days, when the first flush of enthusiasm suffused us all, and when confidence in the men on top made every junior do and dare.

Captain Frederick Johnson, our district supply officer, was kept busy shipping supplies to newly organized units. Distances between stations in Mindanao were vast compared with those in northern districts and taking into account means of transportation, which was almost wholly by water. In 1903 there were not more than fifty miles of roads in all Mindanao.

From Zamboanga to our remotest station at Baganga on the east coast of Mindanao was a matter of three or four hundred miles by water, which meant ten days' or two weeks' travel by the monthly mail steamer, while many other stations were almost as difficult to reach. Either Colonel Harbord, Captain Johnson, or myself was always on the go, inspecting, supplying, and paying our growing forces. Good old Johnson, carried away by the enthusiasm which pervaded all, worked himself beyond one man's limit in efforts to keep supply abreast of organization.

One day I started hastily for remote stations on Mindanao—I suppose that a steamer was making an unexpected voyage—when at the last moment Johnson appeared on the wharf followed by half a dozen Moros carrying an iron safe which he turned over to me as the vessel's ropes were cast off from shore.

"Here, White," he panted, "there's seven thousand pesos in bills and silver in this safe, and for goodness' sake pay those men at Davao, Baganga, and the rest, and take up any vouchers they have. Here's the key. Adios!"—as the steamer pulled away—"keep track of what you pay out and don't get me stuck for a thousand or two by the auditor!"

Johnson wasn't "stuck" by any carelessness of mine on that trip, but, poor fellow, he was finally "stuck" for a lot of property issued without proper receipts during the haste of organization. I think that he told me in 1911, when I relieved him as governor of Agusan Province, that his generosity and overwork in Mindanao cost him about fifteen hundred pesos—deducted from his salary for property shortages unexplained.

The governor of the District of Zamboanga was a ponderous army captain, past middle age, but with a tremendous capacity for individual work that led him to make little use of the Constabulary, especially as he could call upon the Regulars or Scouts for escorts and expeditions. His courage as well as his misplaced confidence in his personal influence over the Moros of his District once came near bringing disaster on one expedition of which I was part.

A Moro chief named Datu Mustapha ruled over the region of Margosatubig on Dumankilas Bay, an arm of the sea on the south coast of Mindanao, some hundred miles or so east of Zamboanga. Datu Mustapha refused to obey the governor's orders and even sent insulting messages to the White Father of the Moros of Zamboanga District, so, for once, the governor called on the Constabulary for an escort and went to reason with his fractious ward.

By some chance I had a holiday from my adjutant duties and took command of the twenty Zamboanga constables, embarking with the governor on the little government steamer Borneo. With us went Datu Mandi of Zamboanga, the Moro-mestizo chief who loyally served the American Government at Mindanao until his death in 1913, several other friendly Moro chiefs and hadjis, and another army officer who desired to see the fun.

The Borneo, a craft of about a hundred tons, flew the English flag, as she hailed from Sandakan, North Borneo, and was only chartered by the Moro Province Government. She was commanded by a typical English sea-dog, Captain Pfort.

On arrival at Margosatubig, we anchored a hundred yards from shore opposite a massive old Spanish stone fort situated on rising ground and in which Datu Mustapha with his two-score armed retainers, his harem, and his slaves considered himself safe against the interfering world outside. A message from the governor requesting Mustapha to come aboard and pay his respects sounded to that hostile chief like, "Ducky, ducky, come and be killed!"

For an hour or two, while messages went to and fro, he remained in his secure retreat; but finally came aboard, sullen and resentful. After a short bichara (powwow) with the governor, Mustapha returned to his fort, and the governor, declaring his intention of returning the call, directed me to accompany him ashore and pay respects to the datu. It looked to me like a repetition of the "Ducky, ducky, come and be killed" proposition—with us as the ducks.

But I was anxious that the Constabulary should earn the governor's approbation, and I said nothing. When, however, he told me to leave my men aboard, I gently demurred; and we compromised by letting them ashore to stretch their legs. Captain Pfort and the army officer accompanied us, curious to see a Moro datu in his stronghold. Within a few minutes they were to wish that they had remained aboard to view it from a safe distance.

Before we walked up the green slope to the fort, I took the precaution of calling my sergeant aside, told him to wait until we were inside the fort in the datu's quarters, then to enter the fort with the detachment, place the men with their backs to the wall of the fort, and await developments, being careful to give the Moros no cause of offense and to appear cool and careless—but to be ready. From the attitude of Datu Mustapha, from hints dropped by Datu Mandi, the other friendly chiefs, and by my own soldiers, I was disinclined to trust ourselves to the sullen chief of Margosatubig.

When we reached the fort whose stone walls rose up a forbidding score of feet, we found the heavy wooden gate shut. For a moment I feared that we were to be assassinated then and there by fire from above. My soldiers were still near the beach, waiting according to my orders until we entered the fort. However, the gate was but lightly propped and yielded to pressure.

We entered the fort to find that the Spanish stone buildings constructed within the enclosure were in ruins, while Datu Mustapha had erected a rambling edifice of bamboo and palm-thatch against the further wall. Up to the chief's quarters led a flight of rickety bamboo steps. As none came to greet us, we climbed up, the governor in the lead. We were a procession of flies buzzing into a sticky spider's web.

The room we entered was packed with armed men. There were no women or children, always a suspicious sign when an American finds himself among the wild peoples of the Philippines. Datu Mustapha squatted on a mat and cushions at one side, while around and behind him were massed half a hundred as fierce-looking Moros as I had ever seen, armed to the teeth and all scowling and casting glances that were an eloquent "Hymn of Hate" for the white men.

Near Mustapha was a stand of twenty or more Remington and Mauser rifles with belts of cartridges pendent from their muzzles. Men lounged against the stand of arms so that we could not move without brushing against the ready weapons of Moros hostile in every attitude and movement. Furthermore, Datu Mustapha made no move to greet the governor.

After some maneuvering, we seated or squatted ourselves near a door on the further side of the room which opened on to the broad battlements of the fort. Scarcely were we seated when an order from the datu closed the one possible avenue of escape, while several of the retainers with hands on their half-drawn krises stood between us and such safety as flight might have afforded us.

If anything started we were in the position of so many chunks of meat in a meat-chopper—and I breathed a prayer that my sergeant with his men might be inside the fort with their backs against the wall, from which position they commanded our death trap and might cause the Moros to weigh chances before they turned the handle of the meat-chopper.

I was the only member of our party to carry arms; a .45 revolver was at my hip, while across my knee was my .44 carbine, but my head would have been off before I could press a trigger, for just behind me stood a Moro whose wrinkled leather face was carved in a diabolical grin, and whose right hand grasped the ornamented hilt of a razor-edge kris half drawn from its scabbard.

In this perilous situation the governor, either unconscious of danger or by exhibition of iron nerve, began to harangue Datu Mustapha, his words being interpreted by Datu Mandi, who with other friendly Moros accompanying us, was ashy-gray with fear. I helped the interpretation by rendering the governor's words to Mandi in Spanish.

But Mandi was interpreting for his life and needed little assistance, nobly rising to the occasion. The words of the drama went something like this. The governor spoke in English, I translated roughly in Spanish, toning down a little, and Mandi conveyed a further diluted version in the Maguindanaw dialect to Mustapha.

The governor: "Tell Datu Mustapha that he must get out of this fort. It's government property and he has no right to occupy it."

Datu Mandi: "The governor says, most honorable Datu Mustapha, that he is pleased that you should occupy this old fort, for which the government has no present use."

The governor: "Tell Datu Mustapha that he must release his Subanun slaves and stop exacting tribute from the tribes around Dumankilas Bay."

Datu Mandi: "The governor says that under the American law there must be no slavery, but he understands that you have no slaves—only servants whom you treat well. Anyhow [sotto voce], the Subanuns are fit for nothing but to be slaves for the Moros."

Thus the powwow went on for an hour or more. Whether the presence of the soldiers inside the walls or Datu Mandi's mollifying translations diminished Mustapha's ire, it would be difficult to decide.

But when we left the fort and breathed the clean air outside with deep, grateful inspirations, the governor said nothing about the presence of my soldiers within the walls, which, perhaps, he had not even noticed. And not until we were on the good ship Borneo, streaming out of Dumankilas Bay did he broach the matter of Mustapha's attitude, about which we felt some delicacy in approaching him.

Then, when Datu Mandi had supported my estimate of Mustapha's hostility, the governor suggested that we turn back and have another talk with him. But as a little reflection determined that my Constabulary could make no impression against those massive walls, we proceeded to Zamboanga for reinforcements.

A day or two later the governor returned to Margosatubig with a full company of United States infantry and a piece of field artillery. Datu Mustapha, willing enough to die fighting but anxious to have a fighting chance, took one look at the cannon, then gathered together his retainers, slaves, and women of his harem, and left the fort.

However, he continued his recalcitrant attitude toward the American Government. A few months later, when I was far away in Cotabato District, he attacked Captain Platka of the Constabulary, and died with many of his men in a hand-to-hand fight. Platka said that Mustapha died game and almost reached him, kris in hand, when a load of buckshot took the chief of Dumankilas Bay full in the chest, sending him to the Mohammedan paradise to lie in the arms of countless houris and receive his reward for defying Unbelievers.

Another experience while I was adjutant will show that organization of a Constabulary among the Moros was not accomplished entirely without friction, although it was produced rather by inefficient American officers than by the Moro recruits, usually docile under proper treatment.

The Moro was quick to recognize the qualities he expected in an officer. Courage—that was indispensable—kindness, patience, and intelligence. There was a certain officer of the Constabulary who had the first three, but whom isolation and responsibility unnerved. He was stationed at Tucuran, which is by way of being more of a geographical expression than a place; a few stone buildings erected by the Spaniards on a dominant hill overlooking the Illanun Gulf and commanding the narrow neck of Mindanao Island.

The cable to Manila came ashore and ran a few miles overland there, then into Panguil Bay on the north side of Mindanao on its way to Manila. To protect the cable operators from the Moros of that neighborhood, we sent Captain Z. with twenty raw Moro constables and a few Filipino non-coms to Tucuran, where he could drill his men, hunt deer and wild hog on the grassy plain behind his hill, or admire, while looking for the smoke of the monthly mail steamer on the horizon, the glorious panorama of a twenty-mile, curving sandy beach a few hundred feet below his bedroom window.

This was the kind of a job that either molds a man's character into firm stuff or gets on his nerves; it was an experience that scores of Constabulary officers have been through. Captain Z. was a clean-cut young fellow and of a good family, but he had been promoted too fast. He was a relative of the wife of the Chief of Constabulary—and Mindanao was a poor place to send a relative unless there was something behind the blood tie.

Z. forgot to buy or requisition food and supplies for his men, he mislaid orders and circulars from headquarters, and he messed up the discipline and organization of his company by every form of omission. Now, an officer can leave a lot undone if he will only feed his men well; but the stomach of a Moro soldier revolts just as quickly at bad treatment as that of an American. They want but little, with rice and dried fish as the staples of diet, but that little must appear regularly and in sufficient quantities to satisfy hunger; while if it leaves a feeling of repletion, the officer will find his company easier to manage.

One day at Zamboanga, we received a cable message from lonely Tucuran saying that the Constabulary company had mutinied and had locked up Captain Z. in his quarters. Colonel Harbord put me aboard the little Coast Guard cutter Ranger with instructions to work her speed up to the maximum of seven and a half knots, and find out what "that idiot Z." had been up to.

Over the Celebes Sea we wallowed until the white buildings of Tucuran dotted the green mountains at the head of Illanun Bay. The sight of a steamer had operated to release Captain Z. from durance vile, and he met me, a natty figure in well-starched uniform with collars and cuffs showing to the prescribed degree. But all the starch was in his uniform. Isolation had bred fear, and fear had taken the stiffness from his backbone. Within an hour or two he was bundled aboard the Ranger and was on his way to Zamboanga, while I remained at Tucuran to straighten out the comic mutiny.

When questioned about their wrongs, the Moro soldiers grinned and said, "He gave us no food—he did nothing."

Regular meals, regular drill, and enough discipline to operate like fleas on a dog and keep them from worrying about being soldiers, quickly straightened out the detachment. However, despite plenty of work, during the two weeks or more that I was at Tucuran, I learned to tire of that interminable vista of beach and mountain and to appreciate the fact that man, a social animal, cannot live by view alone.

Incidentally I had a taste of my chief's mettle. On arrival at Tucuran I did not like the look of things. A number of the mutinous soldiers were related to semi-piratical Moros living along the shores of Illanum Gulf within a few miles of the Constabulary post.

I cabled to Colonel Harbord recommending that the mutinous element be transferred to another district. Promptly came the reply, "You keep them there and put the boots to them"—or words to that effect. I did—and nothing happened except improvement in the company.

But one thing happened which gave me a momentary scare. I had been at Tucuran a day or two and was passing under the projecting second-story veranda of the soldier's quarters when "BANG!" went a gun above my head and a bullet struck the gravel just in front of me. It required little flight of imagination to believe that a mutinous soldier under discipline desired to end my promising career.

Revolver in hand, I turned and bounded, three steps at a time, up the stairs of the building, eager to have it out with the supposed assassin. In the room full of excited soldiers I found one of my Filipino sergeants stretched on a bamboo cot, groaning and holding his leg between thigh and knee. He had been cleaning his .45 revolver while holding it muzzle down on his leg, when it exploded and the bullet passed clean through the flesh, just grazing the femur, then on through bed and floor to give me my scare below.

I did a little first-aid work and then went over to my own quarters for a drink—which I needed.

XXVII - Riflemen from Mud

EARLY IN JUNE 1904, GENERAL WOOD CALLED upon Colonel Harbord to organize a Constabulary in the District of Cotabato, the largest and perhaps least-known division on the Moro Province, where a prominent Moro chief named Datu Ali had recently started on the war-path.

Colonel Harbord relieved me as adjutant for assignment as Senior Inspector of the Constabulary of Cotabato with instructions to recruit as rapidly as possible among the tribes of friendly Moros and organize a force that could be used as Scouts, accompanying expeditions of United States troops against the hostiles scattered throughout the length and breadth of the valley of the Rio Grande de Mindanao.

Cotabato District consisted of the valley of this broad, deep, muddy stream, a valley some two hundred miles long and from ten to fifty broad. This watershed contained large areas of swamp and lakes, with villages of Maguindanaw Moros sparsely scattered along the banks of the river and its tributaries or amid the almost trackless and impassable swamps. Back of the valley rose forbidding ranges of mountains, culminating in Mount Apo, eleven thousand feet in height. In the jungles of these mountains were legendary pagan tribes, rejoicing in the names of Tirurayes, Manobos, Bagobos, Bilanes, and many more such.

The Maguindanaws were the largest tribe of Moros. They controlled practically the whole of the mainland of Mindanao. Although more agricultural and less piratical than their cousins in Sulu, they held almost as tightly to their ancient privileges of slavery and control of the pagan tribes, while the situation of their bamboo villages and earthen cottas (forts) on the shores of the mountain lakes, as in Lanao, or amid the swamps, as in Cotabato, made campaigning against those chiefs who refused to recognize the authority of the United States both difficult and costly. The Spaniards had sent many an expedition up the Rio Grande, and with shallow-draft gunboats had shot their way into the heart of Cotabato District. They obtained concessions from Datu Utu, the Maguindanaw chief who then ruled that swampy land.

But the control exercised by the Spaniards extended little if any further than the range of cannon shot from the toy men-of-war, while the price they paid in men and blood for even such victory was heavy. Furthermore, every inch of ground wrested from the Maguindanaws must be controlled by stone-fort or blockhouse.

When, in 1899, the Spaniards withdrew before the advancing Americans from the north, anarchy reigned in Cotabato. Datu Utu had gone to the voluptuous reward of good fighting Moros, and his nephew, Datu Ali, ruled in his stead.

The American troops came to Cotabato. A wise officer, Colonel Febiger, was appointed governor of the District. Datu Ali paid his respects to Colonel Febiger and for a while all went pleasantly along the Rio Grande.

The military government was busy subduing Aguinaldo's insurrection in the northern islands and was quite willing to let the Moro hornets alone as long as they refrained from stinging American soldiers. Colonel Febiger cemented friendship with Datu Ali and at one time even made tentative arrangements to send him on an educational tour to the United States.

The cautious governor shut the other eye at such exhibitions of Moro customs as slavery, an occasional raid on the pagan hillmen, or a little intertribal bloodshed by way of keeping the young braves fit.

It is likely that had Colonel Febiger remained at Cotabato, gradually enlarging his influence and control of the Maguindanaws and especially of their fighting chief, Datu Ali, the bloody chapter of our campaign in Cotabato, of which I shall sketch but the highlights, might never have been written.

It is safe to say that nine-tenths of the trouble in Mindanao has been due to the impermanence of officials; no sooner did an officer like Febiger get to know his Moro men and manners than military orders carried him to some other sphere of usefulness; and his successor came with no fund of stored-up experience upon which to draw.

Of course, it was not to be expected that the feudal conditions of Moro misgovernment in Mindanao and Sulu could be replaced by an administration modeled on American ideas of the rights of man without a certain amount of friction and even bloodshed. But the amount of each might have been much reduced by a policy which used personal influence rather than the Krag to enforce necessary and wholesome changes.

General Wood recognized this. He soon appointed civilian understudies as District secretaries under the army governors; but before many years the general himself, after having become skilled in Moro administration, was spirited away to another command.

Colonel Febiger left Cotabato. Datu Ali heard of the new laws passed by the legislative council of the Moro Province, which prescribed penalties for slave-holding, together with other new and altogether hateful restrictions on the authority of proud Moro chieftains.

As a matter of fact, these laws, designed to bring order out of chaos, were sufficiently benevolent; what was lacking was a corps of officials experienced in Moro affairs to explain the laws to the chiefs and to drop oil on the creaking joints of the new legislative machinery. The Moro is proud, touchy, and quick to resent abridgment of his rights and ancient customs, and to him those laws seemed designed to upset all that made life worth living.

Had they been explained and toned down by a District governor in whose friendship the Moro placed confidence, they might have been swallowed without other result than a slight stomach ache; otherwise administered they were a violent emetic—and the convulsions of Moro vomiting were to spell blood and disorder over Mindanao and Sulu for years to come.

Of course, it is easy to be wise after the event. I do not pretend that any of us participants in the making of Mindanao history possessed the power of vaccination. Yet, a year or two later, on the island of Tapul, when for twenty-four hours I was in the power of a band of hostile Moros and talked to them for my life, I came nearer an understanding of the Moro point of view than I did when, in June 1904, I first set foot in Cotabato to organize my Constabulary among the sulky and semi-hostile Moros of the lower part of the Rio Grande Valley.

Datu Ali was then some distance along the trail which ultimately led to his grave. From his point of view a good beginning had been made when in May 1904, he ambushed a company of the Seventeenth Infantry and killed two officers and seventeen men. It was a bloody little affair, typifying the difficulty of campaigning against hostile Moros in that part of Mindanao.

The small company of about forty soldiers had hiked through the almost trackless swamps at the mercy of a faithless Moro guide, the officers ignorant of the terrain and language, yet gallantly leading their men into the heart of a hitherto unexplored country. Mile after mile the trail led through the high tigbao grass, impassably interlaced on either side and often overhead, while underfoot was the vicious black mud of a churned-up trail with occasional holes where the men sank to their waists.

Then there was a sudden spurt of rifle fire from ahead, from either side, from an invisible enemy secure behind the maddening wall of matted, cane-like grass. The men in advance fell dead and dying in the stinking mud. The officers pressed forward, and, in like manner, were mown down without seeing the foe. The remnant of the expedition withdrew in disorder while the victorious Moros with vicious kris and barong completed their work by beheading and disemboweling the dead and dying Americans. Yet even then Datu Ali showed some spark of chivalrous warfare. Two captured American soldiers were cared for and later returned to Cotabato.

This ambush happened in the far interior of the District, and when I arrived at Cotabato several companies of American soldiers and Filipino Scouts were campaigning to revenge the "Simpetan Massacre."

The Moros of the lower valley, though doubtless sympathizing with their cousins up the river, professed friendship for the Americans. As their villages were mostly on the banks of the river or its tidal delta lands, easily reached by gunboat or launch, it behooved them to be good. Datu Baki and Datu Balabadan were leaders in the lower valley.

From them I solicited recruits for my Constabulary—and such specimens of Moro manhood they sent in! Kipling's pungent phrase about "making riflemen from mud" would have been less a figure of speech than a reality in Cotabato in 1904, for some of my recruits were so encrusted with scales of dirt and filth that several preliminary baths were necessary before we reached the human material for our soldiery.

At first the men sent to me were slaves of the lowest class, enlisting at the orders of their datus as they would have done anything else, from laboring in the rice fields to lopping off an enemy's head. But in every Moro is the germ of a good fighting-man, so that with the assistance of my able lieutenants, Furlong and Gilsheuser, it was a matter of days, or at the most weeks, before a mud-encrusted slave became a natty, self-respecting soldier.

Moreover, I had one or two of my old Negros soldiers as non-coms, and they were adaptable devils of great assistance in drill and discipline, who quickly picked up the Moro customs, especially in the matter of the plurality of wives.

Our barracks and quarters at Cotabato were situated half a mile from the town, on the summit of a rocky knoll which rose straight up two hundred feet above the surrounding rice fields.

One or two old Spanish stone buildings were supplemented by temporary constructions of bamboo and palm thatch. From the hill the view across the paddies and swamps of the Rio Grande Valley, of the red-tiled or tin-roofed town half hidden by groves of coco palms and avenues of flaming acacias, of the river winding down to the Celebes Sea and of distant ranges of stern mountains, was something to soothe an officer after hours spent in teaching recruits how to march and how to hold their guns.

Tantawan, meaning "extensive view," is the Moro name for the Constabulary hill at Cotabato. It could not be better named.

Also, Tantawan is for the Moros a sacred spot and connected with their mythology which attributed the origin of their race to an egg carried through the air by a gigantic bird—doubtless the roc of the Arabian Nights and Sinbad's adventures.

For the Mohammedan Moro is by tradition, blood, and even language connected, tenuously but no less certainly, with that race of Arabian adventurers of whom Mohammed was the militant prophet and Allah the complacent God.

So, while the United States troops campaigned in the "Valley after Ali," as soldier-poets soon began to sing, we worked away with our scaly recruits until we had a detachment that could take the field without bringing discredit on the corps.

Lieutenant Furlong was the first to lead a Maguindanaw Moro against his fellow Moros. General Wood had arrived at Cotabato to direct operations, and he wanted a few Constabulary to scout through the swamps of the upper valley and feel for the hostiles who were hard to find when a powerful expedition of a hundred or two American soldiers felt its way carefully along the trails through the long-grass country but could be quickly located by a force small enough to make an engagement a sporting event, with the odds favoring the Moros.

That was one reason why the Constabulary proved so successful in bushwhacking warfare throughout the archipelago. Its strength lay in the very weakness which invited attack. How often have Constabulary officers calculated the number of men that it would take to "do the job" without showing sufficient strength to scare the enemy!

Furlong took fourteen constables, including several Moro recruits who still handled krises better than carbines, and he scouted back from the river at Kudarangan, where several hundred infantry and Scouts were assembled for a blow at Datu Ali—when he could be located.

Furlong's orders were to "get in touch" with the hostile Moros. He did more than that. He touched them up, hiking for miles through the heart of Ali's preserves, and with his fourteen men kept up a running fight with forty or fifty Maguindanaw Moros led by Bapa-ni-Manakup, Ali's best fighting man.

When the odds pressed too heavily against him, Furlong withdrew in good order, carrying his wounded, and striking back hard when the exultant Maguindanaw Moros led by Bapa-ni-Manakup thought to annihilate his little band, until he found shelter behind a company of American soldiers sent out to succor him. General Wood highly commended Furlong's conduct on this scout, while the American troops embraced the red-fezzed Constabulary as brothers-in-arms.

After that first essay we were kept busy cooperating with the army in the Valley campaign, an officer and a handful of men accompanying an expedition of United States soldiers to act as scouts and advance guard, an honorable and dangerous position when creeping along grass-hidden trails against an enemy ever lying in wait to spring, but rarely visible until he struck; and the knowledge of our Moro constables of the traits and tricks of their Moro brethren doubtless saved the lives of many Americans in that campaign in the "Valley after Ali."

XXVIII - Bullets and Bees

CAPTAIN VAN HORN OF THE SEVENTEENTH INFANTRY, a young, able, and energetic officer, was then governor of the District. From the first, he generously helped the organization of the Constabulary. Van Horn was a fighting governor who often laid down the reins of office to take up the whip of a military expedition.

His District secretary, F. J. Dunleavy, an Australian by birth but a cosmopolite in experience, was a frontiersman of the world who had mined for gold in the Rand, in Madagascar, and the Klondike; run a sugar plantation in the Fiji and Hawaiian Islands, and who, when I last heard of him, was administering a rubber concession at Sorata, Bolivia, near Lake Titicaca, fourteen thousand feet above sea level.

Always active and full of plans, Dunleavy was planting rubber on the slopes of Tantawan Hill behind the Constabulary quarters and laying out a large sugar plantation in the vicinity of Cotabato.

General Wood had organized for the campaign against Ali's "provisional companies" of Infantry, taking the most active young officers and men from every company of a regiment to make an organization of fighting, hiking American Scouts about 150 strong. Van Horn commanded the provisional company of the Seventeenth Infantry. He invited me to accompany it on an extended expedition through the Talayan country, a part of his District some fifty miles southeast of Cotabato, where the swamps ran into foothills and the foothills into the unknown mountains.

A few days before we started for Talayan, a disgrace befell the Constabulary of Cotabato. Two of our Moro recruits deserted, taking with them their belts of ammunition and carbines. That was a serious blow to our pride. For several nights after the desertion, Furlong and I took turns lying in the long cogon grass behind our soldiers' barracks in wait for other deserters, ready to give them a load of buckshot to carry in addition to their own arms and ammunition.

We had no more desertions. When it is considered that the possession of a modern rifle raised a Moro from slave to chief among his fellows and perhaps gave him the woman of his desire, it was a tribute to the general loyalty of our men that more did not return wealthy and influential to their clans. The two who deserted were tempted by relatives among the hostiles of the upper valley.

The carbines were worth several hundred pesos each, and the women of Talayan who could be purchased by the price of a gun were brown, yet fair, in the eyes of two Moro soldiers, erstwhile slaves. They deserted and we learned that it was to Talayan they fled. I was overjoyed, therefore, at the chance to accompany Van Horn's expedition into that unknown land, where even the Spanish troops had never penetrated.

We embarked and sailed up the river by launch. The wash of the boat swept ugly crocodiles from the mud batiks. Then we hiked for days through the swamps when our only desire was to find a passably dry spot on which to throw our blankets and rig our mosquito bars. There were hours when with two or three Moro soldiers ahead I crept along the tunneled trails through the long grass, peering for signs of the hostiles, and momentarily expecting a volley from an unseen foe.

Let me take up the thread of the yarn one night when we had emerged from the swamps on to higher ground where groves of bamboo and forest trees appeared among the matted, blanketing tigbao grass. There the expedition of more than 150 men with as many or more cargadores camped near a stream on a meadow-like spot surrounded by higher grass and cane-brake.

All day the Moros had fired at us from every point of higher ground that commanded the trail out of the swamps; and on one occasion when the hostiles came within hailing distance, my soldiers said that they distinguished the voices and taunts of the two deserters.

We expected an attack during the night, so Governor Van Horn disposed the expedition in a hollow square, with sentries every few feet along the four sides.

My handful of Constabulary stopped a small gap in one side of the square. Behind them I made a bed in the damp grass, fixed my mosquito bar with four sticks, and, after supper, composed myself to sleep. But there was little rest for anyone that night, as the Talayan Moros were thick around our camp, and their shouts and yells were answered by the calls of our sentries and the crack of Krag rifles.

From time to time, when the hostiles became too annoying, Van Horn would take a detachment of soldiers and volley through the long grass toward the red flashes that showed the discharges of the Moro guns. Then there would be comparative silence, broken perhaps only by the groans of a wounded Moro in the long grass. The Constabulary part of the line was comparatively free from attack.

Perhaps this was in part due to the fact that my non-coms and myself were armed with short-barreled repeating shotguns which scattered loads of buckshot through the grass and made our front too unpleasant for the human mosquitoes who buzzed around us in futile attempts to sting.

When, after one particularly vicious spurt of fire, I returned to my mosquito bar, it was to find it spread and torn upon the grass. During my fortunate absence, a bullet had struck one of the supporting sticks and pierced the gossamer fabric. It was as well that I had been away!

While I was patching up my mosquito bar as best I could in the dark, an American soldier who had bedded near me was groping around and cursing because he could not find his rifle, which was by his side when he went to sleep.

Nor did he find it. Some venturesome Moro had crept through the cordon of our sentries, and in the darkness and confusion had stolen the rifle and then sneaked back to the outside world and the plaudits of his comrades. It is impossible not to admire the courage and steady nerves of a man who could thus slip between our sentries and into the midst of an armed camp.

After that experience the soldiers slept above the rifles, hollowing out a place for them beneath their blankets, or tied empty tin cans to their arms and to the mosquito nets around them—a sort of field burglar alarm.

Thereafter, also, we took steps to round up the Moro cargadores before nightfall and to account carefully for each man, as it seemed possible that the theft had been committed from within the camp. Precautions sometimes failed.

On another expedition, there was a squadron of dismounted cavalry that lost, in similar fashion, four or five carbines in one night. For that matter it was just as well that a soldier should not awake while the theft was taking place as instead of merely losing his rifle, he might also lose his life by a knife-thrust from the predatory prowler.

The morning following our night of alarms, we penetrated the heart of the Talayan country, through deserted Moro villages scattered under groves of cocos and bamboo along the banks of the Talayan River.

At a place where the river made a hairpin turn, we ran into a carefully prepared ambush, and were lucky to escape as lightly as we did. With two or three American soldiers and half a dozen of the constabulary, I was scouting along the bank of the river, here deep, swift, and about a hundred feet wide.

On the opposite bank were some Moro huts, apparently deserted. Suddenly a rattle of rifle fire burst from the opposite shore. The bullets which combed around us issued from the bank of the river, where the Moros had dug trenches and loopholed through the bank.

As best we could, we sheltered behind coco-palm trunks or lay below bushes of oranges and lemons of which there was a considerable grove on our side of the river. One American soldier was killed—shot through the heart. He had pitched down on his face just to the right of me, and seeing him lie there so quiet, I thought the surprise of the ambush had perhaps shaken his nerves.

I went over to speak to him. When I caught the sleeve of his shirt, the deadweight told the story.

My Moro constables were pumping away at the puffs of smoke which showed the enemy's loopholes. They seemed to be enjoying themselves in true Moro style, yelling between shots at their friends, and perhaps relatives, on the other side of the river, when a diversion was caused by a swarm of bees which had doubtless been disturbed by a stray bullet.

The infuriated insects first attacked my constables, who, heedless of the more deadly but less immediately painful bullets that were buzzing in unison with the bees, danced around in full exposure to the enemy. A moment later we were all careless of the bullets and only anxious to withdraw from the range of *Apis mellifica*, the common honeybee, but an uncommonly inconvenient insect to meet when engaged in other combat.

The allies of the Moros of Talayan won that fight. We withdrew from the field but not before a soldier of the Seventeenth Infantry, who was firing near me, made one of the prettiest shots I have seen.

Beyond and above the enemy's trenches was a large, well-foliaged mango tree, in the branches of which a Moro sharpshooter had established a perch. The soldier saw him, and before firing called my attention to the blur in the foliage which he believed to be the sharpshooter. Then crack went his Krag, and out of the mango tree fell a Moro, spread-eagling down like a dead crow.

However, we ran away only to fight again. We found a ford over the Talayan River a mile or so below the ambush, crossed over, and came around behind the trenches, whose occupants scurried over the rice fields to the nearest hills, turning to give fight at every dike and giving us a run for our money—or our ammunition.

As we skirmished over the rice fields, Private Taguetal of the Cotabato Constabulary found a relative among the bodies of dead Talayan Moros sprinkled somewhat freely over the landscape. Taguetal was a tall, flat-footed Maguindanaw Moro with a head shaped like the small end of an egg and features resembling the shape that an intelligent child of three might produce from a handful of brown clay.

When he enlisted, he was not young, and his joints were stiff from years of work in waist-deep rice paddies so that his military motions were always jerky and automaton-like. But he was as faithful as a dog and appreciated the fact that the Constabulary had raised him from a toiling slave to an independent man-at-arms.

At Talayan he approached the corpse of a Moro with the intention of relieving the deceased of no longer needed weapons together with such trifles as the brass betel-nut box, quids of tobacco, or whatever might be concealed in the twisted sash around his waist.

On turning the body over, Taguetal recognized what he called a "tungud-minsan," which is about the Maguindanaw equivalent for our word cousin. He grunted the information to me, and then quietly continued the search for family heirlooms.

It was old Taguetal who on return to Cotabato from an expedition came at nightfall secretly to my quarters with the information that one of the other Moro soldiers was going to kill me because I had administered a little field discipline during the expedition. Supplementing his information with advice, the faithful old soldier calmly proposed that he lop off the head of the intended assassin.

However, I thought of a better plan to maintain discipline, and the following morning I interviewed the sullen soldier in the presence of my non-commissioned officers. His grievance was that I had hit him on the back of the head with the butt of my revolver because he was holding back during a skirmish.

He said that the reason he held back was that there were relatives of his among the Moros with whom we were fighting. He was a higher-class Moro than old Taguetal and others and therefore more loyal to his clan and less loyal to his officers. It was a delicate situation.

I knew that I was at fault for striking a soldier no matter what the provocation or under what stress of excitement. But I managed to adjust matters by proposing that instead of assassinating me he could get even in more honorable manner by accompanying me to the rifle range where at three hundred yards we would exchange shots—and let the best man win. That appeared to all the Moro soldiers as a square and sporting proposition.

My offer was not accepted. But that sulky and mutinous man became one of the best soldiers and a trusted non-commissioned officer.

I am sure that no senior inspector in the Constabulary had a better lot of officers and men that I had at Cotabato. Lieutenants Furlong and Henry Gilsheuser, my junior officers, later rose to responsible positions in the service; the former was a gallant and dashing cavalier, loved by the Moro soldiers for that fearlessness and justice they most admired; while Gilsheuser had German thoroughness and method tempered by American experience and tolerance.

Among my soldiers were some Sulu and Samal (Zamboanga) Moros, but the bulk of the company was recruited in the Cotabato District. On first enlisting the Moros we were somewhat obsessed by the idea of following the British example in India and other colonies and taking the men of one tribe or district to serve elsewhere than in the vicinage of their homes and relations. That was also the Spanish method in the Philippines.

Their native army and Civil Guard used Tagalos in Bicol and Ilocano provinces. Ilocanos and Visayas in Tagalo provinces, and so on; and any Filipinos in Mindanao against the Moros. In the American way, we disregarded precedent. The organic act of the Constabulary provided that constables should serve in the province of their enlistment, and on the whole this policy has been fully justified by events.

The few cases of desertion or venality due to nepotistic influences have been as nothing compared with the contentment of the enlisted men as a whole and the utilization of their knowledge of local conditions.

XXIX - Life at Cotabato

Life at Cotabato differed from that of Negros. There was practically no social intercourse with the Filipinos and Moros of the district. For one thing, the Filipinos of Mindanao were less cultured than those of the northern provinces; there were but few of them, scattered along the coast towns, and the Spaniards alleged that they were the descendants of convicts sent from Manila and the Filipino provinces to settle in Mindanao and form a barrier against further Moro encroachments.

Then there were many American women at the army posts with which Mindanao was studded, and wherever the American woman reigned no officer dared associate socially with Filipinos or Filipinas, Moros or Moras, under pain of instant and complete ostracism, petalism, and social annihilation.

Rajah Brooks used to say that until Englishwomen came to Sarawak there was no difficulty in administering that state; also, there are not lacking old Anglo-Indians who lament the days when, in default of white women, British officials mingled socially with the Indian peoples. Part of the success of the Dutch in Java has been due to their social intercourse with the ranking Javanese and to the fact that a half-breed is embraced as a member of the ruling class, not treated as the Eurasian pariah.

But in the Philippines wherever an American woman has had her say—and she has had it almost everywhere—a massive dam of social prejudice was built across the stream of that mutual intercourse between the races which was necessary to a complete and proper understanding. The American women who did not help to build that dam were honorable exceptions to the rule of prejudice—needless to say they were women of the highest type and ideals—but they were too few to pull down the barrier that their sisters built and sustained by every means in their power.

That attitude of American women is natural enough. Fear motivates us all, and the American woman, whose charms often faded under the tropical sun, might well fear the seductive little brown women who blended so well with the heat and the palms and the white-hot nights.

The arrival of the bimonthly transport from Manila usually brought a bevy of army and civilian girls and wives, making the round trip, and also making the quartermaster of the transport old before his time, as he had to allot space, needed perhaps for officers traveling on duty, to the female relations of some officer with a "pull."

When the transport anchored in the mud off the mouth of the river we had a "hop" in the club at Cotabato; and pretty girls and matrons would visit our quarters on the Hill of Extensive View and graciously deign to accept from youths, to whom a pretty American girl looked like an angel from heaven, such offerings as brass trays, copper chow-bowls, betel-nut boxes, or other loot from the last expedition.

As the Constabulary increased in numbers, we took over from the army several blockhouses that protected strategic points on the Rio Grande. I had to visit and inspect such posts. Sometimes I managed to get passage on one of the army launches or navy gunboats that plied up and down the river. But more often I made my journeys in a big dugout canoe paddled by six or eight of my Moro soldiers. Then I could stop to shoot a crocodile basking himself in the early morning sun, or land on the muddy banks, walk a short distance inland guided by one of my men, and shoot the ducks and ibis that abounded on the pools and swamps bordering every rice paddy.

Usually I traveled at night or in the early morning, thus avoiding the full glare of the sun as well as offering a less conspicuous mark to any Moro sharpshooter from the hostile bands that roamed along the river banks.

Those night journeys on the great river of Mindanao, the chunking of my soldiers' paddles, the chanted epic of some Maguindanaw Homer among the paddlers, the splash of crocodiles taking to water, the flickering lights of smudge fires beneath huts of the river bank, a coco palm assuming queer shape through the mist at sunrise—those are hours held in tender recollection, when the toil and sweat and bloodshed of the campaign in the valley are almost forgotten.

The little gunboats that patrolled the river were oases of solid comfort for their officers and men compared with the desert of army and Constabulary existence ashore. Sometimes at the end of a long hike, covered with mud and wet through with perspiration, we would reach the bank of the river to find a clean white gunboat gracefully floating on the muddy tide, and a white-uniformed, bathed and shaven young ensign ready to extend the hospitality for which the navy is honorably famed.

What a contrast that was to pass in a moment from the heat and filth of the trail to the coolness and comfort below the double awning on the after deck of the gunboat and, after the lukewarm water and canned food of the hike, to get an iced cocktail or mint julep, followed by a meal cooked by a skillful Chinaman.

About fifty miles up the river was the large Maguindanaw village of Kudarangan where Datu Piang reigned. This wise old Moro-mestizo—his father was a Chinaman—read the signs of the times better than the pure, hot-blooded Moro chiefs who followed Ali's lead against the hated American intruders.

Piang was allied by marriage and other ties with the hostile Moros, yet he managed so to handle both sides that he constantly acted as go-between. He executed the difficult role so skilfully that he maintained the friendship, and even the respect, of both sides until, upon the death of Ali, he succeeded to that unhappy chieftain's hegemony over the tribes of the Rio Grande Valley and became the wealthiest and most influential Moro in Mindanao.

Piang made presents to every American officer who came to Cotabato. He had a carefully graduated scale of gifts that ran from an engraved lantaka or valuable piece of brass for a general, down to half a dozen eggs for a second lieutenant. As a captain of Constabulary, Piang found difficulty in adjusting the question of my relative rank, but usually thought I was entitled to a small and scrawny fowl.

With Piang lived Datu Inuk, a Moro chief reputed as a good fighting-man but whose chief recommendation in the eyes of the American soldiers was the fact that one ear grew upon his neck where it had been bound with crude Moro surgery when the kris of a rival sliced it away from its proper position. The ear hole thus left naked to an interested and inquisitive world was stoppered by a short section of bamboo which Inuk often removed in contemplative manner, and which he used to scratch his nose.

Datu Inuk was supposed to have a grudge against Datu Ali. He often served as guide to our expeditions. On one occasion I was with him in a small canoe for several days. I was accompanying a provisional company of the Twenty-third Infantry on an attempt to reach Datu Ali's stronghold by water.

We embarked in a hundred canoes and for days wandered around the further shore of Lake Liguasan, a vast tract of swamp and water where crocodiles, pelicans, ibis, duck, and myriads of other waterfowl furnished the only incidents of monotonous days when we paddled over open stretches of water or pushed with difficulty through masses of sud-formed of swamp grass, water-cabbages, and water-lilies.

It was the Mohammedan feast of Ramadan when good Moros do not take food between sunrise and sunset. Datu Inuk slept through the long daylight hours, only awakening to direct the course of the flotilla or to remove his earplug for a comforting scratch.

Several days passed thus. We explored Lake Liguasan and finally lost ourselves in tortuous canals between dense groves of wild sago palm.

It was on one of these canals that an incident happened in my canoe that proved the old adage that a gun is always loaded. An American soldier next to me in the canoe was lying sprawled on his back in such comfort as could be obtained on the narrow concave bottom of the craft. His hat was over his eyes and a short briar pipe served to while away the leaden hours and protect him against consuming swarms of mosquitoes.

In the canoe that followed ours, prow to stern, sat another American soldier who was cleaning his Krag rifle. Bang! went the supposedly empty gun and the dozing soldier in my boat jumped up, yelling blue fire and murder. The bullet had smashed the bowl of his pipe, creased the side of his face, and bored a hole through his campaign hat.

We were cramped up in those canoes for a week. When at the end of a fruitless quest we returned to Kudarangan and stretched our legs ashore, we reeled and staggered like drunken men.

XXX - A Night Alarm

ONE DARK NIGHT WHEN I WAS SLEEPING peacefully in my quarters on top of Tantawan Hill, Governor Van Horn awakened me with a vigorous and un-gubernatorial shake. He had rushed up from town with news brought by friendly Moros that a band of Ali's hostiles under the leadership of our old friend Bapa-ni-Manakup had circled around the upriver military expeditions with the intention of attacking Cotabato that night.

The plan was to assault first the cotta of Datu Mastula, whose mud fort was situated about three-quarters of a mile above the town, and to capture from the princesa of Cotabato her horde of some thousands of silver pesos.

Datu Mastula was a friendly Moro chief, and the princesa, who was the widow of Datu Utu, was reputed very wealthy by Moro standards—that is, in brass and in silver pesos. She lived on the other side of the river almost opposite the town of Cotabato. Van Horn explained that the post of Cotabato had been drained of soldiers for expeditions and that only by mustering the bandsmen of the Seventeenth Infantry could he make up a force to protect the American women and children against an attack. Consequently, it was necessary for the Constabulary to cross the river and protect Datu Mastula and the princesa against Ali's men.

My junior officers were absent on expeditions with most of my best men. In the barracks were about a dozen recruits and second-raters of whom I took eight out into the black night. Down the hill we hurried, through the streets of Cotabato where lights were appearing in the houses of Americans and Filipinos as news of the expected attack spread, to the river bank.

We embarked in a large canoe and paddled out into the mist which was low upon the water. A few minutes of swift and silent paddling brought us across the river and opposite the village of the princesa, a mere cluster of huts beneath a grove of coco palms.

The flare of torches showing yellow through the mist dimly illumined the moving figures of men and women, the shiny trunks of the coco palms, and a flotilla of canoes with bows thrust into the muddy shore. Over the water floated a babel of confused and hurried speech. We backed water and watched. Men were carrying heavy boxes, trunks, brasses, and the other lares and penates of the princesa from the huts to the canoes.

Had the hostiles already raided the village and were they making off with the plunder? Keeping our canoe just outside the circle of glare from the torches and ready if danger developed to back further into the sheltering mist, we challenged the men ashore. Answer came in friendly tones.

We quickly paddled in, to find that the princesa was moving with bag and baggage in fear of an immediate assault by Ali's warriors, who were reported not far distant. Her chief wealth consisting of some thousands of Mexican silver pesos, was already aboard the canoes.

There would be little left for Bapa-ni-Manakup if he arrived, and the princess village was not to be easily defended by my small band. So, I started through the grove of coco palms, bordering the river bank, toward Datu Mastula's fort a few hundred yards further upstream. In that fort were many rifles and much ammunition which could not be allowed to fall into the hands of hostile Moros.

But as we moved away from the village a Moro boy, who spoke a little English, learned from the American soldiers at Cotabato, plucked me by the shirt sleeve and haltingly said: "No go that way, capitan! Many bad men there—men of Datu Ali."

The boy's warning probably saved us from a dark and bloody death. I learned a few minutes later that the space between the princesa's village and Datu Mastula's cotta was alive with hostiles. We reembarked and paddled up the river, were challenged by Mastula's men from the walls of his fort, and were admitted through the river wall.

Then I placed my detachment to reinforce the friendly datu's men guarding the fort, and heard the demands of Ali's Moros issuing from the impenetrable night that the fort be surrendered, and the arms and ammunition delivered to men who could make good use of them. Safe behind the walls, we shouted defiance to Bapa-ni-Manakup and urged him to open the ball. For some time, taunts and defiance were bandied across the walls.

My Moro soldiers lied freely and vociferously about the number of American soldiers who had reinforced the fort, while my own voice gave verisimilitude to their exaggerations.

After a time, as no attack developed, I retired to Mastula's bamboo hut in the center of the fort to resume my interrupted slumbers. The women of his little harem furnished me with grass mats and greasy kapok pillows. The last I saw before dozing off was a buxom Moro girl who was readjusting her scanty wardrobe before reclining on a mat near my feet.

My sleep was fitful both because I had a touch of malarial fever and because it was often interrupted by calls from outside when an attack seemed imminent. Therefore, I welcomed the dawn and doubly welcomed a little naval launch which chugged up the river bringing to the rescue a chubby-cheeked midshipman, a Colt automatic, and a dozen husky American sailors.

When that Colt was mounted on the walls of the fort, Mastula's arms and ammunitions were safe. The dawn mist had not risen from the rice fields behind the fort before we were further reinforced by a company of Infantry from upriver. Then we issued forth against Bapa-ni-Manakup and his band. But that wily chieftain had fled with the dawn, and a scout of several miles revealed nothing more than *carabao* grazing in the rice fields and a string of probably hostile Moros disappearing over a grassy rise half a mile or more ahead of our perspiring column.

Soon afterward I received a letter of commendation from the department commander, General Wood, for my "fine conduct in proceeding so promptly at midnight to the cotta of Datu Mastula and thereby preventing Datu Ali from obtaining large quantities of ammunition."

I felt like endorsing the communication on to that little Moro boy who caught me by the sleeve and warned me not to go overland from the princesa's to Mastula's cotta.

XXXI - Saved by Cicadas

I THINK THAT IT WAS IN SEPTEMBER 1904, that I made the first of three expeditions down the coast of Cotabato District, south from the mouth of the Rio Grande River to Lebak, a harbor and abandoned Spanish settlement distant some sixty or seventy miles from Cotabato. It would have been an easy matter to reach Lebak in a few hours direct by launch from Cotabato.

But Governor Van Horn wanted me to inspect the Moro fishing villages on the little bays and river mouths along the length of the coast that the Moros called Biwang, or Left, because it was to the left as one emerges from the delta of the Rio Grande.

Consequently, I embarked with half a dozen Moro constables in a sapit, or sloop-rigged Moro craft built on lorcha lines, without outriggers. One or two of my men were Sulu Moros and professed to know how to sail the boat, which was about thirty feet long, of two- or three-tons burthen, and equipped with a pair of long sweeps for propulsion when wind failed.

As we glided swiftly down the Rio Grande on an ebbing tide it seemed to me that the sapit was a bit cranky or what sailors call "tender." She careened quickly to the slightest breath of wind or movement among the crew. Perhaps we had insufficient ballast aboard, yet we carried provisions and equipment for a two weeks' trip.

We floated out of the river mouth as the sun was setting behind the rim of the Celebes Sea and caught the light swell set up by the southwest monsoon which had, however, died with the sun. We were expecting to make most of our southing by night when a land breeze usually blew offshore from the cooler mountains over the warm sea. There were black clouds beneath the orange and topaz afterglow that painted the sky almost to the zenith, yet the weather seemed set fair and a light breeze wafted us slowly on our voyage. In order to make clear the details of the adventure that was awaiting us, I must briefly describe the topography of sea and land in that part of Mindanao.

A few miles above its mouth the Rio Grande divides into two streams which empty into the Celebes Sea four or five miles apart. Between the two mouths is a rocky promontory, while a little to the south of the southern entrance is another rocky point.

The remainder of the shoreline is mud flats and sandy beach. I knew the region fairly well because I had frequently fished for sea perch from the rocks at the entrance to the southern arm of the Rio Grande.

We were a few miles offshore when the black clouds in the west rose higher and obscured the stars which had rushed out after the brief tropical twilight. The land breeze died. We floated idly on the sea, the boom swinging and clanging back and forth with every roll of the boat.

A soldier was at the helm, taking advantage of every puff of wind that helped us on our course. I was preparing my bed on the latticed bamboo floor beneath the nipa awning on the poop. Suddenly an ominous soughing of the wind startled me and caused the soldiers to murmur in alarm. The distant moaning swelled to a roar as through the semi-darkness a white line of foam was seen approaching. We had barely time to turn the sapit stern on to the storm and lower the mainsail before the vicious squall struck us, almost without warning.

There was nothing to do but run ahead of it and pray that we might make the southern entrance of the Rio Grande or drive up on a sandy beach. It did not do to think of those jagged rocks to north and south of the entrance. On we rushed through the night, a soldier crouched at the helm and I clawed on beside him, giving a helping hand on the buffeted tiller. The squall increased in violence and the helmsman left me alone to steer the leaping sapit. The jib blew away, but without showing canvas we rushed at tremendous speed toward the dangers or safety ahead, depending on where we struck the shore. It was now pitch dark and the howling of the wind with the waves foaming on either side and often curling over the stern, as well as the mad motion of the boat, made up a terrifying experience.

When it seemed that we must be near shore there was a sudden lull, the comparative silence contrasting strongly with the previous riot of the elements. The sapit, losing headway, pitched drunkenly in the trough of the seas and with difficulty I made the frightened sailor-soldiers take the sweeps to keep her stern to the waves.

Out of the black void ahead and a little on our starboard bow I heard the shrill call of cicadas, those stridulating insects that sing so penetratingly in the trees of tropical forests, and I guessed—rightly, as it happened—that they were in the forest that crept out on the rocks just south of the south entrance to the Rio Grande. I put the helm over, urged my men on the sweeps, the sapit just grazed the rocks, tumbled a moment among the breakers, and rounded the point.

Then the storm began again with redoubled fury and we continued to drive before it. But we were now in smoother water, and a few minutes later we grounded in the surf on a shelving beach of soft sand and small gravel. We were all wet to the skin. The sapit was half-full of water, its rigging a tangled mass of rope, canvas, and poles. Our misadventures and discomforts, however, seemed as nothing compared with our escape from those fanged rocks and boiling breakers, an escape which, fantastic though the recounting of it may seem, I must ascribe to the good offices of those shrill-voiced cicadas.

To this day I never hear a cricket or other strident insect without recalling that black night on the Celebes Sea and the sapit pitching violently toward the dangers of the shore. We lit a fire on the beach, dried our clothes, and slept on the sand, comfortably enough except for the onslaughts of countless nik-niks, an expressive enough name for the infinitesimal, almost invisible, but wholly abominable, sand gnats.

The following morning, I had had enough of sapit voyaging. I bargained with some Moro fishermen for the use of their outrigger sailing canoe, a small kind of parao known to the Moros as an awang. In this we could paddle or sail along close enough to the coast to disembark quickly and drag the awang up on the beach at the first sight of an onshore squall which, I was assured by the Moro fishermen, was an almost daily occurrence at that time of year.

Thus, we voyaged easily and slowly down the Biwang coast, putting ashore at every cluster of huts that marked the official residence of some Moro chief whose claim to authority was in no manner vitiated by the uncleanliness of his person or his surroundings. Half a dozen coco palms, three palm-thatched bamboo huts, two dugout canoes, a few verdigrised brass trays, bowls, and a betel-nut box, a small but choice assortment of spears, krises with, perhaps, a musket of Waterloo vintage, some scaly men and women and naked, pot-bellied infants—such was the stock in trade of a Moro chief along the Biwang coast, the possession of which, however, enabled him to terrorize the timid Tirurayes, those pagan tribesmen of the mountains which rose steeply back from the Biwang beach, and, likewise, to compel them to bring down panniers of sweet potatoes and other tubers or bamboo canes full of wild-bee honey to exchange for a handful of salt.

By reason of his assumption of superior civilization the Moro datu exercised a monopoly over the production and sales of that necessity of life—sodium chloride. The high tides left deposits of salt on the rocks and tidal flats from which it was scraped by Moro women and children. The demand for salt among the Tiruraye villages of the interior was steady; its supply was entirely controlled by the coast Moros.

Thus, was established an economic basis of life extremely agreeable to the latter. A Tiruraye man or woman would carry a pannier of sweet potatoes weighing from fifty to one hundred pounds many miles through the mountains, descending perhaps four or five thousand feet, and would receive in exchange but a few ounces of salt.

Much as I disliked to disturb the idyllic existence of these petty datus, I was compelled to investigate some cases of abuse that had been reported to the governor and handed on by him to me. Many hours I spent in bichara, adjusting the scale of exchange between salt and sweet potatoes, warning of condign punishment if the governor heard any more tales of abuse of the Tirurayes, explaining the attitude of the American Government toward Mohammedan customs, and acting as judge, jury, and sheriff in cases of petty and grave crimes reported to me. Of course, my Moro constables were invaluable, both as interpreters of language and of ideas.

Often at low tide I hiked along the beach from village to village, mapping the coastline and obtaining data useful to the District government and the Constabulary. In places huge almendra (wild almond trees) overhung the strip of sand left bare by the ebb-tide, and on the nuts fed flocks of huge fruit bats.

Strange-shaped crabs and other crustaceans scurried away from us; monkeys came out of the jungle to play on the sands, but saw us and fled back to their arboreal home; Tiruraye hillmen and hill-women, trudging along the beach, also fled back into the jungle unless they were close enough to be reassured by the shouts of my soldiers. Then they would draw near, trembling with fear and excitement, which were only partly quieted by gifts of salt and hardtack. Once we came on a Tiruraye man engaged in hiding a pathetically small canoe in the jungle that ran down to the high-tide mark.

My soldiers asked him why he was so carefully hiding his craft. He answered that he lived in the mountains, and came occasionally to the coast to fish. He usually fished at night, so that the Moros of the vicinity might not see him and be offended at the trespass on their preserves.

Not infrequently we met, either on the sea or anchored near shore in some sheltered cove, a fleet of Bajaw vintas, the light sailing craft of the sea-gypsies of the East Indies.

The Bajaws rarely set foot ashore. They are born, they live, and they die in their tiny high-sided outrigger canoes that float like petrels on the water. In those eggshell craft they voyage thousands of miles between the islands of the East, always keeping south of the tracks of the dreaded typhoons, wafted south by the northeast trades and north by the southern monsoon.

With never a fixed abode on land they trade spoil of the sea for such land-food as they need. Rather are the Bajaws kin to the seagulls than to other human beings. A low-browed, long-haired, evil-faced crew they are, with their dirty, brown, half-naked bodies ringed by all manner of skin diseases, their graceful canoes stinking so strongly of fish and unwashed humans that we gave them a wide berth. Yet it was impossible not to admire them, as seamen.

A scene that is indelibly impressed on my memory is a fleet of Bajaw vintas off the Mindanao coast, rising and falling to a long southwest swell which sometimes curled in ugly whitecaps and caused the steamer on which I was passenger to roll and pitch most uncomfortably. The Bajaws rode the waves without fear and calmly fished while their little boats, no more than chips on the water, tobogganed down one watery hill and up the next.

Often, they were invisible in the trough of a big wave, but always they bravely rose to the crest of its successor. After several days of this hiking, paddling, and investigating, we brought up one evening on the beach at the mouth of the Taran River a mile or two from my destination at Lebak.

Our landing was hurried and lacked ceremony, for another onshore squall caught us half a mile from land and tumbled us in the surf before we could seek a cove or river mouth. Again, we were wet through and again the minute nik-niks wrought evil against each exposed inch of epidermis. When I crawled out of the surf, I found that I was clutching in one hand a quart bottle of Rioja claret and in the other a tin of crackers. These I shared with my men while we huddled around an unwilling driftwood fire.

The next morning, we dragged along the beach and around a rocky point into Lebak, finding there a perfect little harbor, a grove of coco palms, a decayed Spanish blockhouse, a still further decayed Moro datu, and a fever-racked Chinaman who kept a trading store. The Chino and I soon became good friends, for I was also developing a nice malarial chill and fever, doubtless brought on by exposure and involuntary baths.

We shivered, sweated, drank gin, and swallowed quinine pills together. From him and from some timid Moros who spoke with bated breath, I learned more of Datu Matabalao, a great Moro chief who lived a few miles inland from Lebak and who laid tribute on the Biwang coast for many a mile. Before leaving Cotabato the governor had told me that Matabalao was a powerful Moro chief, suspected of being in alliance with his cousins in Talayan, over the mountains, and, also, of having instigated the assassination of a Syrian merchant who had established himself at Lebak a year or so previous to my visit.

This Matabalao was evidently a gentleman with whom the District government and the Constabulary must reckon. My inquiries elicited the information that he possessed about a hundred men-at-arms, a nice stand of old muskets, with few modern rifles, a cannon or two, as well as a vast quantity of brass. The latter showed his great wealth and influence.

Of little use for a Moro gentleman to bank his money and have to show for it nothing but a bit of paper with which he could not impress his followers or the ignorant hill tribes; but if his worldly possessions took the form of cannon, guns, and brass, above all, brass, why, that was something tangible, something to which he could point with pride and which would impress his ignorant public.

It is easy to imagine a datu seated in his combination bedroom-office-harem, giving audience to a messenger from another chief, and saying: "What? You dare to doubt my word? Look at that pile of brass in yonder corner—look at it!—twenty-two trays, seventeen cuspidors, forty chow bowls, and much more. Go! And tell your master that I am a man of wealth and that my word is good."

I considered, but not for long, paying a visit to Matabalao. I looked at my five soldiers, remembered a certain experience with Datu Mustapha at Margosatubig and the general touchiness of disposition evinced by Moro datus who possessed abundant men and arms, and forbore the pleasure of an afternoon call.

Moreover, I was full of malaria. My head rang with quinine and my stomach was upset by calomel. Now, a man's courage and a man's stomach are in some way intimately connected. I had no stomach for a game with Matabalao—as long as he held all the trump cards.

That only goes to show how long residence in the tropics and continued attacks of malaria will weaken a man's fiber. If my orbit had crossed Matabalao's a few months or a year earlier than it did, there would have been an even chance that with my five men I could have given him "cards" and "spades" and have come out winner in a nice little game of casino down there on the Biwang coast. Intrinsically, the situation was not perhaps more difficult than that Mansalanao fight of mine in Negros.

As it was, I sent word to Matabalao that, as representative of the District governor, I would be glad to see him at Lebak. Answer came, after an insultingly long interval, that the datu was sick and could not leave his village; but, taking one thing with another, I guessed that his sickness was not serious enough to rob him of his sting.

After devoting a little more thought to the odds of five against one hundred, and with as much dignity as the situation and a malarial chill permitted, I embarked my little expedition and paddled out of Lebak harbor into the Celebes Sea, headed back to Cotabato. The southwest monsoon that had hampered our southern progress now wafted us north at several knots an hour.

Spreading the patchwork sail of the awang, we fairly leapt over the waves.

The day after leaving Lebak we sailed into the mouth of the Rio Grande and then upstream between the banks covered with mangroves and nipa palms, home to Cotabato wharf.

That was the first of three expeditions down the Biwang coast, each of which, owing to the increasing severity of malarial attacks, was more disastrous for me than the preceding one. Doubtless I should have applied for leave and the opportunity to get the fever out of my blood. But I still had a bank account of health and vitality and was not to be satisfied until I had overdrawn it.

XXXII - Datu Matabalo

The news I brought back about Matabalao confirmed Governor Van Horn's suspicions that he was supplying the hostile Moros of Ali's bands with salt, dried fish, and other supplies that they could with difficulty secure by the customary river route.

It was determined by the governor of the Moro Province and the District Chief of Constabulary, that a strong Constabulary expedition should land at Lebak, interview Matabalao, and with guides secured from that reluctant chief, push through the unknown mountains between the coast and the Talayan district of the interior.

I was to command the expedition and as reinforcements for the thirty men I could muster from my own Constabulary, Colonel Harbord sent me from Zamboanga a company of General Service Constabulary. In each Constabulary District there was organized one or two extra companies for service wherever additional forces were necessary.

The General Service company sent to me was commanded by my old friend Captain Johnson, now relieved as District supply officer and trying his hand at commanding troops in the field; it had been recruited from the pagan Subanun hillmen of the Zamboanga hinterland and was therefore by way of being an experiment. Those hill-men were craven souls who had long been preyed upon by the more warlike Moros. It was an experiment that failed. The Subanuns could not be nerved to fight against their ancient oppressors, as I was soon to learn.

With Captain Johnson, Dr. Farrow, and about seventy men, I embarked on the cutter Ranger and comfortably journeyed to Lebak, contemplating from the deck of the steamer with a certain satisfaction the coast along which I had so lately voyaged in perilous and arduous manner.

From Lebak we hiked the few miles to Datu Matabalao's village on the banks of the Taran River. When that astute chief had taken one look at my impressive command, he sulkily complied with my request to be supplied with sixty cargadores for the journey through the mountains. But as for guides to Talayan—why, he knew nothing about a trail to that remote region!

Cajoling, followed by threats, did not change his attitude of obdurate indifference. After a delay of twenty-four hours to secure a sulky and semi-hostile lot of Moro and Tiruraye cargadores, I left Lebak in the direction of the mountains—and with Matabalao as an unwilling guest of the expedition. I did not care to leave him in my rear.

Even before we left Matabalao's village complications had arisen with the General Service company of timid Subanun comrades. Several times I had to interfere when the worm turned and a Subanun constable came to blows with a Moro. The first night we posted guards, the Subanuns fired at imaginary assailants, an unhappy augury of which might occur when we were across the mountains and had to encounter the fighting Moros of Talayan.

Two days I hiked my hodgepodge command into the mountains, compelling as guides Tiruraye hillmen who dreaded Matabalao's future wrath but little less than my immediate punishment. At last we reached a pretty saucer-shaped plateau two or three thousand feet above the coast, where there were level stretches of grassland and some rice fields cultivated by men of Matabalao. Out of the plateau led several trails into the still deeper mountains. But now the Tirurayes and Taran Moros obstinately declared that they knew the trails no further. This was as far as Datu Matabalao's authority extended, they declared, and beyond were trackless mountains and fierce tribes of Manobos and Bilanes. They were positive in affirming that there was no trail to Talayan.

Matabalao, a picture of sulky dignity, refused to use his influence to procure us a guide. One nod from him and the mountains would have been an open book for us to read. But he refused to give that nod. Indeed, there was no doubt that his messengers had already traversed the mountains and warned all Tiruraye hillmen from their clearings. I was sure that this was the case, because my scouts, sent in every direction on the chance of capturing a guide, returned only with tales of recently deserted settlements.

With a few men, I went ahead by compass course along the trail that seemed to run in the direction of Talayan. A few miles through dense jungle brought us out on the grassy slopes above the upper reaches of the Taran River where the trail ran out in the cogon grass.

Vainly I tried such old tricks of the trail as taking two Taran Moros out ahead of the column and telling them they would be killed if they did not guide us to Talayan, then sending one ahead still further with a patrol of soldiers who fired a shot when out of sight of the other obstinate one, who, imagining that his companion was killed, should have promptly offered to show the trail and escape similar fate.

But the influence of Datu Matabalao was such that his men preferred possible death at our hands to certain death and probable torture at the hands of their chief when the temporary irruption of Constabulary had passed.

The week's rations with which I set out had been diminished by four days' consumption. There were at least five days of mountain hiking ahead of us even if we secured a guide, which seemed highly improbable. The attitude of the Subanun company was disquieting and seemed likely to result in disaster to the Constabulary when we met resistance in force. And I was full of fever, my head ringing with quinine. So, after consultation with the other officers, I determined to turn back to the coast.

Even then it took as much courage to make that decision as to go forward, and what finally decided me was the fact that the Constabulary prestige would suffer more by a debacle at the hands of the Talayan Moros—a debacle that in view of the condition of the Subanun company I considered almost certain—than by failing to accomplish the purpose of the expedition.

We turned back. But first I gave Matabalao a last chance to furnish a guide, warning him that if one was not forthcoming, I would take him prisoner to Cotabato. Nevertheless, he maintained his attitude of ignorance and indifference, and we retraced our steps.

At Matabalao's village we impressed a number of his awangs and embarked for Cotabato. But first we loaded the obdurate chief's cannon, rifles, and ammunition, and replenished our stock of provisions from his storehouses. The journey up the coast took us several days. For me it was a miserable trip, as I was racked by fever and disgusted at the result of the expedition.

It was my first failure in years of hiking and fighting. At one point I landed with about twenty men and Dr. Farrow and hiked overland, back in the mountains, through a series of Tiruraye villages, descending again to the beach. Matabalao, under close guard on my own awang or hiking along through the mountain homes of Tirurayes, remained silent and Sphinx-like.

He was served by one of his own Moros whom I allowed to accompany him.

One night when we camped on the beach, the awang aboard which Matabalao was prisoner anchored a stone's throw from shore, three Moro constables being left aboard as guard. I slept on the beach.

Just before daybreak shots rang out and there was a great hubbub and clamor aboard the awang. My soldiers called out that Matabalao had attempted to escape and that they had shot him. Flinging guards along the beach, I waited for the day and when the sun rose inspected the awang and found bloodstains on the prow. The soldier who was sentry at the time said that he had shot Matabalao as the chief sprang up to leap overboard. The datu's servant had also disappeared. Careful questioning and the testifying bloodstains convinced me that Matabalao had been killed.

Not until years later, when all the actors in the drama were scattered far and wide, did I learn the probable facts of the case. Matabalao had escaped sometime before the sentry missed him. The soldier, finding his prisoner gone, shot the datu's servant, who was sleeping near the spot from which his master had fled, spattered the murdered Moro's blood over the boat, fired a few more shots, threw the body overboard, and swore his companion soldiers to the tale which deceived me.

A few months later I learned that Matabalao had come to life again. But the probable facts in the case I learned only by piecing together hints and evidence and knowledge of Moro character gleaned through the years.

We arrived safely at Cotabato. General Wood and Colonel Harbord determined that as an object lesson to the Moros an expedition must go through from Lebak to Talayan. A force of nearly one hundred American soldiers was formed, and I accompanied it with my company of Constabulary.

The General Service company of Subanun tribesmen, however, returned to Zamboanga, and its Subanun members were gradually discharged. That was the last attempt to make soldiers of the pagan hillmen of Minadanao. In a measure I sacrificed my health and endangered my reputation in the attempt.

For the third expedition we took with us friendly Moros who knew the trail over the mountains, at least from the Talayan end.

Though I was rotten with fever, pride and the determination to reestablish the prestige of the Constabulary of Cotabato compelled me to accompany the expedition. But when three days into the mountains, not far beyond the high-water mark of my previous expedition, I keeled over.

We had reached the upper Taran River and some clearings of Manobo hillmen which here jutted into Tiruraye territory. As usual, we were anxious to capture a guide.

To the army captain commanding the expedition I volunteered to ascend a grassy hill toward some Manobos who could be seen on the crest a mile or so away. With a soldier interpreter I advanced toward the Manobos, holding my hands above my head in token of friendship.

But the pagans stood watchful, with spears poised and arrows ready strung on their bows—poisoned arrows. For half an hour or so I powwowed with them in vain attempt to bargain for the services of a guide. It was dreadfully hot in the full glare of the sun on the bare hillside and that put the finishing touch to my fever-racked body.

I scarcely remember how I stumbled back down the hill toward the expedition resting in the valley below, and of the incidents of the next week I remember nothing. The fever went to my head and I rode for days in an improvised stretcher of a blanket between two poles.

Thus unconscious—as I later learned—I was carried over a mountain range several thousand feet high, through almost trackless jungles, and down the opposite slopes to the Rio Grande Valley at Talayan. Hostile Moros attacked the column. But I knew nothing of it. Recollection returned to me only when I was beneath the nipa awning of a canoe, floating down the Rio Grande to Cotabato. The doctor who accompanied the expedition said that most of the time while I was borne on the stretcher through the mountains my fever was from 104 to 106 degrees.

At Cotabato, Captain Heard of the army medical corps took me into his own house and nursed me back to life. I acknowledge this debt to him.

Subcutaneous injections of quinine in my arm and hip, followed by liberal doses of arsenic, finally conquered the malarial germ. But it was not for weeks that I was strong enough to resume my Constabulary duties. A fortunate sea voyage to Iloilo, where I had been subpoenaed as witness in an old Negros case, did much to help me toward convalescence.

In May, I was granted accrued leave of absence for six months, and sailed on a North German Lloyd liner from Manila via Singapore and Europe for the United States. I had been in the tropics continuously for six years, almost all the time on field service involving exposure and hardship. I badly needed the rest and change of climate.

Not long after my departure from Cotabato, the campaign against Datu Ali closed with the death of that Maguindanaw chief who, betrayed by his own men, was killed by a detachment of American soldiers in the heart of Cotabato District, near the Davao border.

Datu Piang then reigned supreme in the valley, conciliating American officials with gifts of brass, chicken, and eggs. The opportunist merchant chief lives and prospers. The proud fighting chief died. Yet I doubt not that when the Maguindanaw Moros gather for the rice planting or harvest, songs are sung and tales are told of Datu Ali—last, and perhaps not the least noble, of the Maguindanaw chiefs.

XXXIII - Oriental Eden Isles

I sailed from the Philippines early in May 1905. Five months later, in October, I was back again, eager to return to Mindanao and the enticing Constabulary work among the Moros, Filipinos, and pagans. My leave had still a month to run. Yet no sooner were my red corpuscles slightly multiplied by sea travel and the colder weather of Europe and the United States than the "call of the East" rang loudly in my ears.

In those stirring times I suppose that a Constabulary officer, removed from the scenes of excitement and danger which his work afforded, was, in a measure, like a Chinaman without his opium or a professional gambler deprived of the excitement of the tables. However, it is only fair to us to say that the craving to be back in the game was also stimulated by the knowledge that we were taking part in a work of constructive administration that reflected vast credit on our country.

Doubtless we magnified the part we were playing. There were few Constabulary officers who went on leave who did not think their prompt return necessary for the continuance of good conditions in their company, province, or district. Most of our officers returned as I did before their leave expired. Egotistical we undoubtedly were; yet, after all, our egotism was tinged with some of the finer qualities of patriotism and loyalty.

Five glorious months I spent running around the world. There were weeks on a North German Lloyd liner from Singapore to Naples, when I chummed with a young Russian naval officer returning home on parole following his capture by the Japanese while he was running a torpedo boat out of Port Arthur, with the jolly little bespectacled German ship's doctor, and with a Danish civil engineer on leave from the Siamese railways.

The four of us—Russian, Dane, German, and American—held high revelry on the steamer and ashore, and the Russian dug deeply into an apparently inexhaustible sack of English sovereigns in an attempt to learn the great American game of poker.

Then there was England in the month of June, bowered almost as green as the tropic isles I had left behind, and some idle days upon the bosom of old Father Thames; an Atlantic voyage on a fast liner, five and one half days from shore to shore; New York in August when the Philippines seemed cool compared with the subways; San Francisco and the first flavor of the returning Orient; an idyllic month across the Pacific on a Pacific Mail boat; a few days in old, yet new, Japan—and I was back in Manila, striding up the broad stairs of the Oriente Building, which now housed Constabulary Headquarters, eager to be reassigned to duty in Mindanao, land of alluring dangers.

Disappointment awaited me, for I was assigned to duty as Assistant Executive Inspector. However, before the end of October, a shuffle of officers in Mindanao gave me my opportunity, and I went south again, this time as Senior Inspector of the Constabulary of Sulu, our farthest-south outpost.

While I was on leave, my old friend Captain Hayson, then Senior Inspector of Sulu, had been murdered in his sleep in his palm-thatched bungalow at Siasi. One of his own Moro soldiers, posted as sentry over Hayson's quarters, thrust his carbine through the open window by the gallant Kansan's bed and shot him through the body, killing him instantly.

The assassin, who had revenged an imaginary injustice, fled with one or two other mutinous Moro soldiers to the interior of the island. Hayson's junior officer, Lieutenant De Witt, was absent on an expedition. When he returned that morning to find his captain dead, he patched up the hole made by the bullet in the cane-bottomed bed on which Hayson was slain and slept there that night, defying his mutinous company to do its worst.

Captain George D. Long had been sent to Siasi as senior inspector and had reorganized and disciplined the company. But he was now under orders to proceed to Misamis, where another Constabulary was in bad condition, so I fell heir to the situation in Sulu. The Sulu District of the Moro Provinces embraced the isles and islets, stretched like a chalice of emeralds, from the southwest point of Mindanao at Zamboanga to within a few miles of huge, mysterious Borneo. There are a Sulu Archipelago, an island of Sulu, and the Sulu Sea.

On Sulu, the largest island and as much as three hundred square miles in area, is the only sizable town in the District, Jolo, a word which is a Spanish corruption of the Moro "Sulu." The sultan of Sulu lived at Maimbun on Sulu Island. He exercised nominal authority over the hundreds of lesser chiefs scattered through the islands which extend over two hundred miles north and south. In 1905 there was no Constabulary on Sulu Island, but the District had two stations, at Siasi and Bongao.

Siasi Island, where I commanded the Constabulary, is some forty miles south of Sulu. A narrow channel divides it from Lepak Island. Beside the channel, over coral reefs and tidal flats, and under coco palms and ylang-ylang trees, sprawls the little whitewashed town of Siasi. The islands of Siasi and Lepak are twin cones of tropical verdure rising a few hundred feet above the Sulu Sea that laves their shores. They are the distilled essence of the tropics, the very "Oriental Eden Isles" of the poet's imagination. And they are but two of the pearls to be found in the string of the Sulu Archipelago, where Nature seems to have lavished on land and sea her richest colors.

South of Siasi lies the long, narrow island of Tawie Tawi, forming with its coral reefs and outlying islets the barrier between the Sulu and Celebes seas. Through the narrow channels between the reefs and islands the tidal currents flow swiftly and often cause dangerous whirlpools, overfalls, and tide-rips.

The islands were inhabited by the Sulu Moros, a race of distinct language and characteristics from the Maguindanaws in my former District at Cotabato. Chiefs ruled in feudal style. Their lack of men and arms was atoned for by the magnificence of their titles—rajahs, maharajahs, hadjis, panglimas, sahips, and datus were as plentiful as blackberries on a summer's bush. Some islands were uninhabited: their jungle interiors or the lagoons and reefs around them offered attractive shelter for pirates, smugglers, and other evil-doers. The Bajaw sea-gypsies roamed the Sulu Sea, fished for shark and dried their fins for sale to Chinese merchants, or gathered bêche-de-mer (sea slug) and pearl shell from the coral reefs exposed at low tide.

To such a district I came toward the end of October 1905; a sea of sparkling blue rarely lashed by storms; islands so lovely that they seemed destined for a race of fairies; and a people in general so unlovely in appearance and disposition that they were as satyrs in the garden of paradise.

Captain Long had done much to improve conditions on Siasi, on the neighboring islands, and in the Constabulary company which was mutinous and sullen at the time of Hayson's death. The murderer, Private Sariol, had been captured and was in the guardhouse at Siasi, awaiting the arrival of the official hangman from Manila.

However, conditions on the whole in the Sulu District were bad, and near Jolo the stage was setting for the bloody drama of Bud Dajo. Engagements between United States troops and recalcitrant Moros on the islands to the north of Siasi were becoming increasingly frequent, and, despite patience shown by the governor of the Sulu District, Major Hugh L. Scott, United States Army, the Sulu Moros were getting out of hand.

These conditions were reflected in the surly attitude of the Moros on Siasi and the neighboring islands, while agitators did not fail to try to seduce the Moros in our Constabulary company from their allegiance to the United States. Luckily, I found at Siasi, Corporal Baynudin and some of my old Cotabato soldiers who had been transferred to the company to stiffen it after the murder of Captain Hayson.

The presence of these loyal men made me feel sure that no mutiny would get underway before information reached me. Lieutenant De Witt, my junior and the only other officer at Siasi, had served for some years in Sulu. His nerves were either proof against the many alarms and dangers that surrounded us, or he had them under fine control.

He consumed prodigious quantities of strong black coffee, slept little at night, but prowled around the towns and island with a pair of .45 revolvers pendent from his belt and a nose quivering with scent for trouble. A few days after I arrived at Siasi, De Witt showed me an exhibition of cool nerve—and perhaps wished to test that of his new senior inspector.

The Constabulary buildings were situated on rising ground just behind the town. There were some old and much-decayed Spanish stone buildings and blockhouses that we used as offices, storehouse, and jail. A wooden barracks with palm roof housed the company of fifty men.

De Witt and I lived in a bamboo and nipa bungalow a hundred yards across a grassy plaza from the barracks and storehouses which fronted on the town.

On the west was the town; on the south and north the land fell sharply down to mud and coral flats partly bare at low tide, and to the east rose gradually toward the green hills in the center of the island. Our bungalow stood alone, under coco palms and ylang-ylang trees. There was nothing between us and the mud flats or the interior hills.

After Hayson's experience, we did not care to post a sentry over our quarters. There was a certain bravado in living thus alone and daring the hostile Moros to do their worst. Of course, we slept with our revolvers ready, or rather I did. De Witt slept little; and if I had remained long at Siasi I might have acquired his nocturnal habits.

Although Private Sariol, Hayson's murderer, lay in our guardhouse, heavily ironed and fettered, there were still two or three other Constabulary deserters at large with their arms and ammunition. Soon after I arrived at Siasi they or other hostile Moros began to amuse themselves at night by firing on the Constabulary buildings from safe vantage points in the long grass, the brush, or the mud flats around us.

The first time this happened I was lounging in a long chair on the porch of our bungalow after the evening meal. De Witt was in another chair. Between us on a table was our reading lamp, lighting up the porch and the vines which clambered up the front of the porch, screening us from the road and plaza.

All was black outside. The quiet of the tropic night only interrupted by the whirring of insects, the stridulation of cicadas, and the subdued murmur of the soldiers' play and conversation in the barracks across the plaza. The air was heavy with the scent of ylang-ylang blossoms. Suddenly the peaceful night was rudely disturbed by several rifle shots. Bullets, evidently intended for us, whistled overhead. Naturally enough, I started up and reached for my revolver, lying handy on the table.

De Witt, however, scarcely moved in his chair but looked up from his book and said quietly, "It's those deserters, captain, they often amuse themselves this way." So, I lounged back again, not to be outdone in calmness by a junior officer. Another shot or two and the murmur from the barracks increased to a loud buzz, while the rattle of arms could be heard as the guard turned out.

Then De Witt coolly and composedly arose and said rather disdainfully, "Shall I give them a volley, Captain?"

I gave assent. He took the guard out into the bush, fired a few volleys in the direction of the interrupters, and soon returned to his reading and smoking.

It was useless to chase the hostiles. A needle in a haystack would be a conspicuous object compared with a Sulu Moro loose on the islands and seas of the South on a dark night.

The above incident carries a companion with it. A few nights later, when De Witt was absent from Siasi, chasing pirates or interviewing obdurate chiefs, I was alone on the porch. The conditions were otherwise the same: black night, circle of lamplight on the veranda, whirring of insects, and scent of ylang-ylang.

I was deep in an interesting book. I became slowly conscious that there was something unusual in the darkness outside. A vague and not unnatural feeling of apprehension was intensified when the unusual defined itself as the low murmur of Moro voices, for it was certain that nobody would approach the bungalow stealthily with honest intentions.

I lay still, but strained my eyes to see through the vines that enclosed the front of the veranda. There were men on the path a few yards away, but from where I sat, they were invisible. It was not a pleasant situation. Six months before, Hayson had been killed within a few feet of the chair. No soldier on business would approach the bungalow without a warning call. No civilian Moro had any business there at that hour of the night unless escorted by soldiers or announcing his coming most clearly.

For all friends knew the custom of the Sulu Sea—approach openly and give ample warning. It was customary for a visitor to strike a match, light a cigarette, and hem and haw loudly when near the house. Nerves were too keenly edged and revolvers too handy, to make quiet approach the usual thing down Sulu way.

When satisfied that there was someone there my hand stole toward the table, feeling for my revolver. Although the night was hot and close, I broke into icy perspiration when my fingers failed to close upon the gun. I realized that for once, and when I might most need it, I had left my revolver in the room inside.

Instead of rising from my chair I put one hand on the floor and rolled out, then crept into the room and found the revolver on an old billiard table left at Siasi by some Spanish commandant and on which De Witt and I were wont to knock about some horribly chipped balls on a bare slate bed. When my fingers touched the trigger, I felt my nerves steady, and determined to find out who had such business with me that stealthy approach was necessary.

Cautiously circling the room, I came again to the open door on the veranda, but on the other side so that I could see down the steps and out on the path where the lamplight filtered through the vines. After a while I made out the figures of three men, and fancied that I could distinguish rifles.

They were still talking in low tones. Although it has taken some time to tell, I don't suppose that two minutes elapsed from the moment the alarm was raised until I was back at the doorway, revolver in hand, peering out into the night.

I was now convinced that the men wished me ill. It was not difficult to imagine them discussing who should do the killing. Should I fire at them—they were within fifty feet and despite the obscurity offered a fair target—or should I challenge them? The question was answered when one of the figures moved and the lamplight glinted on a polished row of cartridges in his belt.

They were Constabulary soldiers and I sharply challenged them. Answer came that they were the patrol that made nightly rounds of the plaza and buildings and they drew near the steps. I slipped my revolver in my hip pocket—but kept it ready.

The soldiers, whom I recognized as doubtful characters, said that they wanted to *reclamar* (complain) about some trivial matter of discipline, food or women, I now forget which. And to this day I do not know whether their *reclamo* was genuine or invented on the spur of the moment because of my preparedness.

XXXIV - Talking for My Life

One day in December 1905, the plaza beneath the walls of the Spanish fort at Siasi was a scene of interest to hundreds of Moros who had come from out the Sulu Sea on paraos, vintas, sapits, and other craft. Private Sariol, Philippine Constabulary, was to pay the penalty of his crime. The official hangman had arrived from Manila that morning, bringing with him the sinister instruments of his unpleasant trade. In the center of the plaza the hastily erected gallows glared out stark and naked against the blue sky and whitewashed buildings.

Around it a company of American soldiers and part of the Constabulary company formed a hollow square. Governor Scott brought the American soldiers from Jolo to ensure that the hanging should be free from interruption by the hundreds of visiting and sympathetic Moros. This was probably wise, although we of the Constabulary would have preferred to do our own job in our own way. When the stage was set, the hangman, as leading man, mounted the gallows platform. With a squad of four constables I escorted the villain, ex-Private Sariol, from the guardhouse and marched him across the sun-washed plaza to his death.

When the shackles were knocked off, he was given an opportunity to speak to his assembled brethren and we hoped that he would express contrition for his crime. But without a tremor he faced the crowd and shouted, "What I did, I did—and now I will pay my utang (debt)." The drop fell, his body seemed almost to reach the ground, then fetched up short with a jerky thud, quivered a few seconds, and was still. Captain Hayson was avenged.

How well in the month or two that I was at Siasi I grew to know the sun-bathed plaza and the one street leading to the wharf between wooden, whitewashed buildings that housed the Chinos' stores, in front of which, drying in the sun and emitting an unspeakable stench, lay sharks' fins, bêche-de-mer, pearl shell, and other fruit of the sea.

At sunset, when the day's drill and office work were over, I would don a bathing suit, slip on a pair of rope-soled slippers, and, accompanied perhaps by many of my soldiers, run down to the wharf for a dip in the sea.

It was just as well to have many companions of the bath, because crocodiles and sharks abounded. The crocodiles at night often crept beneath the houses built on piles along the beach, and on at least one occasion took a Moro girl from the slatted back porch of a house. At high tide the floor of the houses was but a foot or two above sea level. After the swim I soused with fresh water, put on white uniform, and visited the Moro market and Chino stores. At the latter I was shown the latest consignment of pearls bought cheaply by the trading Chinos from the Moro fishermen and divers. Wonderfully fine pearls were sometimes to be seen in those humble Chinese stores.

Once I was shown a perfectly matched pair, larger than the common white bean, which the Chino said were worth fifteen hundred pesos ($750). In New York they would have been worth many thousands. I bought a few small pearls and had I possessed the trading instinct I might have become wealthy while commanding the Sulu Constabulary, as my position and authority gave me special opportunities. One pearl that I bought for sixty pesos was later priced in Manila at six hundred. But I was more interested in the discipline of my company and in running down the many pirates and smugglers who in their swift vintas sailed the seas and channels between Siasi and Bongao.

Before telling of my own voyage by vinta to the southernmost settlement in the archipelago, I must relate an incident that happened on Tapul Island, a few miles north of Siasi, an incident which ended happily enough, but which furnished all the necessary accompaniments for a first-class tragedy.

For several hours one day I talked for my life beside the Sulu Sea. Tapul is about ten miles in circumference and lies between Siasi and Sulu. It was inhabited by several thousand Sulus under many chiefs, whose only common interest was sullen and scarcely veiled hostility to the American Government. Governor Scott had appointed Datu Pangiran of Siasi, a weak and opium-smoking chief but of good lineage, as headman of the Siasi subdistrict, of which Tapul was a part.

Soon after I arrived at Siasi, some of the young bloods of Tapul, following time-honored custom, made a piratical cruise to the outlying islands of Sulu. Datu Pangiran, spurred thereto by Governor Scott, imposed a fine of seven rifles on Panglima Baladji of Tapul, the chief of the offending clan.

Panglima Baladji told Datu Pangiran to go to the Moro equivalent of Gehenna, and if he really wanted the fine of seven rifles, to come and collect it. That would be something like collecting the sting from a wasp, and well did Datu Pangiran know it. At last Governor Scott's patience was exhausted, so he sent me a launch with instructions to run over to Tapul with Datu Pangiran and extract that fine.

My predecessor, Captain Long, had paid a friendly visit to Tapul and had told me something about the number of fighting-men and arms possessed by the Tapul chiefs, so I took along all the Constabulary that could be spared, about twenty men, and started out to get the sting from the wasp.

Perhaps it will furnish an illuminating commentary to state that this visit of mine to Tapul occurred about two months before the famous Bud Dajo fight near Jolo, in which nearly one hundred American soldiers and Constabulary were killed and wounded in an assault on that fortified hill where six hundred Moros died defending their positions, literally to the last ditch. Many of the Moros whom I interviewed at Tapul later found their way to Jolo and died in the Bud Dajo fight.

The launch sent me by Governor Scott boasted a machine-gun with which to awe the Tapul braves. But owing to the coral reefs, the launch could not approach within two or three hundred yards of shore. I had to disembark in a small boat with my men, and landed on the beach beneath a huge balatig, or banian tree.

Datu Pangiran and an interpreter, Moro Jalmany, were with me, and they did not look at all happy. I picked out a nice open spot near the beach so that my small detachment could not be rushed by hostile Moros. Back of the beach the interior of Tapul is hilly and densely covered with coco palms and fruit trees, bamboo and brush, among which are the many Moro villages.

Then I sent Jalmany inland to look for the obdurate chief Panglima Baladji. He went up a trail into the brush, slowly and unwillingly, like a poor-spirited cur into a rat hole. However, after a while he returned with Panglima Baladji and his following of armed Moros, who much outnumbered my Constabulary.

I greeted Baladji and led him to a comfortable spot beneath a banian, a couple of hundred feet from my detachment. I had given orders to the men to keep together with carbines loaded and handy, but without showing signs either of fear or hostility toward the Tapulites.

As a sign of good faith, I left my own arms with the detachment and mingled with the Moros as nonchalantly as the sight of so much cold steel might allow. They were a picturesque lot, with their tight-fitting trousers and Zouave vests of many colors, their brilliantly turbaned heads and their gay sashes thrust full of krises and daggers. As many of them carried muskets and rifles, it was apparent that Panglima Baladji could pay the fine of seven guns, if the spirit or my persuasions moved him.

Scarcely were we seated on the roots of the banian, when down the beach came a gaily caparisoned throng of Moros afoot and on horseback. Every Maharajah, panglima, datu, and salip on Tapul seemed interested in the business on hand, and from every trail they poured in to witness the first case under American civil law on Tapul Island. American government was at stake that day.

They were ready to rescue their comrade in trouble if necessary. It was not long before several hundred well-armed and ugly-looking Moros surrounded me. I gave orders that they were to keep away from my detachment and this they did, while casting many sullen glances at my soldiers. It was solacing to know that the machine-gun on the launch commanded our position. But it would have been more solacing had I not been in the midst of anything that might happen.

Under the banian tree beside the Sulu Sea, I began a bichara with the Tapul Moros which lasted all that day and until the sun of the next was low in the west. I had to get those seven rifles, or the Sulu Constabulary would become a joke instead of a menace to the lawbreakers of the South. To get them by force was an impossibility. I was outnumbered fifty to one, and many of the Moros carried rifles more modern than the Krag carbines of my own men. One chief who squatted near me ostentatiously placed across his knees a Lee-Enfield rifle of the latest British Army model. I had to secure those rifles by diplomacy and by representing judiciously but not in too irritating a manner the forces of the United States behind me.

Unfortunately, Washington D.C., was a long way from Tapul. The American soldiers at Jolo were few, and, as subsequent events proved, had their hands full on that turbulent island.

The Tapul chiefs were not slow to give me their opinion of the American Government and of what they considered our interference with their ancient customs such as slavery and the right of every honorable Moro gentleman to take up arms against his neighbor, the public weal and order notwithstanding. I listened patiently, and as well as I was able, I answered with conciliatory but not too yielding speech. Always I reverted to the fact that I must have those seven guns from Panglima Baladji.

That wily chief rested his case with his stronger and better-armed fellow chieftains, so that it soon became not the United States vs. Panglima Baladji, but the United States vs. all the chiefs on Tapul. I did a good deal of hard thinking and soft talking.

When night came and the Moros withdrew with the case continued till the morrow, I returned to my detachment more tired than by a fifty-mile hike. That night I slept little, being not at all sure that the camp would not be rushed and the Tapul Moros collect twenty carbines from us instead of our collecting seven guns from them.

In the morning the bichara began again, but with the difference that the Tapulites and I met as old acquaintances. That night had doubtless given opportunity for the wiser counsels of conservative old men to prevail over the fighting instincts of the younger chiefs.

Of course, I had not failed to point out that although they might not pay the fine and might even add to their list of misdeeds by resisting my force and removing my own rubescent head, the island of Tapul lay invitingly open to shell fire from the American gunboats which would later arrive.

All this I hinted rather than threatened, while insinuating that I felt as one of them and that we might settle the affair as a family matter rather than call in the American soldiers and sailors. Were not my men also Moros and had I not one or two Tapulites among my soldiers? That should be a sign of good faith, and that the American Government and particularly the Constabulary wished to understand and sympathize with the Sulu Moros.

But always there was the point about the seven rifles I must take back with me. That was the rub which I was compelled to lubricate with soapy, yet not too soapy, speech.

Datu Pangiran, full of opium and apprehension, could give me little assistance except inasmuch as I pointed to him as the Moro representative of the United States and consequently another guarantee that the Government desired to let the Moros live in their own way.

Would it not, I pointed out, have been easy to send gunboats to collect the fine? Did not the Government show consideration for Moro custom by dealing with lawbreakers through a Moro headman—Datu Pangiran?

Chief after chief arose to harangue the audience. They minced no words. I was at their mercy. Consequently, I learned more of the Moro point of view in thirty hours on Tapul than I had in my previous two years of Mindanao. A summary of the arguments presented was that the Sulu Moros did not want any government except the loose and indulgent hegemony of the sultan of Sulu. More especially did they object to fines imposed by a headman no better than themselves.

"Let us alone!" was their cry. And they might have added "so that we can roam the Sulu Sea as we have always done—looting Chino stores, capturing Filipina girls for concubines, revenging with bloody promptness insults fancied or real, and generally perpetuating in the twentieth century the good old customs of the feudal Middle Ages."

Poor, anachronistic Sulus! The world had been growing up around their beautiful isles, and now the tendrils of civilization were spreading over land and sea. They might lop off the vine here and there, but the plant would continue to grow until it enveloped them. I was witnessing the old, old business of civilization versus barbarism, an encounter which, unfortunately, often at first results in the loss of civilization's finer attributes of mercy and justice, just as it intensifies barbaric stubbornness and savagery.

There on the Tapul beach beneath the banian I felt very much like a tender tendril of civilization that might be easily pruned by Moro knives. However, my arguments finally prevailed. One by one, slowly and reluctantly, were handed me the seven rifles which represented the price paid by Panglima Baladji for the midnight pleasantries of his young braves.

As the guns came in, I refrained from examining them too closely. There are times for minute investigation of details as there are occasions when such would be an impertinence—or imprudence! I strongly felt that this was a moment when it were well to take a comprehensive view of life, men—and rifles.

So, I accepted the seven assorted muskets and rifles without examining their breech mechanism. It was not until I was on the launch, chugging back to Siasi, and feeling lighter and happier than for many hours past, that I found that only two of the seven guns would fire.

Thus, fortunately, ended the case of the United States vs. Panglima Baladji et al. Yet my connection with the Moros of Tapul was not entirely ended, for within a few weeks I was to take part in the Bud Dajo fight and fall wounded at the walls of a cotta in which, rumor had it, many of the Tapul recalcitrants had gathered to support their brethren of Sulu against the hated Americanos. But of that when the time comes.

XXXV - Sailing the Sulu Sea

SOON AFTER MY EXPERIENCES ON TAPUL, I made a voyage by vinta from Siasi to Bongao, a voyage that I would like to be able properly to describe. But such is the color on land and sea that among those islands only the brush of an artist or the imagery of a poet can adequately paint it.

*And thus we sailed
Into the Sulu Sea, smooth as lakes
In some more blessed land, far from this world of strife.
Blue water flashed from keel as south we bore,
And flying-fish athwart our path
Escaped by flight from some pursuing bully.
The porpoise gamboled round our bow or leapt
His shining length clear of the sea
In joy of living.
Lean, hungry fish
Upon their tails skipped yards along
The surface of the water.
Ugly snakes
With painted coils lolled on the waves.
On the horizon a water spout joined sea and sky.
The emerald isles slipped by, each fairer than the last,
With grassy slopes where cattle grazed, and shores
Bordered by coco palms. The Moro fishing boats
With many colored sails and curving prows
Rushed on the tide toward the distant shoals
Where rich spoil of the sea awaited them.*

If, as has been said, the function of poetry is to represent much in little, the above lines may partly serve. In any case they will prove the charm of the Sulu Sea to be such that it could lift a prosaic Constabulary officer to poetic mood.

Over such seas, amid such scenes, I sailed from Siasi to Bongao in a small vinta which just accommodated five small

Moro soldiers and one large American officer. We were three nights and four days sailing and drifting the hundred miles or so between the two Constabulary stations.

The swift tide pouring back and forth between the Sulu and Celebes seas often took us almost out of sight of land and but for the assurance of my Moros that its turn would take us back again, I might have been somewhat uncomfortable floating out to the open sea in so small a craft.

We landed for water and leg-stretching on islets where sandy beaches invited the prow of our vinta, where turtle eggs abounded in the sand and coconuts were to be had for the shaking of the palms or, if that failed, for a well-directed rifle shot at the cluster. The moon was crescent, and the stars were spangled on a black velvet sky. Above the coral reefs the sea was strongly phosphorescent.

Behind us was a wake of milk, and every paddle stroke was a pyrotechnic display. Under the water, fish, snakes, and other marine creatures left slowly fading tracks of ghostly fire. So wonderful were the phosphorescent nights that I stayed awake, but slept in the day beneath a palm-thatch awning, or lolled, idly watching the great albatross and frigate birds that wheeled and whirled around us, recalling almost forgotten verses of the "Ancient Mariner."

We overhauled other craft and searched for opium or Chinamen. We visited Sulu chiefs on little, lone, lost islands. We sailed over wonderful "sea gardens" between Tawi-Tawi and the islands that formed the barrier against the Celebes Sea. A few feet beneath our vinta were vast patches of mushroom-coral, brain-coral, and every other variety of marine growth.

Among them, vying in color with the vegetable life, flitted brilliant fish, the damsel, butterfly, trigger, and other varieties—orange, vermilion, light blue, dense black, every color imaginable. Some were all of one intense blue, others striped harlequinwise, but all so exquisite and so dainty in their subaqueous playgrounds that they seemed part of an Arabian Nights' entertainment rather than real fish in a real sea.

Hours I spent leaning over the side of the vinta to watch the wonderful cinematograph film of marine life unrolled beneath our keel. It was easy to imagine oneself in Captain Nemo's submarine, "twenty thousand leagues under the sea."

Of other adventures than those afforded by breasting a squall or paddling violently to escape from a tide-rip, we had none. Yet there was a potential adventure in each encounter with other vintas, of which we overhauled and passed many, usually stopping them to search for opium or to see whether the crew included a Chinaman entering the high-wage Philippines from low-wage Borneo via the popular Sulu Sea route.

As the wages of a Chino in Borneo or other Malayan islands was about ten cents a day and in the Philippines a dollar or more, there was every temptation for humble but aspiring Mongolians to elude the customs and immigration officers, who were, in any case, few and far between in Mindanao and Sulu.

Moreover, the Chinaman, once safely established in the Philippines, soon abandoned manual labor to become a merchant or trader. What an Oriental business romance might be spun from the adventures of a young Chinaman, leaving Canton or Foochow for Singapore, to work in the tin mines or on the rubber plantations of the Malay States, then, perhaps, to the tobacco plantations of North Borneo; thence, after many adventures in a vinta on the Sulu Sea, landing on some remote point of the Mindanao coast to receive the certificate of a recently deceased Chinaman and, under a new name, to begin his Philippine career!

Each Chinaman in the Philippines was compelled by law to possess a certificate of identity, which was duly visaed at intervals by customs officers. But so prized were the certificates that on the death of a Chinaman his body was smuggled away and another Chino smuggled in from Borneo or elsewhere to assume the protecting certificate of the late deceased.

I once heard Robert Burdette, the California orator-preacher, preface a sermon by stating that a dead horse was worth more than a dead man, as the defunct animal could be turned into glue and soap while the body of a dead man had no other use than to clutter up an otherwise useful bit of soil. The Rev. Mr. Burdette would have been compelled to revise his comparison had he lived in the Philippines in 1906, where a dead Chinaman was worth just about $500, provided his body could be disposed of without interference from inquisitive United States health or customs officials.

"The King is dead, long live the King!" found its echo in Mindanao in "Wun Lung is dead! Long live Wun Lung!"—a new Chino under the old certificate.

However, in later years a hard-hearted government insisted that each certificate should bear the photograph of its owner, a duplicate picture being filed in the customs archives. Consequently, the business in dead Chinamen fell off.

I'm afraid that, although sworn to enforce the law and if necessary assist the customs officers, my sympathies were wholly with the Chinaman, whom I have always found a decent, law-abiding, self-respecting citizen, with a measure of philosophy which should make him the envy of a neurasthenic West. What, I wonder, will be history's verdict on our action in keeping the overflowing millions of China out of the almost unoccupied land of Canaan at their door?

And what people in history have had the luck of the Filipinos to find a protecting nation apparently willing to sacrifice her own interests and put a dam across all economic and racial currents in order to give them a chance to work out their own salvation, un-submerged by the Mongolian flood to the north? Every Filipino boy and girl should nightly kneel at prayers and say, "God bless Uncle Sam and keep him generous for all time."

We also stopped to watch the Moro pearl divers. These men, without diving suits or any apparatus, descend fifteen or twenty fathoms by holding on to a large rock, which they release when they have gathered sufficient shell. I did not see any such deep diving, as the boats we visited were anchored in only a few fathoms.

But an American who has lived years among the Sulu Moros told me that many attain a depth of eighteen fathoms, while at Tandubas, an island off Tawi-Tawi that I passed on this voyage, there is held each year a diving contest at which a record has been made of twenty-three fathoms without suit or helmet. That sounds almost incredible, but I later verified the figures by inquiry among the Moros and found that diving to eighteen or twenty fathoms is not unusual.

At the end of a leisurely voyage, we sailed through the narrow passage fringed by palms and mangroves that is the eastern entrance to the southernmost port in the Philippines, Bongao Islet, stone fort, straggling village, and thumb-shaped peak, all bear the same name, which should be pronounced as if written "Bon-gow," with accent on the last syllable. Mindanao lies between the Pacific Ocean and the Sulu Sea, like a scorpion with its head towards the Pacific and its tail curled round to Borneo; and the very point of the sting is Bongao.

I sat on that point for about a month, my only white companions being a Constabulary lieutenant who under the tropical sun had ripened too quickly and was now going to seed, and the collector of customs, a clever and genial youth who now, I believe, edits a newspaper in his native state.

The collector of customs and I had an extended argument as to who slept furthest south under the American flag. To determine the mooted point, we ran a topographical survey along the beach. I forget to whom the honor went, but the incident will show that despite pirates and smuggled Chinamen time sometimes hung heavy on our hands.

I had expected the monthly mail steamer to rescue me from Bongao, but she skipped a month and I had the more time to whip the Constabulary company into shape. Lieutenant X. was hopeless and helpless, giving daily and faithful imitations of the actions of a man attacked by hookworm. Those isolated stations either make or break a man, and Bongao had badly broken poor X.

With the customs man I climbed to the summit of Bongao Peak, straight up two thousand feet through tangled thickets of bamboo, rattan, and orchids, to a rock pile whence we looked across thirty miles of intervening sea to the dark mountain mass of Borneo—home of the Wild Man of dime-museum fame, but also of the elephant, the rhinoceros, the orangutan, the chimpanzee, the Dyak headhunters, the bird-winged butterflies, the White Rajah of Sarawak, with many other actualities stranger far than the imagination of the owner of a freak museum.

Perhaps on that mountaintop the customs man and I were less picturesque figures than Balboa, "silent upon a peak in Darien;" yet there was a touch of romance about the two young Americans, each with a handful of orchids gathered by the way, gazing across the amethystine Sulu Sea to empurpled Borneo.

The Constabulary officer at Bongao was the official representative of the United States for a hundred miles north and fifty south—from Siasi to Borneo. His District included several hundred square miles of sea and almost as many islands; his subjects were several thousand Sulu and Bajaw Moros; his duty to keep the peace among this scattered multitude of almost professional disturbers of the peace, to assist the customs officer in suppressing the opium and Chinaman traffic, and to be as ready to shoot a smuggler, pirate, or ordinary amok as to bind up the wounds when inflicted.

For the Constabulary hospital at Bongao, merely a whitewashed room in the fort, was rarely without Moro patients, and the officer, who must combine medical and surgical work with his multifarious other duties, soon became expert at treating and bandaging bullet and bolo wounds, with tropical ulcers and other loathsome sores, besides diagnosing and curing beriberi, yaws, malarial fevers of several varieties, together with other assorted tropical diseases.

Some of the diversions for the officer at Bongao were hunting crocodile, wild boar, and python, although during my month there I found time only to indulge in the first and was unsuccessful in that.

Once or twice when the moon was full and the palms, coral reefs, and sandbars of Bongao seemed rather the stage setting for a moonlight scene in grand opera than a place to live, work, and next morning sweat at drilling thick-headed Moro recruits—then, when the moon was high and the sandbar across the bay was dry, the customs man and I paddled over the silver water along the very molten path where the moonlight quivered, to the sandbar whence in pathetic contrast with the peaceful beauty of the night came the agonized howls of a pariah pup fastened on the beach as tempting bait for crocodile.

We hid behind a whitened drift log that glistened like a bone, and pointed our rifles in the direction of the unlucky cur and waited for the kawayan (crocodile). Sandflies and mosquitoes rivaled the cur in attempts to mar the otherwise bewitching night, and it is likely that our efforts against the torments of the air were warning to the scaly bully of the bay. Be that as it may, I shot no crocodile at Bongao.

This lack of luck distressed me little, as I had had plenty of that sport at Cotabato. So, we released the yelping hound and paddled back through the incandescent night to the ghostly buildings and palms of the Constabulary post across the bay.

While at Bongao I suffered from my old trouble, malarial fever, doubtless brought on by exposure to the sun on my vinta voyage. At the first opportunity I reported to the District Chief, Colonel W. S. Scott, who had succeeded Colonel Harbord during my absence on leave, that the malarial attacks unfitted me for duty at Siasi. By return mail came orders relieving me as senior inspector at Sulu, and assigning me to my old position as District adjutant at Zamboanga.

Strange indeed is the manner in which the "moving finger" writes, for my transfer away from Siasi and Sulu enabled me to take part in the biggest event in Sulu history, the battle of Bud Dajo, which, had I remained at Siasi, I should have missed. That was one time at least that the fever did me a good turn.

XXXVI - Amok and Juramentado

VERY GLAD I WAS TO BE BACK IN ZAMBOANGA, which was, at that time, more home to me than any place on the globe. I found my new chief, Colonel Scott, a most courteous and considerate administrator. General Wood was still at Zamboanga, although about to transfer the Military Department of Mindanao and Sulu and the civil government of the Moro Province to his successor, General Bliss.

Many physical improvements were to be noted in roads, buildings, and general upkeep of the town and neighborhood; while the ability and fine personality of the general was reflected in the contentment and confidence of subordinate officials and the general public.

Mindanao as a whole was comparatively tranquil. In Cotabato the warlike Datu Ali was safe in the arms of paradisal houris and the peaceful Piang reigned in his stead. In Lanao the Lake Moros, better known throughout Malaya as the Lanun Pirates, were raiding less and cultivating more than for years past. In Davao and Zamboanga all was peace and prospective plenty. Enterprising Filipinos, Japanese, Americans, and Spaniards were setting out plantations of cocos and hemp. Only in beautiful but bloody Sulu were clouds gathering.

Spencer St. John, whose "Life in the Forests of the Far East" is redolent of the jungle, the tropic seas, and the "smell of fish and wet bamboo," says of his first visit to Sulu in 1858:

"The sun soon dispelled the mist and showed us the lovely island of Sulu. The slopes of the hills presented alternate patches of cleared and grassy land with clumps of trees scattered over its face, reminding one of a noble English park."

And later, like one enchanted, he returns to a description of the physical attractions of the island: "The appearance of the country from the sea is very beautiful, many of the hills rising to a peak some 2,000 feet in height; while others are lower and wooded and form an agreeable contrast. Several of these eminences are forest-covered to the summit, while many present alternate patches of rice cultivation, pasture land, groves of coconuts, palms, gardens and detached clumps of forest trees. It is by far the most beautiful island I have seen."

St. John estimated the population of Sulu as between 100,000 and 200,000. That was in 1858. In 1906, of which I now write, the inhabitants had been so reduced by internecine warfare and by the successive attacks of the Dutch, English, Spanish, and Americans, that there were fewer than 70,000 people on Sulu Island. Sulu is the Tripoli of the Far East.

Many nations took turns at subduing the fierce Balignini pirates, but it was left to the United States to finish the job, and bring them to terms, just as she did those of Tripoli. In their palmiest days, before the introduction of steam gunboats, the Sulu and Lanao pirates terrorized the seas from the coast of China to New Guinea, some 1,500 miles north and south.

The Sulus were commonly known as Balignini and the Lanaos as Lanuns. The former sailed in light outrigger paraos holding less than a dozen men, while the latter cruised in large schooner sapits, manned by a crew of fifty or sixty. But they were equally ferocious and merciless.

Woe betide the sailing ship caught in the narrow straits between the China Sea and the Pacific Ocean, or the Christian Filipino settlements on the islands north of Mindanao! A prominent feature of the Philippine seascape is the number of stone towers and forts, which the voyager might at first take for lighthouses, along the shore of every island. They are the refuges which sheltered the Visayas, Bicols, or Tagalos, when the dreaded Moro sails came up over the southern horizon.

It was scarcely to be expected that a people for centuries habituated to piracy and adventures on the high seas would easily turn to the plow and counter, even though steam gunboats, introduced in Philippine waters by the Spaniards in the late fifties, soon ended wholesale piracy.

It would be as reasonable to expect the England of Elizabethan adventurers to have contented itself within its territorial waters after a taste of the Spanish Main. Young Sulu braves took up retail piracy when the wholesale became impossible; and long after American occupation of the islands raids on remote Filipino villages or isolated Chinese traders were common.

As late as October 1910, I pursued some Lanun pirates who had raided a Filipino settlement in Misamis, killing several Filipinos and mortally wounding others.

Furthermore, hot Sulu blood found outlet in the frequent quarrels and fights between rival chiefs on Sulu and its neighboring islands. When every other excitement failed, there remained always the popular Moro sports—amok and juramentado, which might be translated as ordinary, common or garden amuck and amuck with religious and other frills. Now, a Moro in an ordinary state of amuck goes off, so to speak, by spontaneous combustion.

One moment he is an apparently sane and respectable citizen, the next he is a dancing, frenzied, fiend rushing frantically about to slay, blindly, and indiscriminately, friend, relative, or foe, until he himself is slain. But a Moro who "goes juramentado" makes careful preparation for his bloody part, works himself into a state of religious fanaticism, is shaven and shriven by a Mohammedan priest, secretes weapons about his person, then quietly and methodically seeks the spot where Christians are most thickly gathered before beginning his business of beheading and disemboweling.

An amuck is a bomb-dropping Zeppelin; but a juramentado is the submarine that kills by stealth.

I took part in but one case of amok, while I was at Cotabato. A Filipino soldier, disappointed in love, stood on the public plaza and shot everyone within range of his Krag until he was killed by an American sentry, a rather pretty shot which drilled the amuck through the head at two hundred yards. My own part consisted in sneaking up an open sewer, revolver in hand, to get within range of the frenzied Scout soldier.

But I have several times followed the path of an amok or juramentado, gathering up the bloody remains or making investigation of the facts for an official report. A typical incident or two will perhaps illustrate one of the difficulties experienced by American officials in dealing with the Moros.

When a man disappointed in love, trade, or family affairs, is likely to go amok or juramentado it behooves an official to handle carefully such sticks of human dynamite. The Filipinos, further from the pure Malay strain than the Moros, run amuck much less frequently.

At Zamboanga in 1903 or 1904, I went to Taluksungay to investigate an affair which had resulted in several deaths and more wounds. Three Yakan Moros from Basilan Island, across the straits twenty miles from Zamboanga, set sail for Taluksungay market with a cargo consisting of a sack of unhulled cacao (cocoa) pods, the value of which was perhaps a dollar, perhaps less, certainly not much more, and surely a small sum to cause the death of seven people. But seven Moros and Filipinos died because of that sack of chocolate beans.

On the voyage across the straits a squall arose which almost swamped the vinta of the three Yakans and carried overboard the sack of cacao with their other few belongings such as a handful of rice, a cooking pot, a few sweet potatoes, some dried fish, all, in fact, except the keen-bladed weapons that hung from their waists.

So, the three Yakans landed on the Taluksungay beach, wet and poverty-stricken. One who did not know the Moros might well think that they had reason to be thankful to have escaped with their lives. Not so. Life to them had suddenly become not worth living; they would run amuck.

It was evening in Taluksungay. The sun sank behind the coco palms that fringed the village, a community of mixed Moros and Filipinos, the former fishing along the coast and the latter cultivating the rice fields inland.

From the beach, up the one street of the village between the huts of bamboo and nipa, strolled the three Yakans, perhaps with despondent mien, but with nothing otherwise direful in their bearing. From the rice fields, down the street, came many Filipinos returning from the day's toil and bearing bundles of golden, ripe rice; ahead the women and children; behind, bearing heavier burdens, the men, but all chatting cheerfully or humming snatches of a harvest song.

The two parties drew nearer—the embittered Yakans and the cheerful Filipinos. It was the opportunity that the former, despite their maniacal intentions, still possessed control enough to await.

Out flashed the murderous Yakan knives—slash, cut, slice, a child's head here, a woman's arm there, and in as many seconds as it has taken words to tell, the peaceful village street became a place of massacre and wailings. The Filipino men rushed up to protect their womenfolk and children, and by superior numbers finally succeeded with their working *bolos* in hacking the three Yakans into submissive corpses.

Outside of a butcher's shop, I never saw so much red meat exposed as on the bodies of those three Yakans. About every Filipino in Taluksungay had taken a whack at them for luck. They were buried in sacks.

Another case. Near Jolo several Moros were squatting around a campfire after their evening meal when one of them began to hiccup, and his companions made fun of him. But they carried the joke a little too far, the hiccupping one took offense, drew his wavy kris, and carved a companion or two before he was himself cut down.

Those were cases of simple amok—ungovernable temper resulting in bloody but unpremeditated murders. The juramentado, on the other hand, prepared for days or weeks before playing his part. Then, when the time was ripe and the Mohammedan ceremonies fulfilled, he would, if possible, sneak through one of the gates of Jolo town, past the watchful American sentries, down the main street until he found American or Christian Filipino victims in sufficient number.

No armed Moro was allowed through the gates of Jolo or over the wall of the city. But a kris or barong could be concealed beneath wide trousers or flowing sarong so that American sentries, always on the lookout for a Moro who walked stiff-legged, were sometimes deceived. Outside the Jolo gates life always hung by a tenuous thread which might at any time be severed by the blade of a juramentado.

A period of freedom from the scourge made Americans and Filipinos careless. Then one day there would be cries of "Juramentado! Juramentado!" Women and children scurried to their homes and banged doors tight, men issued forth revolver and rifle in hand, a trail of blood and cries showed the track of the fanatic, a few shots rang out, and one more Moro went to the arms of waiting houris.

One morning I landed at Jolo a few minutes after a juramentado had cut down and killed an American officer who was walking with his little daughter but a few yards outside the main gate of Jolo and in full view of the guard there posted. A party of tourists, who were being driven in an army wagon to the Moro market, also saw the murder. It gave them some idea of the insecurity of everyday life among the Sulu Moros.

Given some fertile and prospectively productive "Eden isles" set in a sea abounding with valuable pearl and other fisheries; inhabit those islands with a race proud and warlike, cruel and resistant to civilization, yet not lacking in qualities of courage and racial virility that might under cultivation produce happy results; let the pioneer colonizers and adventurers of three nations deal harshly with that race in attempts to extirpate piracy that interfered with trade—deal harshly but with no fixed policy either of suppression, toleration, or modification—and you have the situation that confronted the United States in Sulu.

One thing, and one alone, might have prevented the years of bloodshed that prevailed when American met Moro in those Oriental isles. If from the first a policy of retaining such officers, army or civilian, as showed interest and intelligence in Moro affairs had been enforced, it is likely that personal influence would have achieved more than force.

But a policy which took every administrative officer away with his regiment, giving him a tenure of two years at the longest, was not calculated to make the machinery of government run smoothly.

Even under the most favorable circumstances, if a well-paid and pensioned civil service had been organized to deal with the Moros, government under the American flag would have been difficult. Moro culture had not advanced to a point at which the pursuits of peace might supplant piracy, slave-holding, and intertribal warfare.

These customs, anachronistic though they may seem in the twentieth century, supplied a necessary outlet for individual and racial emotions. Laws directed against them were resented as bitterly as prohibition in New York or Baltimore. Education should have preceded legislation. It was necessary for the young Moros to have an emotional and physical outlet. They knew no other than the customs of their fathers. Warfare and piracy seemed as necessary to them as baseball and football to us.

XXXVII - Bud Dajo

SUCH WERE THE MEN AND MANNERS OBTAINING in Sulu in 1906.

Colonel Hugh L. Scott, United States Army, governor of the Sulu District, had been fairly successful in dealing with the sultan and other chiefs who controlled the thousands of fanatical tribesmen.

Nevertheless, there was an irreconcilable element which gathered on the summit of Bud Dajo, a bluff-sided, conical extinct volcano, 2,100 feet high and a few miles inland from Jolo town.

For months Governor Scott treated with these people who refused to pay their cedula taxes or in any way recognize American authority. They lived in the crater summit, descending in the daytime to cultivate their fields or obtain supplies. With the passage of time and immunity from attack, they became bolder and more insolent in their attitude toward the government. From a few score their numbers swelled to more than six hundred and included many outlaws whose crimes were unpunished.

Finally, they built around the crater's edge a series of earthworks and cottas which, from a Moro viewpoint, made the mountain impregnable, and from any point of view made its assault a difficult and costly undertaking. The sultan and other Moro chiefs at least simulated friendliness and disavowed the Bud Dajo hostiles. But throughout Sulu there was natural sympathy for the defiant ones, making a last stand against the American invaders.

So, it became an unavoidable test of strength: six hundred Sulu Moros, men, women, and children, on the summit of Bud Dajo, against the United States, represented at Jolo by about as many hundred American soldiers.

In March 1906, Governor Scott decided that persuasive methods were no longer useful and were indeed a menace, as further delay in dealing strongly with the outlaws might be interpreted by other Moros as weakness and result in a general uprising. The crater fortress must be attacked.

I was in my office at Zamboanga when a telephone message came from General Wood, asking whether a company of

Constabulary was immediately available to accompany the army in an attack on Bud Dajo. As a matter of fact, there was no company ready.

But Colonel Scott wanted the Constabulary to get into the fight and we patched up a detachment from the First Zamboanga Company and the First Sulu Company, the latter having just arrived from Bongao for a change of station which might benefit its discipline and instruction.

No experienced officer was available to command the provisional company thus formed of twenty Filipino and thirty Moro soldiers, so I begged Colonel Scott to let me take charge of the expedition.

He detailed me and I had about forty-eight hours to whip my hybrid outfit into shape before taking part in one of the bloodiest little fights that the Philippines have seen.

Fortunately, two or three of the men had served with me before, while I had recently spent a month with the Bongao detachment of the First Sulu Company. Lieutenant F. M. Sowers, a brave and intelligent young officer, was assigned as my junior, and two Filipino staff-sergeants from District headquarters helped to swell my force. We sailed for Jolo on a little army transport which carried also regular troops for the expedition.

On March 4, 1906, we arrived at Jolo, which was even more military than usual. Additional troops were pouring in from Malabang, Parang, and other mainland posts; squads and companies of armed men tramped under the acacias planted by some thoughtful Spanish commandant; wagons and ambulances were being loaded, mule trains assembled, and packs selected; everywhere was that bustle and suppressed excitement, that rattling and snapping of weapons, that hot smell of sweaty men, horses, and leather accoutrements, that accompanies a campaign.

In the evening I was supervising the distribution of ammunition and field rations to my company when a Filipino addressed me. I turned to recognize Ex-Sergeant Eduardo Fernandez of the Constabularies of Negros and Cotobato, a brave soldier who had been with me at Mansalanao and other fights, but also a proper picaroon who was always getting into trouble about women, gambling, or other debauchery. It is sad but true that the moral man is not always the best soldier. A touch of deviltry seems to help a man risk his life in daring deeds.

"What are you doing here?" I asked Fernandez in surprise. The last I had heard of him was that he had been discharged at Cotabato for having too many wives to support even on a sergeant's pay—which should have been enough for three or four wives in Mindanao.

"Ah! senor capitan," answered Fernandez with a deprecatory smile, "I am now but a servant in the officers' club here—I, who was formerly a sergeant under you," and his emphasis on the pronoun indicated profound regard for his former captain. But I was now wise in the ways of Filipino soldiers. Although I held a real regard for Fernandez, who had shared many dangers with me, I also knew that his next move would probably be to touch me for ten pesos or so in memory of Auld Lang Syne.

But he merely shuffled about until I sharply asked him what he wanted. He confessed that he came to warn me against going up Bud Dajo, which, he said, would be much worse than the Mansalanao fight in Negros. The mountain was as steep, and the Moros were better fighting men than the babaylanes.

"Seguro, senor capitan," said Fernandez, "you'll all be patay (dead) if you go up Bud Dajo." He had many Moro friends who had been up the mountain and had told him of the steepness and of the impregnable entrenchments. As a matter of fact, I wormed it out of him that he had been to the summit himself. He was an adaptable devil, who could pass for a Moro if necessary, despite a strong strain of Spanish blood.

"Well, Fernandez," I responded, "I suppose that you will come along with me? Or now that you are a muchacho, have you forgotten how to shoot?"

Fernandez bravely offered to join the party. I issued him a carbine, belt, and ammunition. He was not far behind me when I was wounded, and helped to carry me down the hill. But I had better finish his story now. After the Bud Dajo fight Fernandez reenlisted in the Constabulary, chiefly by virtue of a splendid certificate from me.

Some years later I arrived at Davao, to find him in the guardhouse charged with trigamy and other crimes which I fear that I compounded when I secured his release and transfer to another province.

Next, he turned up at Zamboanga in 1911, conducting a party of wild Bagobos and Manobos to the Mindanao Fair, and nearly frightened my wife out of her wits by bringing on to the porch of our bungalow a long-legged screeching crane, several Bagobo dancing-girls, and some beknived Manobo warriors. The girls were soft-eyed and round-bosomed, and were, I suspected, the latest addition to his harem. On that occasion he borrowed twenty pesos.

After that meeting my orbit carried me far from Mindanao, to the extreme north of the Philippines; and there at Baguio in 1914 I received a pitiful letter from my ex-soldier friend, saying that while a member of the Zamboanga police force he had been falsely accused of rape and had been sentenced by a hard-hearted American judge, who knew nothing of Mansalanao and Bud Dajo, to seventeen years' imprisonment, a term which he was serving at the San Ramon Penal Colony.

I was acquainted with the superintendent of the penal colony, so I wrote to him a resume of Fernandez's career, and of his virtues. His vices were, I felt sure, well known to the superintendent. My last information was that Fernandez had been made a trusty and was in a fair way to earn his pardon. Perhaps hereafter, as he has no deus ex machina in the islands, he will be more careful. But when I cross the river Styx, I shall not be surprised to meet Fernandez on the other side, in trouble and wanting to borrow a few pesos.

So faithful Fernandez augmented the little company I was to lead up the steep sides of Bud Dajo. On the night of March 5, a consultation of officers was held by Colonel Duncan, and at my own request the Constabulary was assigned to lead one of the three attacking columns.

Before daylight on the next day we moved out from Jolo, under the acacias, through the postern gate where the officer of the guard flung a greeting and a "wish I were going with you," out under the stars, past waiting mule trains and cursing packers, past long lines of American soldiers resting on their rifles and joking with one another somewhat nervously; up dew-wet grassy slopes between groves of bamboo and breadfruit that were now but darker blotches in the night; on through the heavy tropic darkness, until we reached our place near the head of the column that moved out to attack the mountain.

When the brief dawn glared into full day, we were almost within rifle shot of Mount Dajo and could see along the crest, clear-cut against the sky, many flags and banners waving defiance over the Moro forts. The Moros themselves lined the parapets.

Their cries and taunts floated faintly to us down the steep sides of the mountain, and over the rolling grassy upland that billowed to the forests of the steeper slopes.

On closer inspection Mount Dajo seemed twin sister to that Mansalanao peak on Negros on which I had my big fight with the babaylanes in 1902. But there was this difference in my present situation: I was now part of a well-equipped and organized expedition, with doctors and ambulances in the rear, and not, as at Mansalanao, days deep in the jungle without hope of assistance if aught went wrong. This was to be an engagement in the limelight, a novel experience.

For a Constabulary officer accustomed to lonely bushwhacking there were pleasurable thrills about a nice sociable engagement such as Bud Dajo was to afford; Jolo town only five miles astern; surgeons, hospital, and, ye Gods, cool-clad American nurses within cannon shot of the fight; fellow countrymen as soldiers on either side and behind—it was for me a fight deluxe.

The assault on Dajo was to be made by three columns, up the three practicable trails which climbed steeply to the crater. Off the beaten cut-out trail was an impenetrable tangle of bamboo and brush. I was assigned to the post of honor at the head of Major Omar Bundy's column, which, in addition to my handful of Constabulary, consisted of two companies of the Sixth United States Infantry, my old friends of four or five years before in Negros.

We went into camp at the foot of the mountain, in the long grass and in full view of the rim of the crater summit where Moros and their banners were silhouetted against the sky. On Major Bundy's orders I sent Lieutenant Sowers with twenty men a few hundred yards ahead to where the mountain jungle ran into the long grass; and as the last of his blue-shirted, red-fezzed detachment disappeared in the timber, shots rang out. We had disturbed the nest of hornets.

There was a delay of several hours while other columns were taking position around the mountains. About noon orders came for me to reconnoiter up the mountain. I moved out with the remainder of my detachment, picked up Sowers and his detachment, who had been sniping at an unseen enemy in the jungle, and started up the mountain. Steeply up, always up, we crept, seeing nothing at which to shoot, yet subject to an occasional harmless sniping from above.

My orders were not to bring on a general engagement, but to locate the enemy trenches. That would be far from difficult; the mountain was only 2100 feet high, and we soon ascended 1,500 feet without other result than to become sodden with perspiration and sore-muscled in the calves of our legs. The ascent was at an angle of forty-five degrees. It was like ascending the stairway of two or three Woolworth Buildings, piled on top of one another.

Toward sunset when we were two-thirds of the way to the summit, Corporal Sayary, who was on the "point" with another soldier, slid quietly back and whispered that he heard talking ahead. I halted the column, enjoined strictest silence, and crept forward with Sayary to locate the first defensive work.

On hands and knees, on bellies and often almost on our faces, we crept up inch by inch, taking advantage of every bit of cover, hugging the jungle or worming into it when the trail was exposed, scratched by thorns and bamboo, bitten by ants and assorted bugs, but always winning upward and nearer to the trench.

At last I could hear a faint murmur of voices that was less a conversation than an unaccustomed note in the chorus of the jungle birds and insects.

Corporal Sayary, himself a Sulu Moro and less than five feet of chunky brown manhood and nerve, motioned that he could creep still nearer and see what the trench was like; so I let him squirm forward and upward while I lay still under some trailing bamboo, scarcely daring to brush off the ants and gnats which showed by their actions that I had no right to lie prone in the jungle on a mountain in Sulu.

Leaden minutes dragged into half an hour before Sayary slid back and whispered that the trench was a small one between two big trees on either side of the trail and that it was occupied by an outpost of four men. This information exactly tallied with spies' reports, so we retired a little way down the mountain and sent word to Major Bundy.

Then, as it was now nightfall, we prepared to sleep alongside the trail, where it was difficult to find a spot level enough to lie down. However, I made myself fairly snug between the trunks of two fallen trees, with my soldiers close on either side and at my head and feet.

But it was a poor night's rest, disturbed by occasional shots fired by nervous sentries, by the regular beat of brass gongs and chanted war songs in the enemy trenches not far above our roost, by the vicious attacks of warrior ants and other jungle pests, as well as by the brooding thought that the morrow would bring a bloody piece of work and a "five to one against" chance of living through it.

Soon after daybreak of March 6, we started up the mountain again. Captain Bayard Schindel of the Sixth Infantry, whose company was immediately behind my Constabulary, sent up four American sharpshooters under First Sergeant Knox.

These men I kept close behind me. As we neared the first trench, we caught our first glimpse of the enemy since entering the jungle. To the left, across a deep gully, through a break in the trees, was a house on the edge of the crater. On the fortifications around and below it were several figures which tumbled back as we opened fire. With the sound of our own rifles confidence and courage poured through our veins.

The first trench, to which Sayary had scouted the night before, we found vacant. But from it, up the ever-steepening trail, we could see fortifications from which came a sputtering of rifle fire soon answered by our sharpshooters who at a range of two or three hundred yards began picking the Moros off the entrenchments against the skyline—like shooting crows out of a tree. Vainly I tried to find flanking trails up the mountain as a frontal attack on the cottas above looked deadly. But we were on a hogback, and on either side, as at Mansalanao, yawned deep canyons.

There was no other choice than to attack up a slippery bare slope. Leaving the sharpshooters to keep down fire from above, I scouted forward with twelve constables—a mixed detachment of Moros and Filipinos.

Soon we ran into an abatis of felled trees which completely blocked the trail. Sergeant Arasid with half the detachment attempted to climb over the abatis. With the remainder I crawled around one flank, and was greeted with such a fire from above and also from the opposite side of the canyon that I withdrew my small detachment with the loss of one killed and one wounded. Private Diukson, mortally wounded, was hanging in the abatis exposed to fire from the fort. He was shot through the jugular vein.

As I crawled up to haul him down his head fell over and great gouts of warm blood spouted over my face and chest, making me almost sick at the stomach.

I sent information down to Major Bundy and remained in a partially sheltered position under a ledge near the abatis until shrapnel fired by our own batteries at the foot of the mountain burst dangerously near. Then we retreated back to the first trench. Major Bundy and other officers climbed to the trench. It was decided to bring up a mountain gun to blast a way up the mountain. Just before dark, after great efforts, the gun was hauled up to the trench.

That night Sowers and I slept beside the little cannon, expecting an attack. But beyond sniping and the occasional discharge of a lantaka (culverin cannon) which swept the jungle with a miscellaneous collection of slugs, stones, and old junk, the night passed in comparative quiet. I received word that the assault was to be made at daybreak, after five rounds had been fired by the mountain gun point-blank at the trenches above us.

Precisely at full daylight on March 7, stiff after a restless night within stone's throw of the enemy who had beaten gongs, fired muskets and cannon, and yelled defiance all through the hours of darkness, we left the partial shelter of the trench and jungle, soon reached the fortification and abatis which had halted us the day before, and turned the corner of the mass of fallen trees into a hell of fire.

I forced my men through a gap in the bamboo chevaux-de-frise that protected one side of the abatis. It seemed that they were killed or wounded almost as fast as I could push them through. For, once around the corner, we came under the direct fire of the large fort which crowned the summit. Between us and the loopholes which spouted fire, there was nothing that would shelter a rabbit.

At a distance of fifty or a hundred feet even rusty old muskets can do terrible execution, while lantakas loaded with junk are more deadly than machine-guns. Man after man fell dead or rolled back, wounded, down the mountain. Those who were left, shepherded on by Lieutenant Sowers from behind, gallantly followed me as I pushed past the abatis and sprang madly up toward the fort where, paradoxically enough, safety lay.

Once up against the walls, we were comparatively safe from the fire which came through loopholes formed by thrusting large bamboo tubes through the earthen walls.

When I prostrated myself, breathless, against the sheltering fort, Sergeant Knox and other American soldiers soon reached me, and we engaged the Moros on the other side in hand-to-hand combat. I attempted to look over the wall, which was but little higher than my head. A spear parted my hair, and the owner of the spear departed this life with a load of buckshot in his chest.

Time after time the Moros reached over the wall to dislodge us with spear or kris, and we took toll of Malay lives aplenty. When they became more careful Sergeant Knox would raise his hat on the muzzle of his rifle, while I stepped back a little so as to get the man who rose to the fly.

Sowers and the remainder of my Constabulary came up on the right, while the blue and khaki figures of American soldiers and Scouts were ascending in a thin, often interrupted but steady stream and massing against the cotta wall for the assault.

Next to me a Moro constable, eager to see what damage he had done to those on the other side of the wall, looked through a bamboo tube into the fort, and rolled back with his eye blown out. The slope below us was carpeted with dead and dying Constabulary and Regulars. I rose to urge my men over the wall of the fort. As I clambered up, a gaudily dressed chief slashed at me with a big kris or kampilan. I dodged, lost my grip on the wall, and fell back right in front of one of the loopholes.

Although I twisted myself out of the path of death as quickly as possible, I was not quick enough to avoid a bullet which passed through my left leg just above the knee. It was fired from a captured Krag rifle at a foot or two from my knee. The shock paralyzed me. Despite the heat of battle and a tropical sun, I became deadly cold and rolled helplessly away from the fort down the hill. My part in the Bud Dajo fight was ended.

Sergeant Alga and the faithful Fernandez gallantly came to my rescue. They helped me down the exposed area to the shelter of the trench near the abatis, there giving me first aid.

The fight raged a few feet above my head, and wounded men poured back until the trench was full. Lieutenant Gordon Johnston of the Signal Corps came up from below, took my shotgun and belt of ammunition, rushed up to the attack, started the final assault on the cotta, and was back in a few minutes with a load of slugs in upper arm and shoulder.

At last there was an increase of fire, yells even more frenzied—then a slight lull as the fort was taken and the fight moved further away. Sergeant Knox staggered back with one hand hanging in shreds, blown to bits as he tried to climb over the wall.

An American hospital corps man gave us more efficient first aid. He stopped the bleeding of my wound by a tourniquet.

Some of my soldiers returned from the victory and carried me down the mountain—an hour or two of agony that seemed like a week until I reached the field hospital at the base, where a surgeon gave me a shot of morphine. The battering, incessant pain ceased.

The main defenses of Dajo were taken that morning, although twenty-four hours were required to complete the conquest of the mountain. We of the Constabulary were proud that we had reached the crater before the other columns. Over six hundred Moro men, women, and children were killed while resisting to the last. Humanly speaking, the incident was unavoidable.

The proud fanaticism of the Moros had caused them to believe that they could resist the American Government. But, certainly, none of us believed that it would ever be necessary to repeat so severe a lesson.

We thought that Bud Dajo would teach the Sulu Moros that the days of irresponsible government, of piracy, slavery, and cattle stealing, were ended. Yet six years later, in 1912, at Bagsak Mountain near Jolo, General Pershing was obliged to repeat the lesson.

Poor gallant gentlemen of Sulu, with your brilliant carmine, orange, and green jackets, your tight-fitting trousers, your wavy krises and razor barongs, your turbans and jaunty fezzes, your bastard Mohammedanism and contempt for the unbeliever, your fairy boats on a fairy sea amid fairy isles—you are, after all, a picturesque people fit for better things than to fill moldering graves on the summits of your beautiful mountains.

I'm afraid that you needed the lesson that even Sulu courage and daredevilry could not prevail against American numbers and science. But now that you've had your lesson, repeated again and again, I wish you well—even though I carry a constant reminder of your contumacy in a stiffened kneecap.

And then, somehow, I cannot help but feel that if America had sent among you, as governors and other officials, men who would stay not for a few months or a year or two but until they knew your language and your customs and had gained your confidence, and were not at the mercy of truckling, dishonest interpreters and clerks, perhaps then there might have been no Dajos and Bagsaks.

After several months in hospitals and a good many manipulations of my knee, I was back at light duty in Zamboanga in August 1906. One day I received a telegram from Manila headquarters stating that if I felt my leg sufficiently repaired, it was proposed to detail me as superintendent of the Iwahig Penal Colony, on the island of Palawan, at a considerable increase of pay. I was still on crutches. But I felt equal to any job which did not mean hiking and fighting, so I wired acceptance and returned to Manila.

XXXVIII - From Warrior to Warden

ONCE MORE THAT PLEASANT VOYAGE FROM Zamboanga to Manila, past the palm-fringed shores of isles and islets, under the shadow of volcanoes, through schools of flying-fishes and porpoises leaping out of the enchanted seas.

By this time I was so familiar with the coastline of the archipelago that at night I could tell our whereabouts by the lighthouse lights or the faint outline of distant peaks against the stars; or when we had anchored overnight in some harbor I could at dawn locate the port by its distinctive smell: Iloilo was raw sugar, in bayones on the wharf or in the godowns (warehouses); Zamboanga was copra, sickly and oily; Siasi was dried fish and bêche-de-mer—and so on for the length of the coastline.

That alternation in Constabulary life, from the strenuous discomforts and dangers of jungle-hiking and bushwhacking to the deck of an inter-island steamer was, I think, one of the pleasantest features of our work. This time I was able to reflect that my hiking days were about over, and that instead of sending outlaws and assorted evil-doers to jail, either to perdition or to prison, I was now to have the job of looking after them in confinement or partial confinement. Neither the penal colony nor Palawan meant very much to me.

But it seemed like an opportunity to do an important piece of work at a considerable increase in salary. There was glamour in the remoteness and lack of civilization on Palawan Island, close to Borneo and scarcely inhabited except by the wild hill people.

Rumor had it that the penal colony was in bad shape, convicts mutinous and escaping. I naturally supposed that my position as superintendent would be accompanied by a certain amount of risk. Perhaps that thought drew me to the job.

But as I shall try to show, I was never safer or more at ease than when among my convict colonists on the remote island of Palawan, nearer Borneo than Manila, and about as far from civilization as it is possible to get in these days of prying tourist steamers. Yet as to the distance from civilization, that is a matter of interpretation.

There have been times when I felt more nearly civilized among the half or wholly naked headhunters of northern Luzon than in the slums or dives of a large city.

Mentioning the "distance from civilization" conjures up the smoking room of a Nippon Yusen Kaisha liner plying between Kobe and Nagasaki. It was in 1907 and I was returning to the penal colony after a few days' holiday in Japan.

Sitting in the smoking room after dinner, making conversation with half a dozen travelers from as many parts of the world, one of the group said, "Well, I expect that I come from a place further from civilization than any of you."

With my Palawan destination in mind I took up the challenge. But it turned out that the speaker was from the Aru Islands off the coast of New Guinea, where he was engaged in pearl fisheries. I paid for the drinks. On the strength of our mutual remoteness from the refining influences of civilization we cemented a steamer friendship, and he traded me the skin of a bird of paradise from New Guinea for that of a peacock pheasant from Palawan.

On arrival in Manila I was taken in hand by the Hon. W. Cameron Forbes, then secretary of commerce and police, and later the governor-general who gave the Philippines the start in good roads and public utilities which preceded their great economic progress.

As might be expected of a man whose maternal grandfather was Ralph Waldo Emerson and paternal grandfather John Murray Forbes, this Forbes was a practical idealist—a builder of things and of men. He saw not only the economic waste of a prison system which confined men within four walls. But he also sensed the tragedies in the lives of broken men—men who might be reconstructed and of use instead of danger to society.

Mr. Forbes believed that men who had broken society's laws had not necessarily dropped from the level of intelligent human beings to that of debased brutes. He believed that if the Filipinos were capable of self-government in their municipalities, they might be trusted under certain restrictions to govern themselves in a penal colony without the irritating restraint of armed warders.

Mr. Forbes in part based his ideas for the betterment of Philippine prison conditions on the successful conduct of the George

Junior Republic, a self-governing institution of previously refractory boys in New York State. Nevertheless, it took both vision and courage to apply to renegade Filipino outlaws and fanatics, murderers and cattle thieves, insurgents and political intriguers, the medicine that had cured American boys, viz., confidence both implied and applied.

At first it looked as though Mr. Forbes's confidence had been misplaced. The selection of penal colony officials had been unfortunate, with the consequence that the several hundred convicts who were sent to a partially cleared spot in the jungles of Palawan died like flies of beriberi, malaria, and dysentery, wallowed in their own filth until at last the remainder rose in revolt, nearly killing the neglectful superintendent.

Many of the convicts fled to the wild mountain interior of the island where they lived with the pagan Tagbanua tribes.

Yet even then, despite mismanagement and crass stupidity on the part of the officials, the soundness of the plan was shown, because the majority of the prisoners, responding to the confidence placed in them, refused to join in the outbreak, and protected the colony officers from the extreme of violence.

A few months had passed since the mutiny, but conditions had bettered little if at all. Despite the fact that the superintendent was a doctor, disease was rife, comparatively little progress had been made clearing land or erecting buildings, and the colony was a great expense without corresponding benefit except that it relieved Bilibid Prison congestion.

Indeed, it relieved the government of the care of a number of convicts, for the death rate was over 250 per 1,000 when I took charge. One man in every four—and that among men in the prime of life—was doomed to die. Such, in brief, was the situation when on September 1, 1906, I was summoned to take charge of the colony.

Mr. Forbes, with a party of other officials, among whom were General Emilio Aguinaldo and Dr. Victor G. Heiser, director of health for the Philippines, was to make an inspection of the colony, and at the same time install me as the new superintendent. We left Manila in a special Coast Guard cutter, and after two or three days of pleasant voyaging steamed into the beautiful bay of Puerto Princesa.

The voyage gave me an opportunity to become acquainted with General Aguinaldo, whom I found to be a quiet-mannered Malay gentleman, anxious only for the betterment of his people.

From Dr. Heiser I obtained valuable suggestions about tropical sanitation and its application to penal colony problems. Mr. Forbes inspired me with his own spirit of confidence in the possibility of applying the Golden Rule to prisoners of Malay race. Palawan Island is long, narrow, and mountainous, its length perhaps two hundred miles, its average breadth eight or ten.

It is densely forested. To the south, across a narrow strait, bulks Borneo, land of orangutan and headhunting Dyaks. To the north lies Mindoro, a huge, half-explored island. On its western shore thunders the surf of the China Sea. Its eastern beach is laved by the soft waves of the Sulu Sea.

The interior of Palawan is almost unknown, except to the half-naked pagan aborigines, the Bataks and Tagbanuas. Along the coast are occasional villages of semi-piratical Moro fishermen.

At Puerto Princesa, the capital of the island province, are a few hundred Christian Filipinos, descendants for the most part of an abandoned Spanish penal settlement.

Add to the above half a dozen American officials—the governor, the Senior Inspector of Constabulary, the commanding officer of the Scouts, the treasurer—one Spanish and two American merchants; one or two American ex-soldiers and beachcombers married to native women; one white woman, the governor's wife—and you have all the elements of the social structure in Palawan, near Borneo and far away from everything else.

The one link with civilization was the monthly mail steamer. There was no telegraph, cable, or wireless, so our news came in monthly chunks; and the catch of sea bass made by the convict fishermen off the coral reef that guarded the harbor of Puerto Princesa was to all of us more important than the rise and fall of empires beyond our ken and our horizon.

We lacked cities, hotels, streetcars, telegrams, theaters, and movies. We possessed the jungle, a palm-fringed plaza, topaz sunsets, and soft lascivious skies. On the whole it was not so bad.

The anchor plashed into the clear blue waters of the bay. The governor, Lieutenant E. Y. Miller, United States Army, chugged out in his Metz and Weiss engined, kerosene-burning motorboat. We piled aboard and ran two or three miles across the bay to the mangrove-fringed mouth of the Iwahig River, then up the river between mangrove and nipa palm-clad muddy banks, where, as the tide was low, oysters and other crustaceans hung from the boughs.

Ospreys hawked and Ceyx kingfishers flashed like jewels between the palm fronds. Up the river we chugged against an increasing current until dao, ipil, and narra trees replaced the swamp growth, and butterfly orchids instead of oysters hung on the trees.

An hour or more from Puerto Princesa we arrived at the Iwahig Penal Colony, landing haphazardly on a muddy bank. Mentally I immediately built a wharf. We hiked up a muddy trail through long cogon grass, where I resolved promptly to build a road; and on to the central plaza of the colony, a swampish grass- and brush-covered waste bordered on two sides by some ramshackle bamboo and palm-thatched buildings, which housed about five hundred convicts, the commissary, and other stores, and the three or four American officials.

Mr. Forbes made an inspection of the colony and convicts and found conditions bad enough. General Aguinaldo made a fine speech, advising the men of coming improvements and that they should have confidence in and obey the new superintendent. Dr. Heiser pointed out obvious and easily to be effected sanitary reforms. The official party reembarked for Manila. When I saw their boat float rapidly with the current down the river and turned to my jungle swamp and my five hundred convicts, I needed all the optimism and self-confidence I could summon up.

I took quarters with my predecessor, Doctor M——, who was to remain until I had checked over and receipted for the large amount of government property, including the several hundred prisoners. The superintendent's house was little more than a squalid hut; and when I say that we ate our meals on a table made of old boxes while sitting on other boxes, some idea of the crudity and inefficiency of administration may be imagined.

The nearby forests were full of the finest of hardwood trees. There were expert sawyers, carpenters, and cabinet makers among the convicts. All that was necessary to provide splendid furniture was to connect supply with production.

One long building housed nearly a hundred sick men, who were dying at the rate of five or six a day. This was little to be wondered at when the air was alive with flies by day and with mosquitoes by night, breeding in the open cesspools and swampy places around the buildings. The mosquitoes were of the dangerous anopheles family, which carried several varieties of malarial fevers, including the dreaded and always fatal "blackwater" variety.

Scores of the prisoners were afflicted with beriberi in either the dry or wet stages, their limbs withering or swelling as the case might be. It was pitiful to see them dragging themselves about. Although the jungle was full of wild game and the rivers and bay full of fish and shellfish, the staple diet of the prisoners was white rice and canned salmon, both imported from Manila by the monthly steamer.

It was a dolorous settlement, steeped in disease and misery. Yet the very fact that it was so bad made it really easier to achieve something. Anything I might do would be better than what had been done. So almost joyfully I turned to the task ahead.

XXXIX - A Doleful Colony

The first step, naturally, was to establish a more efficient organization among the five hundred convicts, dividing them into squads of about twenty-five men, each under its own foreman or capataz. Then I turned every available man to work digging drains, cutting grass, leveling ground, and building paths and roads around the plaza. About half the men were sick with beriberi, malaria, and dysentery.

But even with about two hundred men an enormous amount of work can be accomplished. Within a few days we could work dry-shod around the central buildings, while the plague of mosquitoes abated slowly but in a steady ratio to the disappearance of pools and swamps. Mosquitoes, which had been more plentiful than leaves in Vallombrosa, were soon a rarity; and flies became entomological specimens rather than pests as soon as we covered up the open cesspits.

As the mosquitoes and flies diminished, slowly at first but soon with encouraging rapidity, the death and sick lists from malaria and dysentery daily dropped. But beriberi persisted. Rarely a day passed but one, two, three, four, or as many as seven men, in the prime of life, died. The infection would reach their hearts, probably already weakened by attacks of malaria and dysentery.

My daily inspections of the shed hospital were often punctuated by the death of a prisoner-convict while I was passing down the ward.

I had a copy of Munson's "Tropical Diseases." Long after all was still in the colony save the distant moans of fever-ridden patients in the tumbledown hospital, I used to pore over his descriptions of diseases which must be combated in Palawan.

Beriberi, a nutrition disease little understood in 1906, hung on for some months until I succeeded in obtaining a supply of mongo beans (Spanish lentils), navy beans, bacon, to supplement the almost exclusively rice and fish diet obtaining on my arrival; and white, decorticated rice at that.

The Japanese later proved that coarsely milled rice would prevent beriberi. As soon as we changed the diet at Iwahig the dread disease disappeared almost overnight. The death rate of more than 250 per 1,000 for men in the prime of life, before I took charge, dropped to less than 8 per 1,000 during the second six months of my tenure.

After the first few weeks I had the able assistance of an intelligent young Tagalo physician, Dr. Florentino Ampil, who was, I am safe in saying, of more assistance to me than many American doctors would have been, proving again the axiom so often forgotten that a good Filipino is better than a poor American.

Dr. Ampil and I established a friendship and mutual confidence which persisted long after I left the Colony. He would call me in for interesting autopsies, and once he showed me a case of the rare lung-fluke or Paregonimus westermanii, and he often showed me under the microscope the malarial bugs in my own blood.

Ampil and I took every measure possible for hygiene and sanitation. I found that the convicts were netting the small creeks and sloughs near the plaza and destroying the fish which preyed on the mosquito larvae: so, we stopped that.

Examination of the shores of the Iwahig River showed that when the tide went down it left pools of fresh or slightly brackish water in which mosquito wigglers were found. I put scores of prisoners to raking the shores smooth and draining the pools. Systematic administration of quinine was recommended.

We lined up the convicts before meals and gave three grains of quinine; and to show that we believed in our own medicine, Ampil and I stood at the head of the line and took the first doses. Mosquitoes and flies became such rarities that if I found them in the barracks or kitchen during inspection a black mark was registered against the man responsible.

A few weeks earlier, the air had been alive with them. It was fascinating to mark the daily physical improvement in the colonist-convicts and to mark the dropping sick report and death rate.

Following organization and sanitation came discipline. Although there had been a mutiny before my arrival, the men were too sick and listless to rebel at any except the worst forms of neglect or ill treatment. Nevertheless, there was a discontented semi-insubordinate element, and during my first weeks at Iwahig I attempted to locate the man or men around whom a possible disturbance might center. Finally, my suspicions focused on a Chinese mestizo Ilocano prisoner named Singson.

Under my predecessor there had been permitted to grow behind the convict barracks a mushroom growth of huts which stretched back along a swampy creek to the ever-encroaching jungle. The place was a regular rabbit warren and so overgrown by climbing vines and flowering plants that it was a perfect hiding place where convicts with sufficient confidence or "pull" might ignore the calls to work or sleep.

Moreover, women either from the Filipino settlements on the fringe of the colony or from the wild tribes which denizened the jungle and steeper mountains, visited these huts for the pleasure of the more influential convicts.

From the points of view of sanitation, morality, and discipline sooner or later I must issue the order to raze the excrescent growth. But as the men's efforts for a little comfort and privacy under the previous regime were in a way commendable, while the growing of vines and flowers was the solitary refining influence in their lives, I stayed my hand until conditions generally were so bettered that the destruction of their little homes would fall less harshly.

Furthermore, daily inspections of the huts gave me valuable insight into the character of my men. The most influential prisoners had the best huts; and the best of all was the hut of Singson, convicted murderer, a brigand chief, who had been sentenced to life imprisonment.

Such a man should never have been sent to Iwahig. But in the early days little care was exercised in the selection of convict-colonists, who were shipped down haphazardly from Bilibid Prison on the monthly mail steamer in batches from twenty-five to fifty.

Singson had gathered around him a gang of the worst men, and it was clear that unless I broke it up and sent Singson back to Bilibid my control of the colony would not be complete. Although it would have been easy for me to call for a detachment of Scouts or Constabulary from Puerto Princesa to make the arrest, I knew that to produce the best effect I must control the situation without outside help. I had already remodeled the colony police force of about twenty convicts of proven good character, and had armed them with long *bolos* in addition to their clubs.

Before my arrival, incongruously enough, the convicts working in the jungle had *bolos*, while the policemen had only clubs.

At the head of the police was a fine old Tagalo, Andres Ascue, gray-haired but still tough and wiry and with a benevolent face and disposition which belied the statements in his commitment papers—"Andres Ascue—Tagalo—Batangas—54—1902—perpetual chains—assassination."

Old Ascue, I felt instinctively, was loyal to me and would lop off a head or two should it become necessary.

The only firearm in the colony was the sixteen-gauge shotgun which I used for shooting the balud pigeon and yellow-crested cockatoos which abounded in jungle clearings. At the colony discipline was maintained by moral rather than physical force.

So, one evening at retreat formation, when all the prisoners were mustered in front of the barracks for rollcall and inspection, I walked down the line, followed as usual by the old chief of police, Ascue, until I reached the squad where Singson stood all unsuspecting that his misdeeds and plottings were known to the superintendent.

Suddenly I whipped out a pair of handcuffs and with Ascue's assistance slipped them over the wrists of the surprised plotter. It was all done so quickly that there was little disturbance, and while Ascue was marching the discomfited Singson toward the improvised guardhouse and gently spurring him with the tip of a bolo when he hung back, I continued my inspection as nonchalantly as might be.

There was a chance that Singson's men might attempt to rescue their leader. But the Filipino is a Malay, and that race is always more impressed by a "grandstand" play than by more solid virtues, which are less attractive to him than the results of some dazzling flight of oratory or the flash of a keen-bladed sword.

Singson's men remained quiescent, and the treacherous Chinese half-breed returned to Bilibid by the next steamer.

I had to return one or two more convicts to Manila, but how easy it was to control them may be imagined by the fact that during my stay at Iwahig there was no jail, any detention cases being placed in a bamboo and nipa building from which escape would have been easy.

None occurred. After all, a jail is but the expression in brick and stone of moral and social failure. It is the protection erected by a community against itself, and we did not need one at Iwahig from 1906 to 1908. I believe that later on a jail was built there.

Another man returned to Bilibid was Felix Almarines, a one-legged convict who had lost a limb during the insurrection. Almarines was well educated in the Latin-Filipino way; that is, in literary and philosophical abstractions rather than the less showy but more useful things of life, and soon after his arrival he began corresponding with the radical Manila newspapers. His articles were at first most laudatory of the colony and its superintendent, but I felt that he might later place me under the ban of disapproval.

Nevertheless, I paid no attention to his correspondence and even gave him a good position in my own office. But Almarines' studies had not extended to the Latin proverb, "Timeo Danaos et dona ferentes,"[18] and he grew bolder. Often in the evenings when I strolled around the plaza while listening to the excellent band which we organized I would find Senor Felix Almarines, orator-convict, addressing a crowd of his companions in tones which became less fervid on my approach.

My office backed upon the Iwahig River. At high tide a boat could row up to the steps which led down a steep bank from the buildings. One day, near noon, the tide was high and Almarines was ripe, so I invited him to accompany me for a little walk which ended at the steps to the river, down which I considerately helped him into a rowboat manned by Chief of Police Ascue and a police crew. While the daily life of the colony flowed evenly on, if with less oratory, Convict Almarines was on his way back to Bilibid Prison, Manila.

XL - The Iwahig Experiment

BECAUSE OF THE RETURN OF ONE OR TWO ringleaders to Bilibid it must not be supposed that we penalized intelligence or ability among the colonists. On the other hand, we made use of many of the educated Filipinos as squad foremen and division chiefs. We soon organized work divisions of which a few were Farming, Forestry, Health, Serving, Police, Fishing, Carpentry, Gardening, etc. One Tagalo convict, Aguedo del Rosario, sentenced in 1902 to ten years for sedition, became chief foreman and, indeed, my right-hand man.

His influence over the men was great, and I am inclined to think that if I had not won Rosario's confidence and support my difficulties would have been almost insurmountable. Rosario was one of the first triangle of the original Katipunan against the Spaniards, a friend of Rizal and of all the leading insurgents and politicians. Just before I left the colony in 1908, I asked Rosario—who was by that time a paid assistant—what more than any other thing had inspired confidence in me.

He answered that my action in sending an American prisoner back to Bilibid had showed him that I was free from race prejudice and that I would treat American and Filipino prisoners alike.

After the first few weeks I am safe in saying that the control of those hundreds of Malayan and half-breed convicts, many of whom were noted brigand chiefs, gave me less anxiety and feeling of responsibility than is experienced by the average kindergarten teacher; and certainly not anything like the trouble I would have had if there had been armed guards and iron-barred cells at Iwahig. The prisoners knew that I wished them well and was doing everything possible for the betterment of their condition.

As I had at night much time on my hands, I occupied it in part by diving into the prisoners' records, often sending to Manila for the original files with record of testimony taken at the trials. What I uncovered of legal entanglement and injustice was sometimes astonishing.

For instance, I found three worthy old Ilocano peasants who were serving life sentences for murder, while the insurgent major who had personally ordered them to kill an "Americanista," and had assisted in the murder, had been pardoned some years earlier owing to political influence.

I noticed the honest-appearing old *taos* working in the tobacco patch. They were from Union province and understood the culture and curing of the pleasant plant. They seemed so honest, dull, and bent by toil that I wondered at their life sentences and, after gaining their confidence, uncovered a story which reference to the official records disclosed as true. They had been ignorant soldiers in Aguinaldo's army.

Their major was an educated politician who made them seize an enemy of his on the pretext that he was a friend of the Americans. The three soldiers had no arms, but the major had a revolver with which he threatened them until they beat the alleged "Americanista" to death with chunks of bamboo.

Later all four were captured and sentenced by an American military court; the major to death, the soldiers to life imprisonment.

The major's death sentence was commuted to life imprisonment; and a few years later, when a civil administration had supplanted the military, the major was pardoned; but the poor peons, without influence or money, continued in jail. I obtained their pardon.

Curious to say, some years afterward when I was chief of the Northern Luzon District, I professionally encountered the major, still a scoundrel and then attempting to stir up a new insurrection. He was one of that class of professional agitators which at times makes the real friend of the Filipino people despair of their future.

My confidence in the colonist-convicts was not misplaced. Only once did an escape occur. Four ignorant prisoners, led by a half-educated Tagalo, were missing one night at retreat. My police force brought back three of the wanderers the following day; the fourth had an unhappy existence among the wild Tagbanua tribes in the mountain jungle for a few weeks and then voluntarily returned to the home comforts of Iwahig.

There was no safer place in the Philippines than Iwahig. My own house was wide open, day and night; my personal servants were convicts, nice-mannered Tagalo and Bicol boys, sentenced to ten or twenty years for brigandage or murder; and during my two years at the colony I did not miss a peso or a button. The reason for such security lay in the fact that the confidence placed in the prisoners was not half-hearted.

Many a penal colony or experiment in penology has been wrecked by tentative measures—an attempt to blend the Golden Rule with warders, shotguns, cells, and bars; whereas the two blend no better than oil and water. Yet I think that the prisoner must always feel that behind the leniency and kindness of the superintendent lies at least the capacity for harsh measures should they be necessary.

At Iwahig I found it just as well to synchronize measures tending to improve the condition of the colonists with disciplinary examples. When they first received small money allowances for continued good work, the order promulgating this innovation appeared alongside the order which returned a bad character to Bilibid, and so on. In the matter of misunderstanding continued kindness the Filipino is no better than most Orientals—and some Occidentals.

When I took charge of the colony, I found two or three American employees of a cheap type, but these soon left. It has been my experience in the Philippines, that a good Filipino is better than a poor American. The failure to recognize that evident fact has caused more friction in government bureaus than any other one thing.

The American who would remain in the islands to work for seventy-five or one hundred dollars a month without promotion or prospects was, more often than not, just the cheap, swaggering sort of fellow least suited to deal with men of different color and race. The prototype of his class was an American dock foreman who was in charge of Moro stevedores on the wharf at Jolo.

The Moros were failing to stack sacks of oats as the foreman wanted, so he exploded like this, "You niggers, you. Porque no pony este sacks of oats donde yo tell you? _____ you. You _____ sons of _____ you. Don't you understand your own _____ language? You're a lot of _____ fools."

Although the convicts as a whole were easily controlled by common-sense methods as opposed to established penal customs of unnecessary repression and restraint, there were times when individual passions were let loose. The Filipinos are largely of Malay blood, and the Malay is noted for the abandon of his passions when disappointed in love or life. There was the case of Nicasio Suavison.

I was at my desk when there came nearer and nearer a hullabaloo which increased until a prisoner dashed up the steps to the sanctuary of my office and only stopped in front of me, panting out, "Nicasio—va—matarme."

And sure enough in rushed Nicasio, naked bolo in hand, and followed by a policeman or two. The pursued one had taken shelter behind me. Nicasio stopped short and I motioned him to sit down on a bench near the door. Then I dismissed the others and went on with my office work and daily routine. Nicasio sat there, bolo in hand; but after a while the bolo dropped to the floor while his face, heretofore convulsed with passion, smoothed into lines of depression and contrition. I knew Suavison and his record fairly well.

He was serving a life sentence for a murder committed in a passing fit of passion such as had now again convulsed him; so I let him sit there for an hour or two until passion had turned to complete humility, when I called him to the desk and, without further investigation, sentenced him to go back a grade and to be confined for a month to the limits of the plaza after work hours. Nicasio took his sentence cheerfully, being only anxious that I did not return him to Bilibid.

Also, I relieved him from work in the bakehouse and put him in the Roads Division, cutting trails through the jungle. Often when making excursions to shoot birds or hunt the wild boar I took Nicasio along to expend his surplus energy cutting out the bamboo and rattan from the trail rather than lopping off the heads of his too irritating friends.

Among the convicts were men whose names had been household words in the Philippines even back in Spanish days. Such was old Capitan Valeriano Gazic of Mindoro, for twenty years during Spanish and American times king of the Mindoro Mountains, perhaps the most noted bandit chief in the Philippines, certainly on a parity with my old Negros friend, Papa Isio.

Capitan Gazic wielded more influence in Mindoro, third largest island in the archipelago, than did the Spanish governor at Calapan; and Spanish methods of pursuit of the bandit band, involving as they did prolonged daily siestas, a great deal of verbiage, and very short journeys into the forbidding jungles and mountain haunts of the outlaws, resulted only in enhancing the brigand chief's prestige.

When the Star-Spangled Banner was hoisted at Calapan in place of the red and yellow flag of Spain, the American Constabulary officers knew no siesta on the trail. And Gazic was getting old and rheumatic. My bright young Cotabato lieutenant, Gilsheuser, then stationed in Mindoro, finally ran him to ground in a Mangyan clearing in darkest Mindoro.

At Iwahig I found the ex-bandit useful and gave him a responsible position in the Serving Division. It was rather pathetic to face the brown old gentleman who once had ruled the Mindoro jungles with a rod of iron supervising perhaps the daily cleansing of the colony garbage cans. Yet he served faithfully, and when he died in 1908, we gave him a funeral that eclipsed all previous interments. The prisoners of his division made a great cross of ipil hardwood which will long mark the burial place of Capitan Valeriano Gazic, bandit chief and amiable old gentleman.

Of the progress we made at Iwahig, of the long avenue of acacias we planted, the flower gardens and the orchid house, the vegetable gardens where we grew nearly every kind of tropical fruit and vegetable, as well as many from the temperate zone, the coffee, cacao, tobacco, tree cotton, papaya, and other plantations—all this progress is told in the reports made to the Philippine Commission.

The colony soon became a show place and tourists dropped in, or prominent government officials. I made trips to Borneo and to Japan and came back laden with seeds and cuttings. Within two years a disease-bearing swamp had been transformed into a little paradise. And it was all so easy, or seemed so at that time.

It was not all work. There were hunts for the wild pig which abounded in the jungle and often did much damage to our sweet potato farm. When the moon was high and full, we would gather a few score convicts on the plaza, some with long stout nets woven in the colony shops, others with spears, and the remainder, who were to act as beaters, armed only with *bolos* to cut through the undergrowth.

Off we went through the warm, still tropic night, over the river with a great splashing and shouting, for crocodiles were in plenty and voracious; through the jungle where we cut or pushed aside the sharp-toothed vines of rattan and other trailing plants, until we reached a grassy clearing in the forest. Here the coarse cogon grass was beaten down so that we could stretch from forest wall to forest wall the stout net which, tight-staked, would stop the rush of even a large boar.

Away off sounded the cries of the beaters, ever closing their circle and approaching the net where we stood with spears ready poised. The cogon grass waved and shimmered in the moonlight as a big tusked boar rushed toward us. Loud rose the yells of my native huntsmen in many a dialect and song; spears flashed as the boar hit the net.

One slain, on came another. It was wildly exciting and there were not lacking occasions when the legs of men were cut by spears or tusked by an old boar. Then home again with the pigs carried on bamboo poles cut from the jungle, and there would be roast pork for dinner next day. The old fellows were tough and only fit for stewing meat, but young wild pig was delicious dark game meat.

Those moonlight nights; the plaza, palms, and buildings gleaming incandescent; the scent of the gardenias and tuberoses; the convict band on the stand in the center of the plaza; the dark line of jungle forest that we had pushed back hundreds of feet beyond the buildings; the barefoot, contented colonists padding up and down the good roads and paths which they had built; paradise in a penal colony, three hundred miles from civilization so-called.

No movies and no soda fountains; no white women and few others; nothing to do but work and improve and make our own amusements; and yet I'm sure that many a convict now free looks back, as sometimes I do myself, to the good old days at Iwahig, while perhaps some of them regret the day when they were set free to battle again with a less well-regulated world.

And should I live as long as a California Big Tree I shall never again receive the perfect tribute that was mine when, in September 1908, I stepped aboard the launch that was to carry me away from my convicts and my jungle. The colony was there to bid me God-speed, and many a wrinkled old Filipino prisoner wept as I said goodbye. My own eyes were not dry.

XLI - THE END OF A TROPIC DAY

ONE OF MY REASONS FOR LEAVING THE PENAL COLONY was that a further stay there meant loss of promotion in the Constabulary. On my return to Manila I was assigned as major and executive officer under my old chief, Colonel Harbord, now acting chief during the absence of General Bandholtz.

Under different circumstances I had again an opportunity to profit by a study of Harbord's executive methods. There was one incident that I remember as proving his independence of thought and action. A prominent American government official had been sentenced to long imprisonment for embezzlement. He had not been long in Bilibid before his many friends in lodges and social life circulated a petition for his pardon.

Colonel Harbord brought it to me, noting that the petition had been signed by almost every prominent government official, by bureau chiefs, justices of the district courts, and cabinet ministers. But after a short discussion my chief said that the man was guilty and the fact that he was prominent and had many friends only accentuated his guilt, and he did not propose to sign the petition.

A vacancy for lieutenant-colonel occurring, I was promoted and assigned as District Chief of the Southern Luzon District, with headquarters at the pleasant town of Albay, under the shadow of Mayon Volcano. During my year in command of the Bicol and part of the Visayan provinces about the only real adventure was an ascent of that eight-thousand-foot active volcano.

We very nearly met our death, Captain Julius T. Knox and I, on that climb. I had picked Knox up on one of my inspections of Constabulary stations when I visited various parts of my district by Coast Guard cutter. He was sick and nervous after too much campaigning against the pulajanes of bloody Samar, so I put Lieutenant Anderson off at Pambujan, I think it was, and thereby signed his death warrant. For Anderson was drowned a week or two later in the rapids of some interior river of Samar. Knox rapidly recovered with good food and a little normal social life, and I took him with me on a reconnaissance of Mount Mayon, which became an ascent to the summit.

The height of mountains is a relative thing. A fifteen-thousand-foot peak that rises from a plateau ten thousand feet above sea level is not apparently as high as a peak like Mayon, which sweeps up sheer from sea level. Mayon is one of the most perfect cones in the world, if not the most perfect. It is even more graceful than Fujiyama.

It is a volcano which has not yet "blown its head off." The lower slopes are covered with plantations of abaca or hemp to about two or three thousand feet, above which level are cogonales of long grass and scrub with some casuarinas; then a zone in which are found delicious blueberries; and then the mountain rises steeper and steeper in slopes that are sliding lava, rocks, and ashes—slopes that are scored here and there by gullies hundreds of feet in depth.

Report had it that the mountain had been climbed only once or twice and that from the side opposite the town of Albay. I reconnoitered a route on several half-day expeditions.

On May 29, 1909, Knox and I rode horses to the 3,500-foot level, and camped there for the night. Just after daybreak on Decoration Day we started our climb, never thinking that we would reach the summit on the first ascent; but at noon, just as the cannon at the Scout post were booming the salute, we reached the crater summit.

The sulphurous steam from many vents and cracks was mixed with a fog which enveloped the summit and through rifts in which we saw half of southern Luzon in colorful panorama below. We spent but a few minutes at the summit, for it was bitterly cold to our tropic-thinned blood, and, moreover, I was a little anxious about finding the way back.

When the mist began to form, I dropped bits of matches along our trail which for the last mile or so had been over a tumbled pile of boulders, insecurely poised on the mountain slope. For a while we followed the broken matches, but soon we came out on an unfamiliar chute of ashes and boulders where we began to slide rapidly down, try though we might to diminish our speed and choose our route.

There was no hold on that steep slope. Down, down, down we rushed in a cloud of ash-dust and with large boulders rolling along with us apparently toward destruction. We dug in our heels and in each hand grabbed small rocks with which to brake our progress, but almost without avail. Time and again we were on the edge of ravines hundreds of feet in depth and into which our accompanying boulders disappeared. Then we rolled away from immediate danger and hurtled on again.

We were about twenty minutes descending two or three thousand feet; and when we managed to control our mad flight and stand erect again in comparative safety on less steep slopes, we found ourselves at some distance around the mountain from our overnight camp, toward which we struggled painfully. So rapid had been our descent that friction had torn off the seats of our trousers, our heavy hiking shoes were worn through at the heels where we had dug into the sharp-edged lava and ashes, and our fingernails were torn and bleeding. I had come through a score of engagements with babaylanes and Moros without any gray hairs; but within a day or two after the ascent of Mayon volcano there were gray hairs around my temples.

Little of special interest occurred during my year in command of the District of Southern Luzon, or for that matter in the next few years as compared with the earlier Constabulary days. Late in 1909, I took several months' leave of absence and made a journey around the world, which was punctuated with malarial attacks as long as I was in a cold climate.

In New York in November I entered a private hospital, and was the center of attraction because doctors found such interesting complicated combinations of malaria in my blood, the inheritance of Palawan, Mindanao, and other islands. In England in December the "blasted English drizzle woke the fever in my bones" again, and I headed south for Spain and sunshine. I was not entirely happy until the steamer headed through the Straits of Singapore toward the Philippines.

On return to Constabulary headquarters in March 1910, I was assigned to command the Constabulary School for cadet officers at Baguio. There under the pines I met Mrs. White to be, and married her in Manila in September 1910. Then there was another tour of duty at Zamboanga, a year as governor of the province of Agusan in Mindanao, and many expeditions among the liver-eating Manobos and other wild tribes.

But those later years, my increasing ill health and final retirement from the Constabulary in 1914, for total physical disability on a pension of $100 a month for five years only—all that, and my return to health and participation in the World War, is another story. I have told something about the Philippines and the Filipinos; and perhaps I have achieved the distinction of writing about the Philippines without expressing an opinion on their inhabitants' fitness or unfitness for independence. The confidence with which the casual visitor expresses his opinion in several hundred pages astonishes us who have spent years among the Filipinos and the Moros. And we usually note how the slightly informed author on Philippine subjects confuses his facts with the theory which he desires to expound.

There was an old Spanish friar who was reputed to be writing a book on the Philippines. After his death his executors found a ponderous tome with the superscription, "What I know about the Filipinos." And the volume was blank. That was at the other extreme. I have tried to hold the middle course and relate my own experiences and a few adventures without too many opinions.

But now, after many years away from the islands, I look back with a kindly fellow-feeling toward the Filipinos and the Moros, the Manobos and the Bukidnon, among whom my lot lay for so many years. When I read the opinions of them held by partly informed authors, the fellow-feeling is intensified so that I often feel like leaping to their defense.

The problem of the Philippines today is scarcely that visualized by President McKinley and his advisers in 1898-1900. Today the fitness of the Filipinos for independence is not the only consideration. But, in fairness to the Filipinos, the general economic and political necessities of the Pacific should be considered on one side; the Filipinos' fitness should be on another page; and future authors will speak more accurately and will be sure of the respect of the Filipinos if they do not mix the two pages, and do injustice to a people of as many virtues as ourselves, and perhaps not more vices.

THE END

Appendix

Footnotes

1. Admiral of the Navy, George Dewey (1837-1917), led the attack on Manila Bay, during the Spanish-American War, sinking the entire Spanish fleet.
2. General Arthur MacArthur, JR. (1845-1912).
3. *Obermann Once More,* Arnold, M.
4. Elegant, French-style open carriages.
5. Ancient Greek courtesans.
6. Puente de España, linking Binodo and Santa Cruz.
7. During the American Colonial period.
8. Revolutionary politician and later Prime Minister of the Philippines, Emilio Aguinaldo y Famy (1869-1964). He led Filipino forces first against Spain in the latter part of the Philippine Revolution (1896–1898), and then in the Spanish–American War (1898), and finally against the United States during the Philippine–American War (1899–1901).
9. Roman philosopher Aurelius Augustinus converted to Christianity in 386 and became the Bishop of Hippo. His philosophical interpretation of the scriptures influenced the early development of Christianity.
10. One who sells provisions to roving troops.
11. Diana, goddess of the moon, rode her bright chariot across the night sky.
12. Mixed or cured with water and oils, and left out to oxygenate, the gum solvent evaporates leaving hardened varnish.
13. *Locksley Hall,* Tennyson, A.
14. *Scotland, Fitz-James and Roderick Dhu,* Scott, W.
15. A mixture of laudanum, tincture of cannabis, and chloroform.
16. A disease among animals that doesn't spread to humans.
17. The Portuguese explorer Magellan was murdered at 41 in the Philippines at the Battle of Mactan.

Magellan's untimely demise ended his much-heralded attempt to circumnavigate the globe.
18. "I fear the Greeks, even those bearing gifts." From Virgil's *Aeneid*, (II, 49).

19.

Made in the USA
Las Vegas, NV
22 August 2024

94258087R00152